ISAAC THE PIRATE
2. The Capital

Also available by Christophe Blain:
Isaac The Pirate, vol. 1, $14.95
The Speed Abater, $13.95
($3 P&H 1st item, $1 each addr'l)

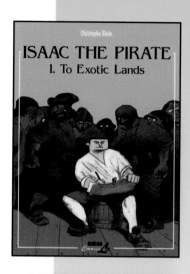

We have over 200 graphic novels in
stock, ask for our color catalog:
NBM
555 8th Ave., Suite 1202
New York, NY 10018
www.nbmpublishing.com

ISAAC THE PIRATE

2. The Capital

Christophe Blain

Library of Congress Control Number: 2004116613

ISBN 1-56163-418-2
© Dargaud, 2002, 2004
www.dargaud.com
© NBM 2004 for the English translation
Published first in French in two parts (*Olga* and *La Capitale*)
Translation by Joe Johnson
Lettering by Ortho
Thank you to Neil Kleid for his help on the Jewish prayers.

Printed in China

3   2   1

Comicslit is an imprint
and trademark of

NANTIER · BEALL · MINOUSTCHINE
Publishing inc.
new york

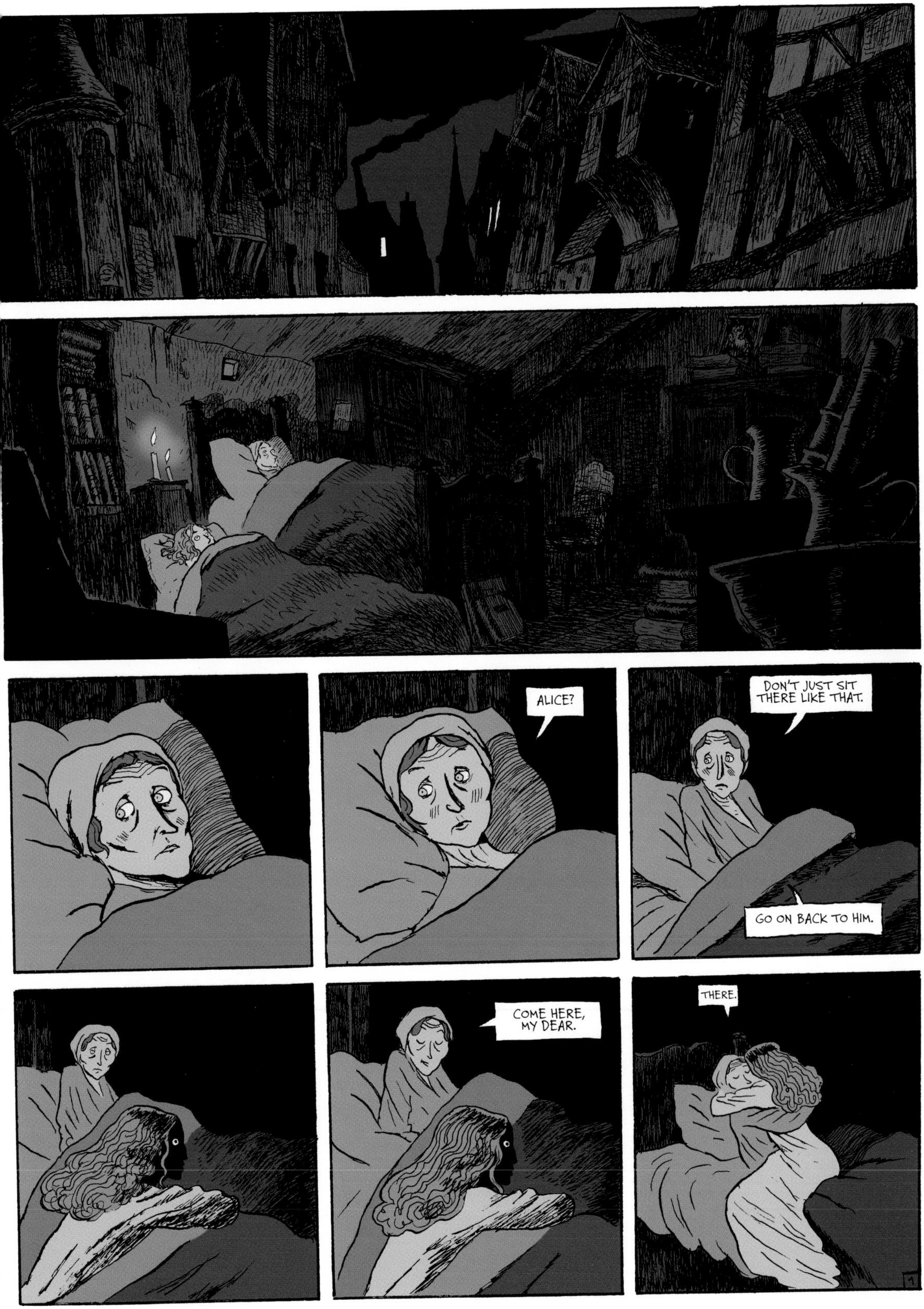
ALICE?
DON'T JUST SIT THERE LIKE THAT.
GO ON BACK TO HIM.
COME HERE, MY DEAR.
THERE.

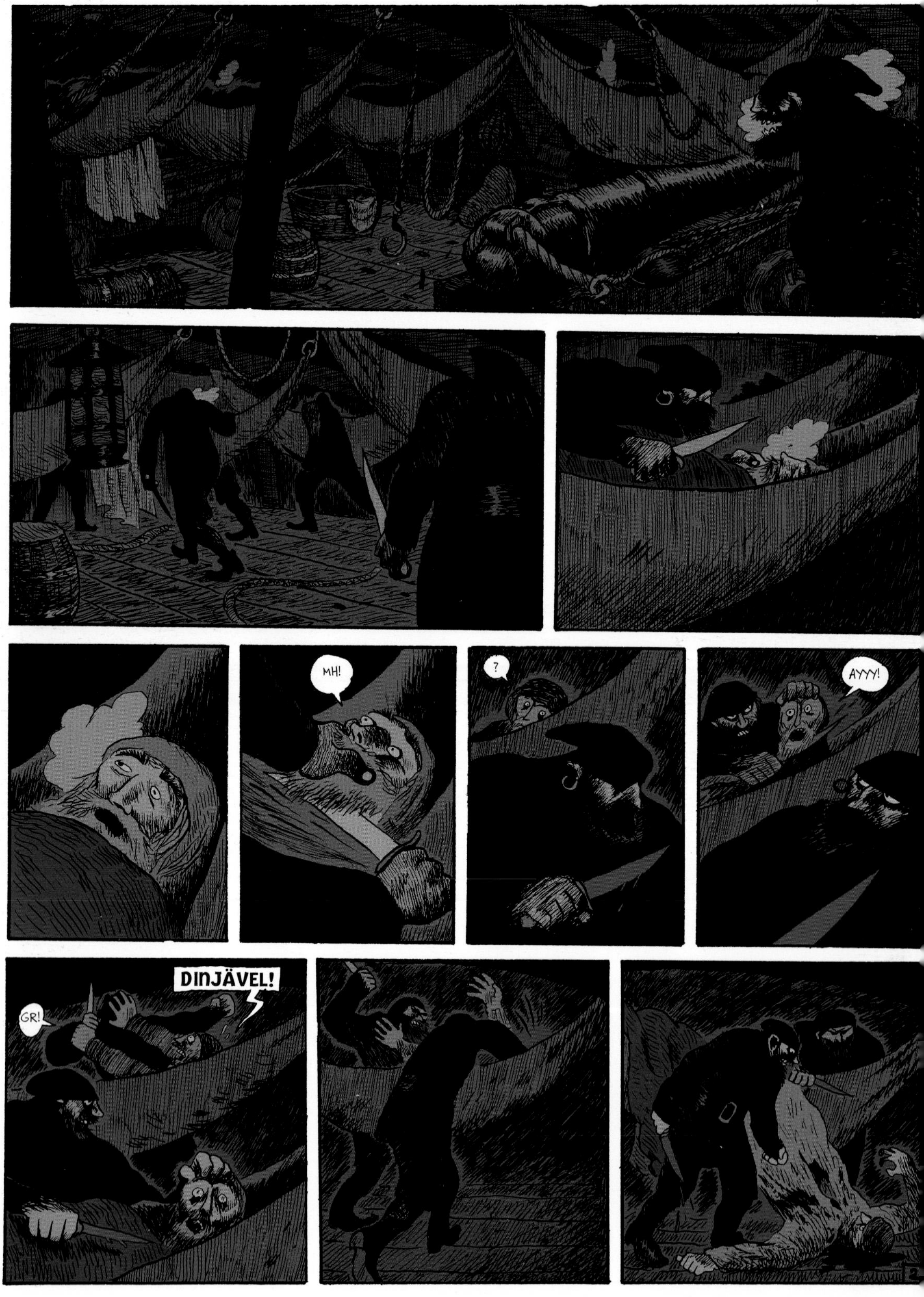
MH!
?
AYYY!
GR!
DINJÄVEL!

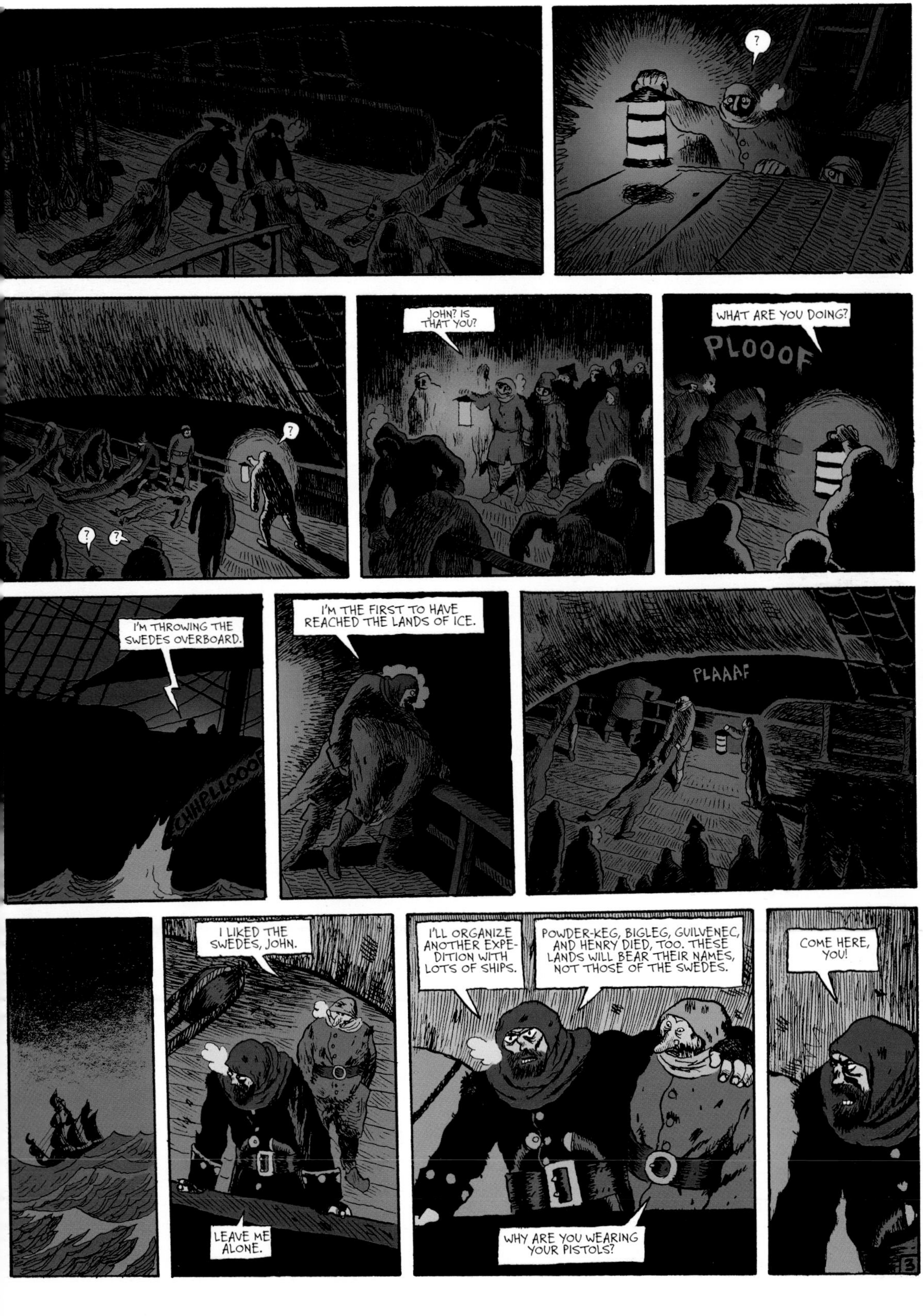

?
?
?
?
JOHN? IS THAT YOU?
WHAT ARE YOU DOING?
PLOOOF
I'M THROWING THE SWEDES OVERBOARD.
CHHPLLOOOF
I'M THE FIRST TO HAVE REACHED THE LANDS OF ICE.
PLAAAF
I LIKED THE SWEDES, JOHN.
LEAVE ME ALONE.
I'LL ORGANIZE ANOTHER EXPEDITION WITH LOTS OF SHIPS.
POWDER-KEG, BIGLEG, GUILVENEC, AND HENRY DIED, TOO. THESE LANDS WILL BEAR THEIR NAMES, NOT THOSE OF THE SWEDES.
WHY ARE YOU WEARING YOUR PISTOLS?
COME HERE, YOU!

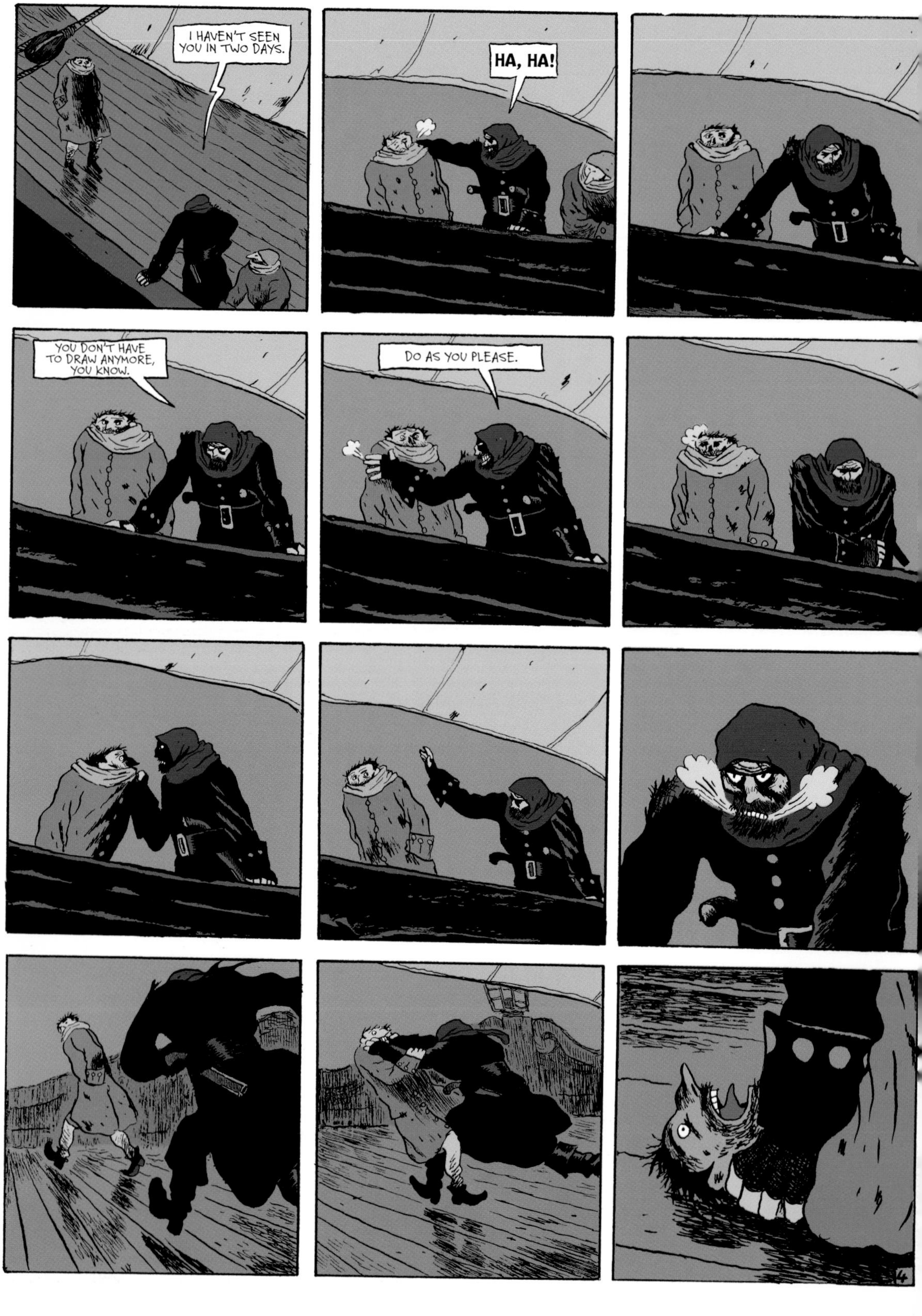
I HAVEN'T SEEN YOU IN TWO DAYS.
HA, HA!
YOU DON'T HAVE TO DRAW ANYMORE, YOU KNOW.
DO AS YOU PLEASE.

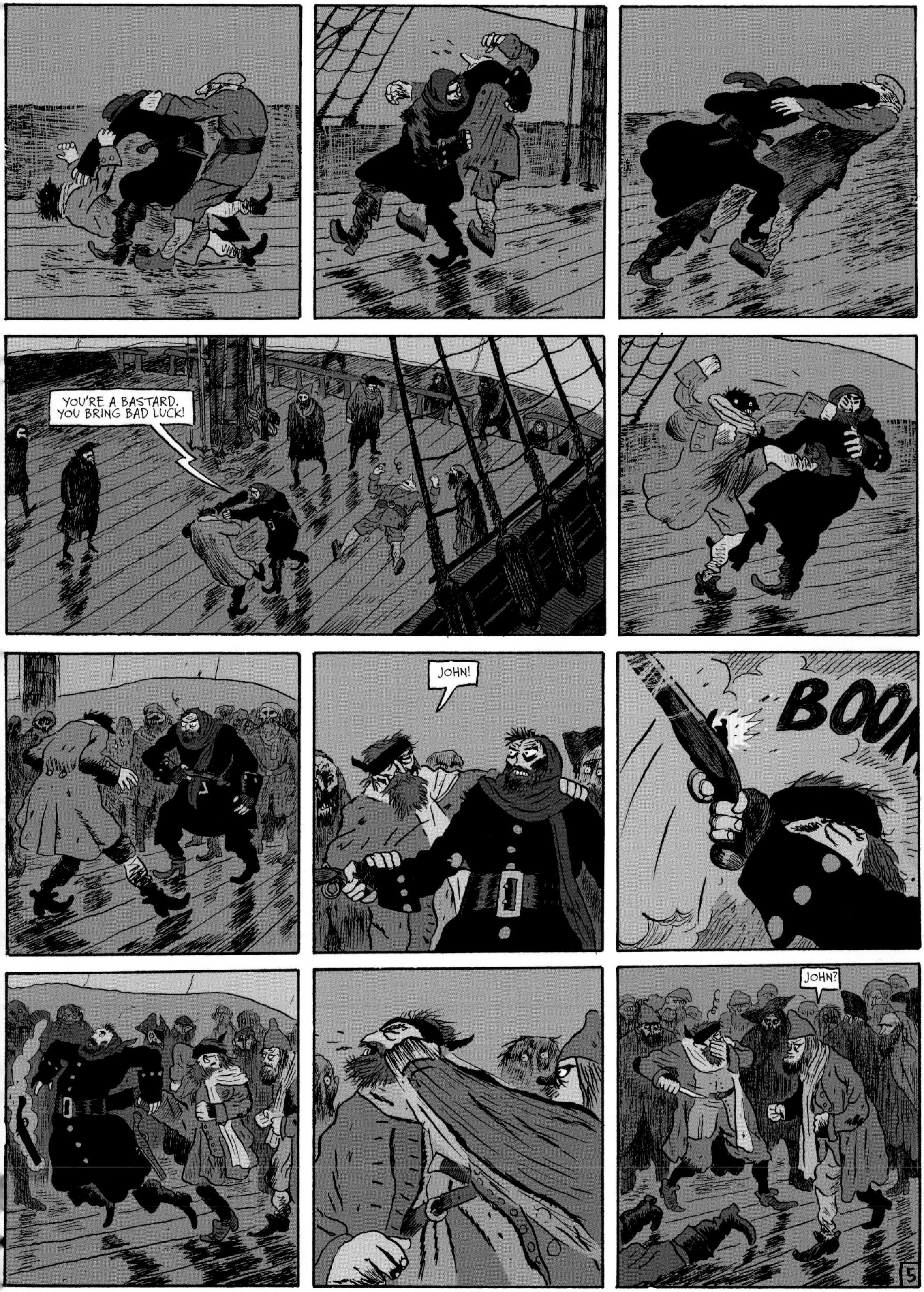
YOU'RE A BASTARD.
YOU BRING BAD LUCK!
JOHN!
BOOM
JOHN?

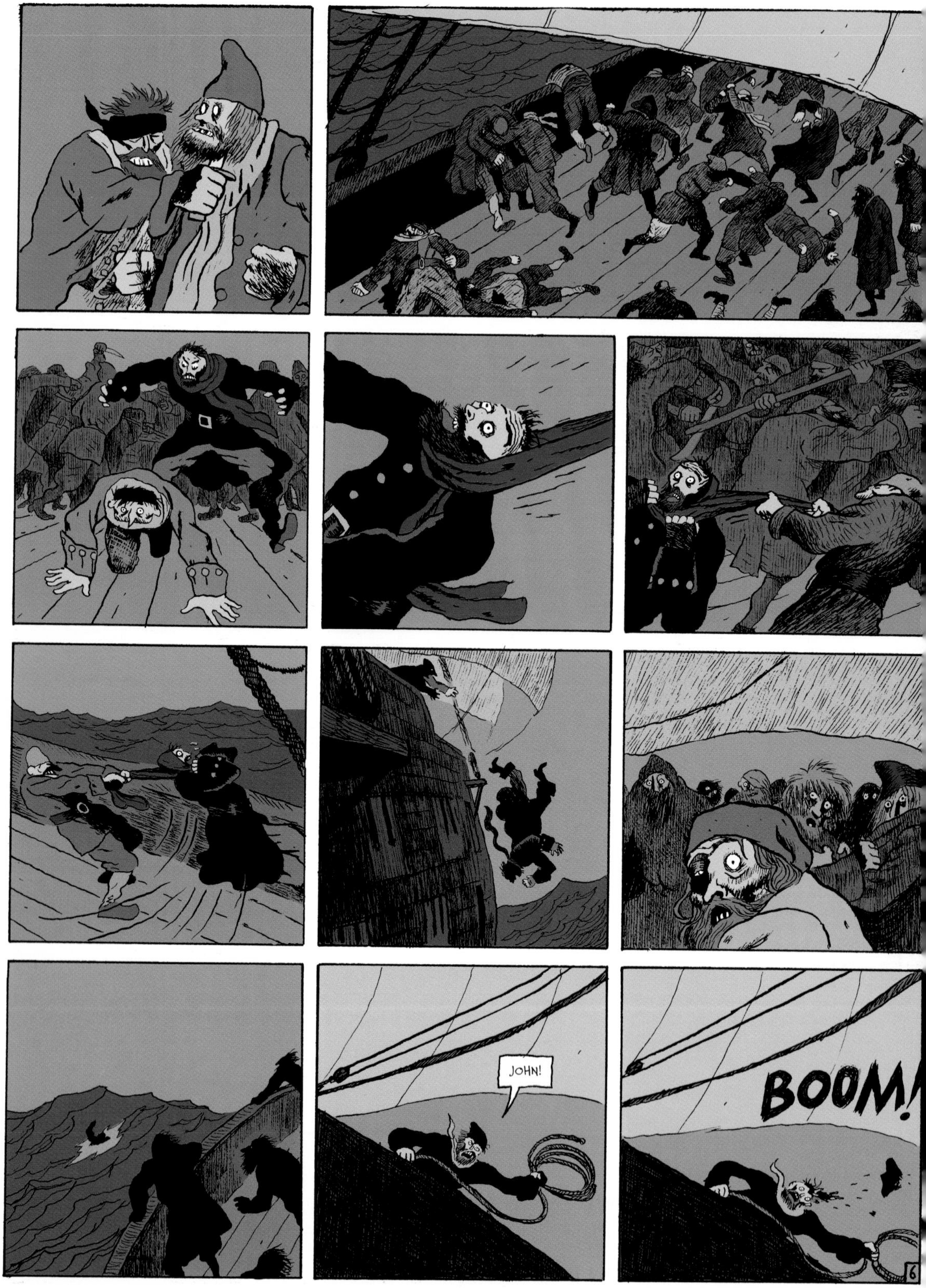
JOHN!
BOOM!
6

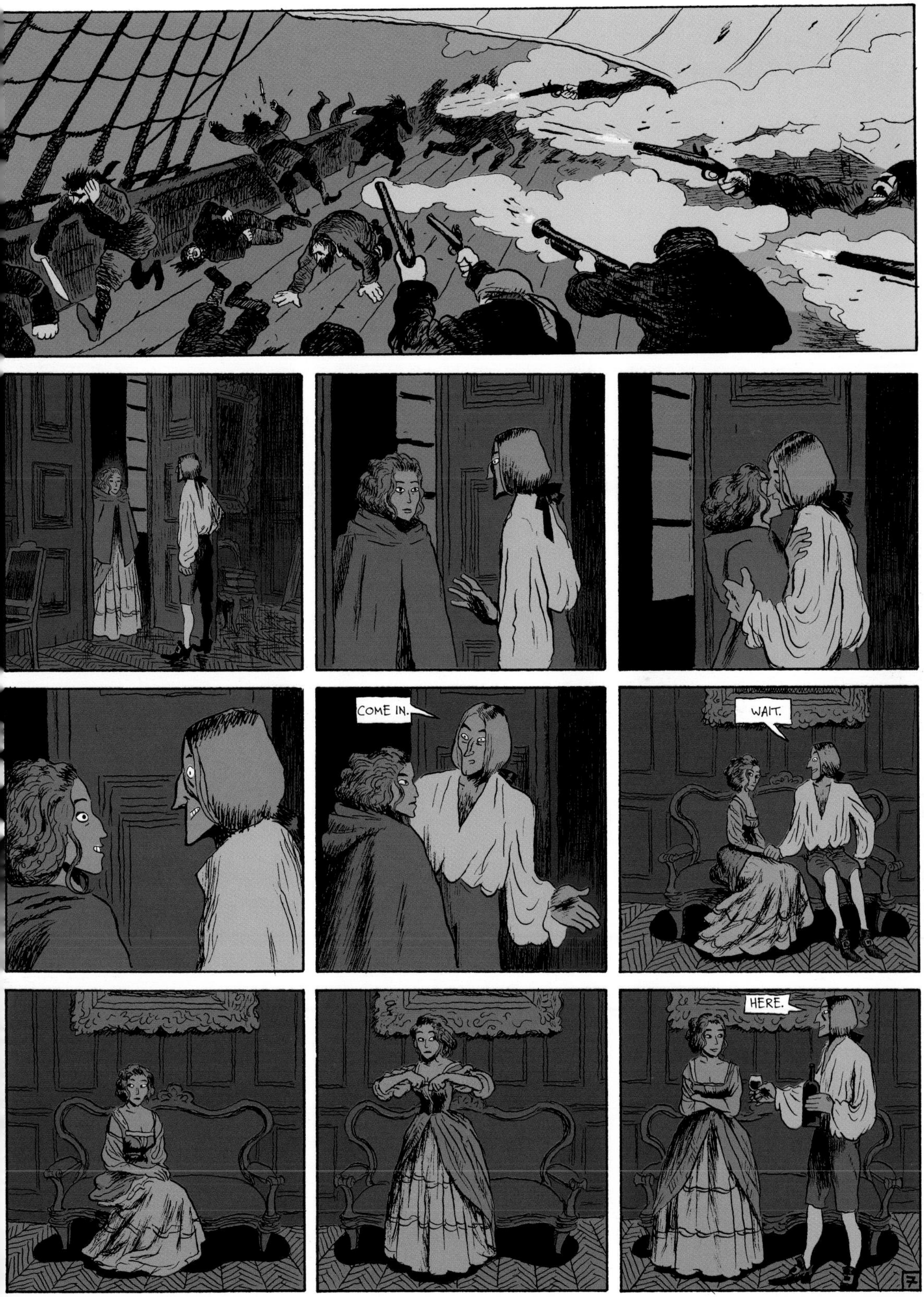
COME IN.
WAIT.
HERE.

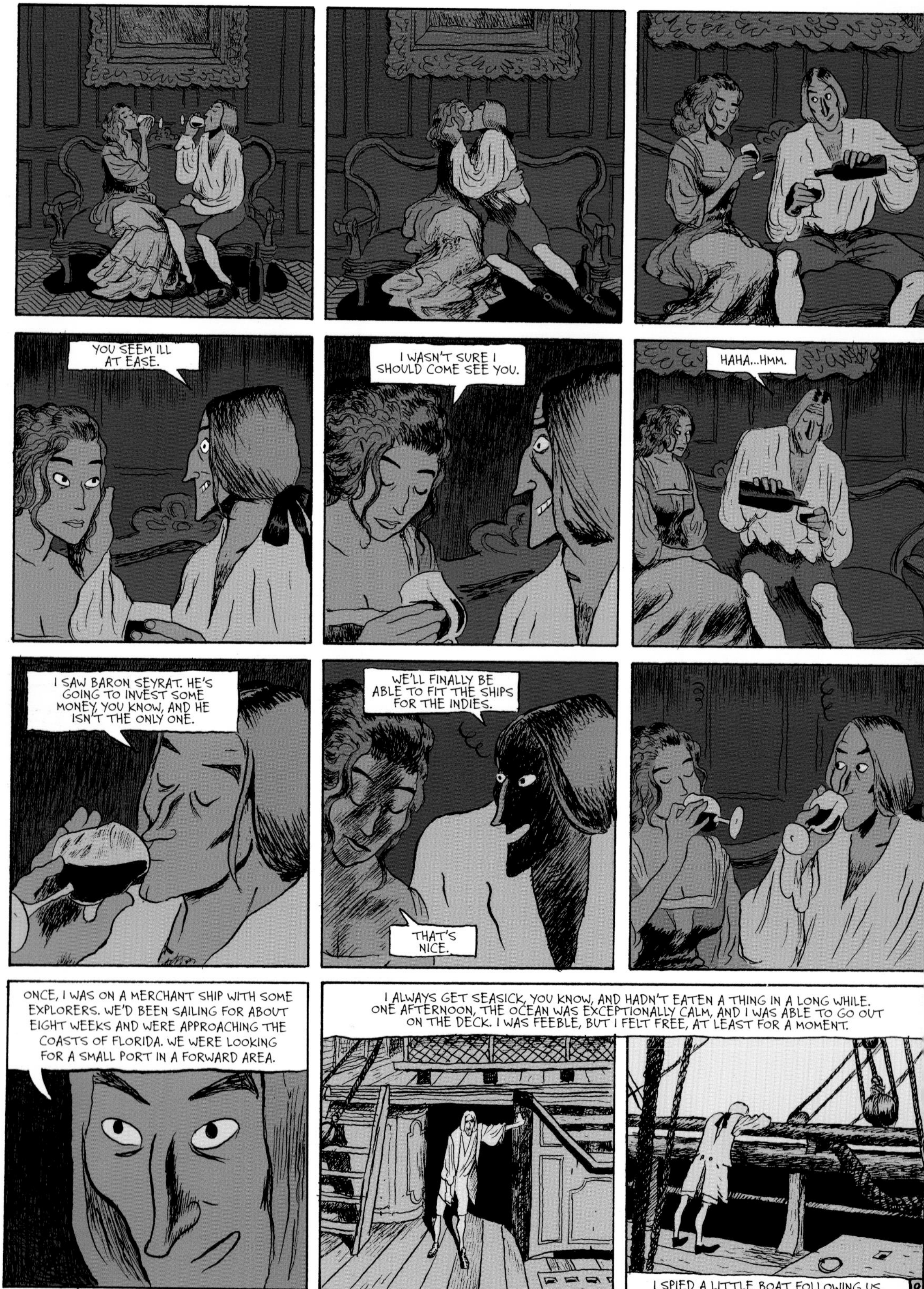

YOU SEEM ILL AT EASE.
I WASN'T SURE I SHOULD COME SEE YOU.
HAHA...HMM.
I SAW BARON SEYRAT. HE'S GOING TO INVEST SOME MONEY, YOU KNOW, AND HE ISN'T THE ONLY ONE.
WE'LL FINALLY BE ABLE TO FIT THE SHIPS FOR THE INDIES.
THAT'S NICE.
ONCE, I WAS ON A MERCHANT SHIP WITH SOME EXPLORERS. WE'D BEEN SAILING FOR ABOUT EIGHT WEEKS AND WERE APPROACHING THE COASTS OF FLORIDA. WE WERE LOOKING FOR A SMALL PORT IN A FORWARD AREA.
I ALWAYS GET SEASICK, YOU KNOW, AND HADN'T EATEN A THING IN A LONG WHILE. ONE AFTERNOON, THE OCEAN WAS EXCEPTIONALLY CALM, AND I WAS ABLE TO GO OUT ON THE DECK. I WAS FEEBLE, BUT I FELT FREE, AT LEAST FOR A MOMENT.
I SPIED A LITTLE BOAT FOLLOWING US.

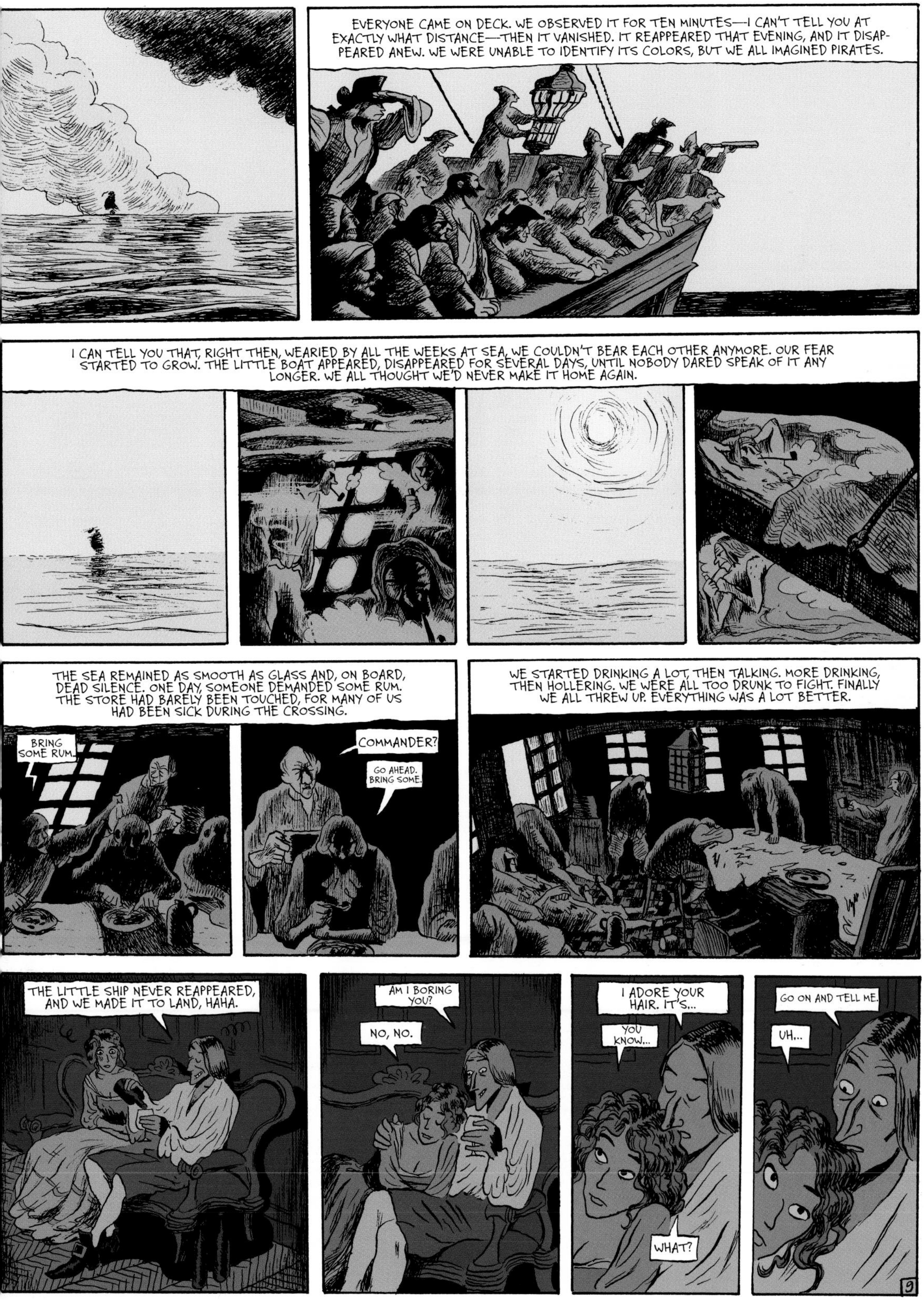
EVERYONE CAME ON DECK. WE OBSERVED IT FOR TEN MINUTES—I CAN'T TELL YOU AT EXACTLY WHAT DISTANCE—THEN IT VANISHED. IT REAPPEARED THAT EVENING, AND IT DISAPPEARED ANEW. WE WERE UNABLE TO IDENTIFY ITS COLORS, BUT WE ALL IMAGINED PIRATES.
I CAN TELL YOU THAT, RIGHT THEN, WEARIED BY ALL THE WEEKS AT SEA, WE COULDN'T BEAR EACH OTHER ANYMORE. OUR FEAR STARTED TO GROW. THE LITTLE BOAT APPEARED, DISAPPEARED FOR SEVERAL DAYS, UNTIL NOBODY DARED SPEAK OF IT ANY LONGER. WE ALL THOUGHT WE'D NEVER MAKE IT HOME AGAIN.
THE SEA REMAINED AS SMOOTH AS GLASS AND, ON BOARD, DEAD SILENCE. ONE DAY, SOMEONE DEMANDED SOME RUM. THE STORE HAD BARELY BEEN TOUCHED, FOR MANY OF US HAD BEEN SICK DURING THE CROSSING.
BRING SOME RUM.
COMMANDER?
GO AHEAD. BRING SOME.
WE STARTED DRINKING A LOT, THEN TALKING. MORE DRINKING, THEN HOLLERING. WE WERE ALL TOO DRUNK TO FIGHT. FINALLY WE ALL THREW UP. EVERYTHING WAS A LOT BETTER.
THE LITTLE SHIP NEVER REAPPEARED, AND WE MADE IT TO LAND, HAHA.
AM I BORING YOU?
NO, NO.
I ADORE YOUR HAIR. IT'S...
YOU KNOW...
WHAT?
GO ON AND TELL ME.
UH...

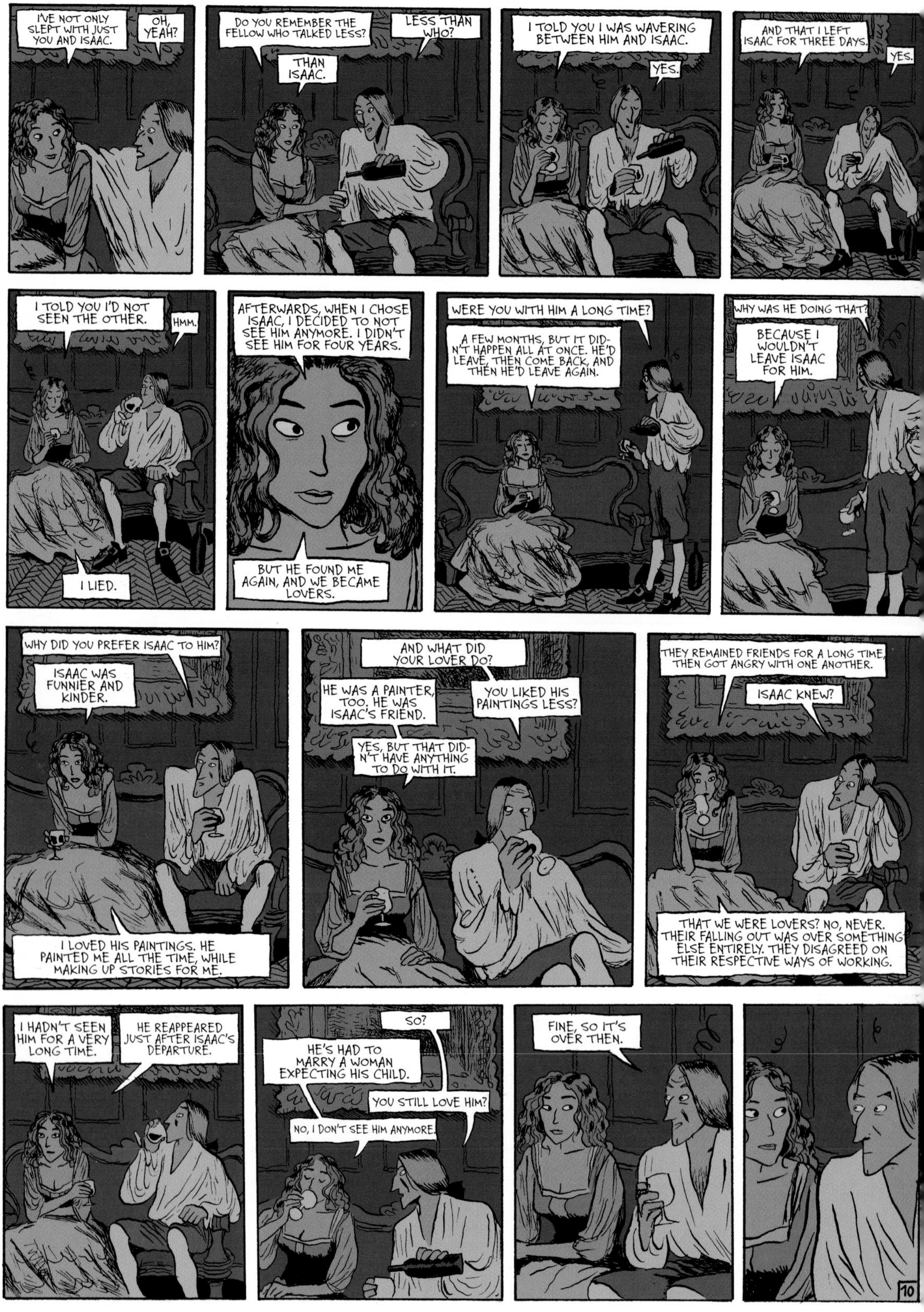

I'VE NOT ONLY SLEPT WITH JUST YOU AND ISAAC.
OH, YEAH?
DO YOU REMEMBER THE FELLOW WHO TALKED LESS?
LESS THAN WHO?
THAN ISAAC.
I TOLD YOU I WAS WAVERING BETWEEN HIM AND ISAAC.
YES.
AND THAT I LEFT ISAAC FOR THREE DAYS.
YES.
I TOLD YOU I'D NOT SEEN THE OTHER.
HMM.
I LIED.
AFTERWARDS, WHEN I CHOSE ISAAC, I DECIDED TO NOT SEE HIM ANYMORE. I DIDN'T SEE HIM FOR FOUR YEARS.
BUT HE FOUND ME AGAIN, AND WE BECAME LOVERS.
WERE YOU WITH HIM A LONG TIME?
A FEW MONTHS, BUT IT DIDN'T HAPPEN ALL AT ONCE. HE'D LEAVE, THEN COME BACK, AND THEN HE'D LEAVE AGAIN.
WHY WAS HE DOING THAT?
BECAUSE I WOULDN'T LEAVE ISAAC FOR HIM.
WHY DID YOU PREFER ISAAC TO HIM?
ISAAC WAS FUNNIER AND KINDER.
I LOVED HIS PAINTINGS. HE PAINTED ME ALL THE TIME, WHILE MAKING UP STORIES FOR ME.
AND WHAT DID YOUR LOVER DO?
HE WAS A PAINTER, TOO. HE WAS ISAAC'S FRIEND.
YOU LIKED HIS PAINTINGS LESS?
YES, BUT THAT DIDN'T HAVE ANYTHING TO DO WITH IT.
THEY REMAINED FRIENDS FOR A LONG TIME, THEN GOT ANGRY WITH ONE ANOTHER.
ISAAC KNEW?
THAT WE WERE LOVERS? NO, NEVER. THEIR FALLING OUT WAS OVER SOMETHING ELSE ENTIRELY. THEY DISAGREED ON THEIR RESPECTIVE WAYS OF WORKING.
I HADN'T SEEN HIM FOR A VERY LONG TIME.
HE REAPPEARED JUST AFTER ISAAC'S DEPARTURE.
SO?
HE'S HAD TO MARRY A WOMAN EXPECTING HIS CHILD.
YOU STILL LOVE HIM?
NO, I DON'T SEE HIM ANYMORE.
FINE, SO IT'S OVER THEN.
10

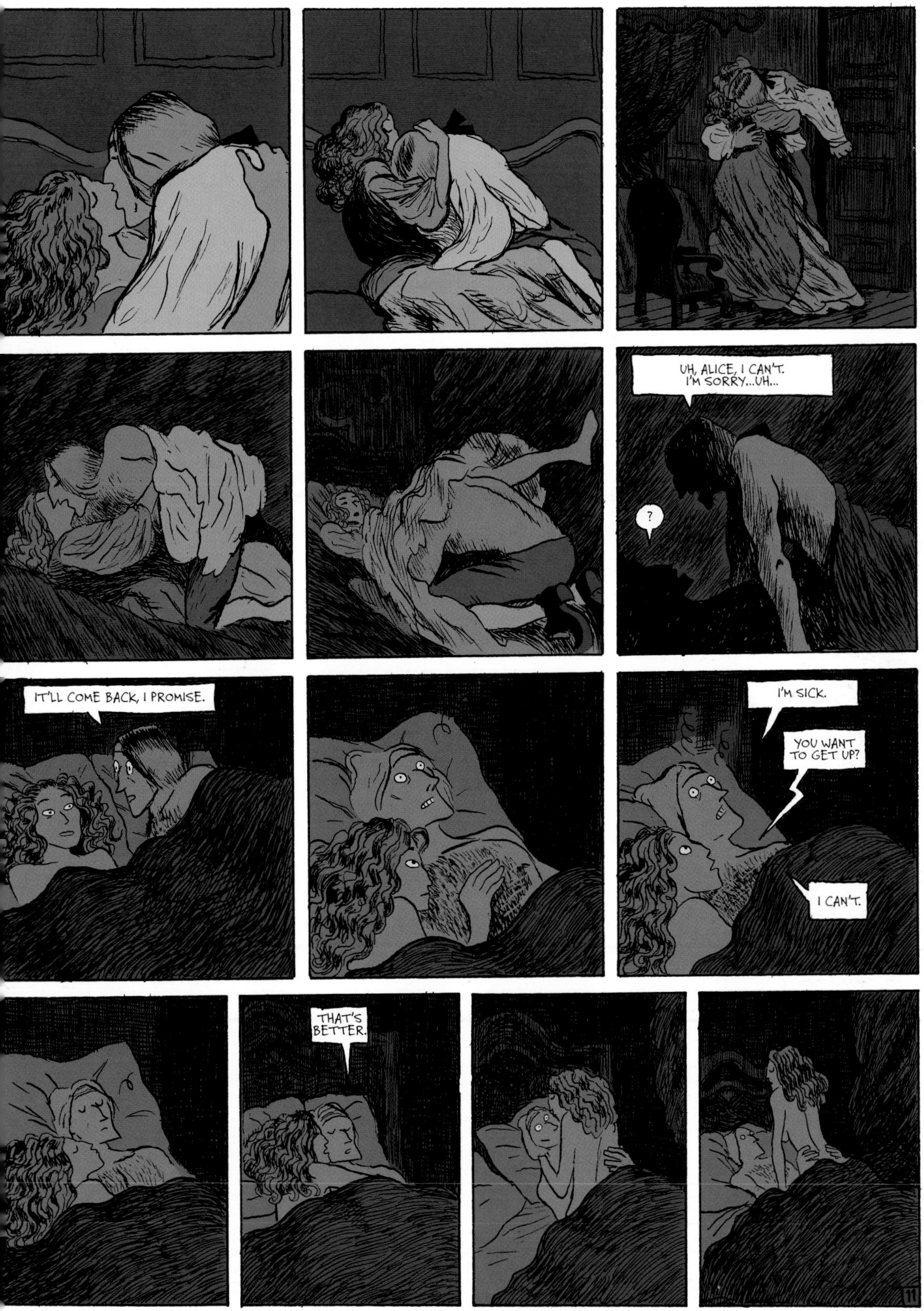
UH, ALICE, I CAN'T. I'M SORRY...UH...
?
IT'LL COME BACK, I PROMISE.
I'M SICK.
YOU WANT TO GET UP?
I CAN'T.
THAT'S BETTER.

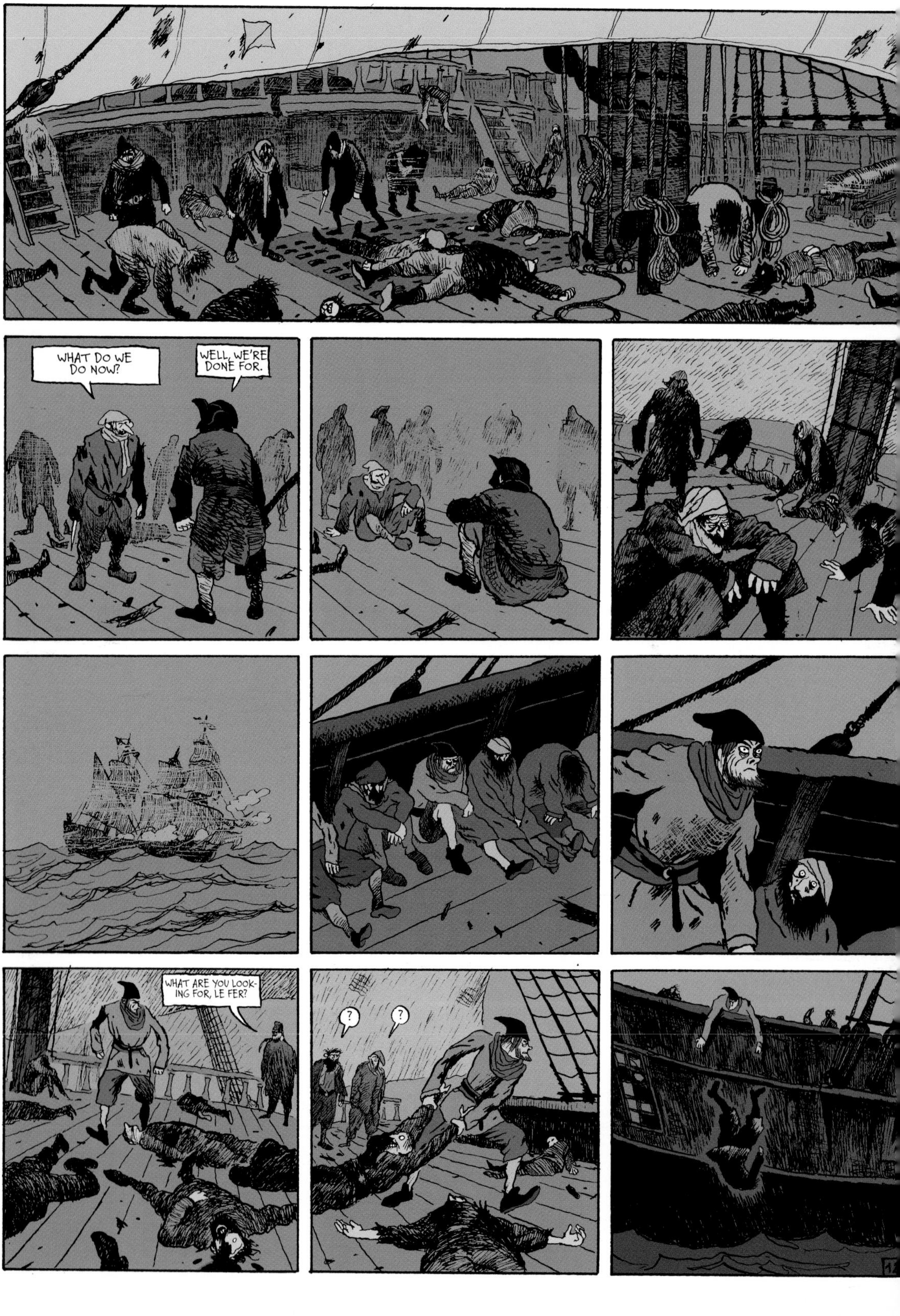
WHAT DO WE DO NOW?
WELL, WE'RE DONE FOR.
WHAT ARE YOU LOOKING FOR, LE FER?
?
?

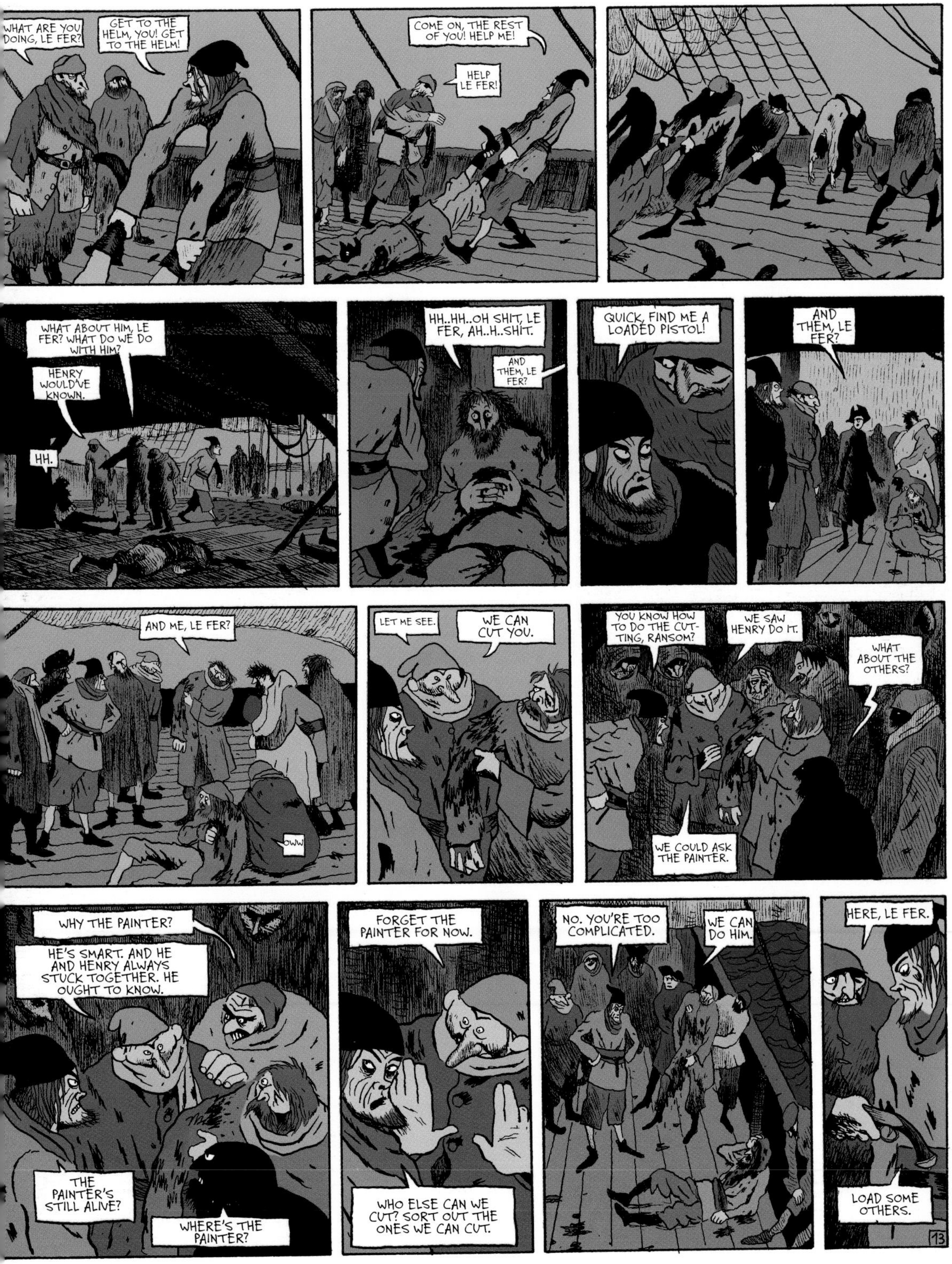
WHAT ARE YOU DOING, LE FER?
GET TO THE HELM, YOU! GET TO THE HELM!
COME ON, THE REST OF YOU! HELP ME!
HELP LE FER!
WHAT ABOUT HIM, LE FER? WHAT DO WE DO WITH HIM?
HENRY WOULD'VE KNOWN.
HH.
HH..HH..OH SHIT, LE FER, AH..H..SHIT.
AND THEM, LE FER?
QUICK, FIND ME A LOADED PISTOL!
AND THEM, LE FER?
AND ME, LE FER?
OWW
LET ME SEE.
WE CAN CUT YOU.
YOU KNOW HOW TO DO THE CUTTING, RANSOM?
WE SAW HENRY DO IT.
WHAT ABOUT THE OTHERS?
WE COULD ASK THE PAINTER.
WHY THE PAINTER?
HE'S SMART. AND HE AND HENRY ALWAYS STUCK TOGETHER. HE OUGHT TO KNOW.
THE PAINTER'S STILL ALIVE?
WHERE'S THE PAINTER?
FORGET THE PAINTER FOR NOW.
WHO ELSE CAN WE CUT? SORT OUT THE ONES WE CAN CUT.
NO. YOU'RE TOO COMPLICATED.
WE CAN DO HIM.
HERE, LE FER.
LOAD SOME OTHERS.

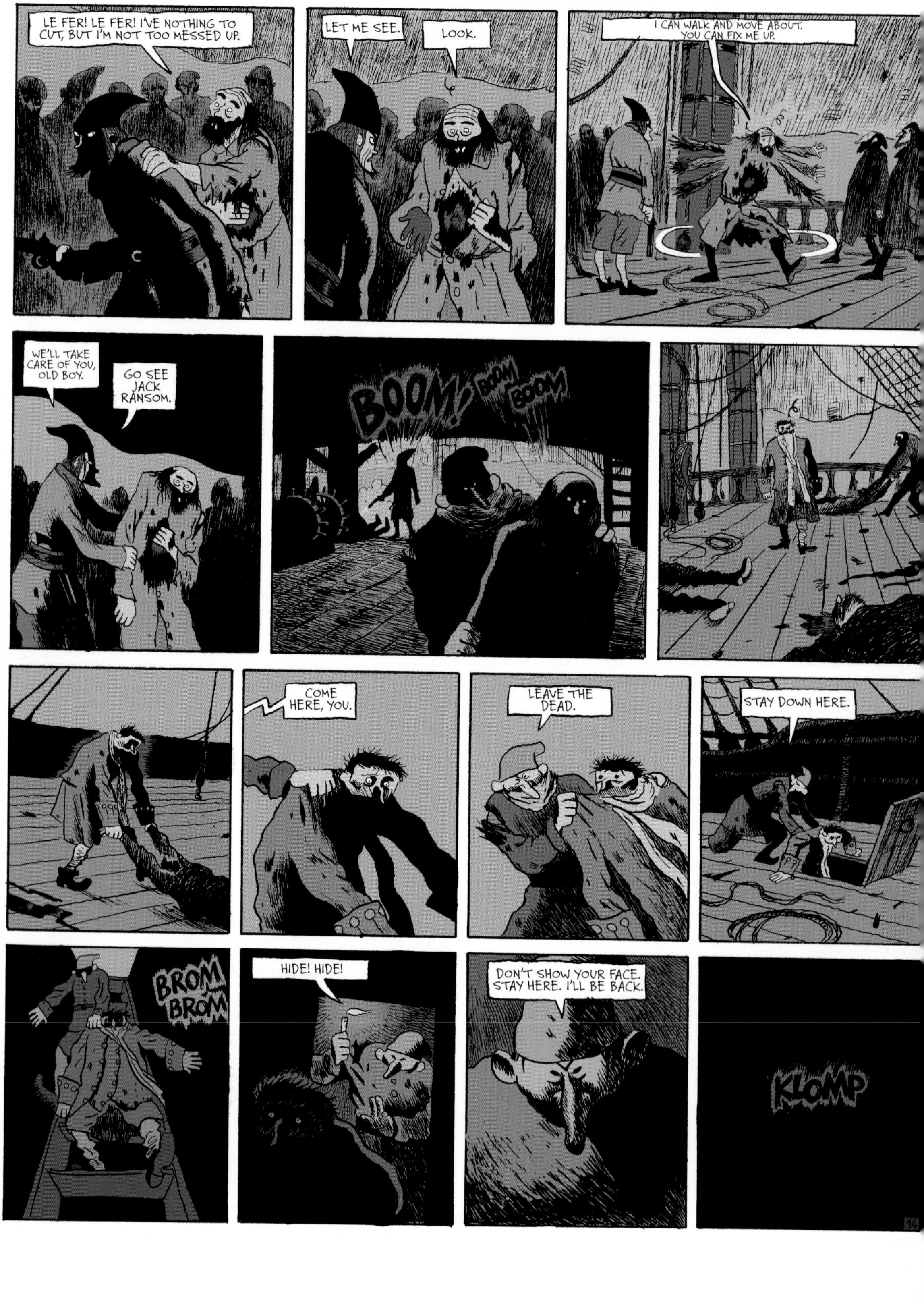
LE FER! LE FER! I'VE NOTHING TO CUT, BUT I'M NOT TOO MESSED UP.
LET ME SEE.
LOOK.
I CAN WALK AND MOVE ABOUT. YOU CAN FIX ME UP.
WE'LL TAKE CARE OF YOU, OLD BOY.
GO SEE JACK RANSOM.
BOOM! BOOM BOOM
COME HERE, YOU.
LEAVE THE DEAD.
STAY DOWN HERE.
BROM BROM
HIDE! HIDE!
DON'T SHOW YOUR FACE. STAY HERE. I'LL BE BACK.
KLOMP

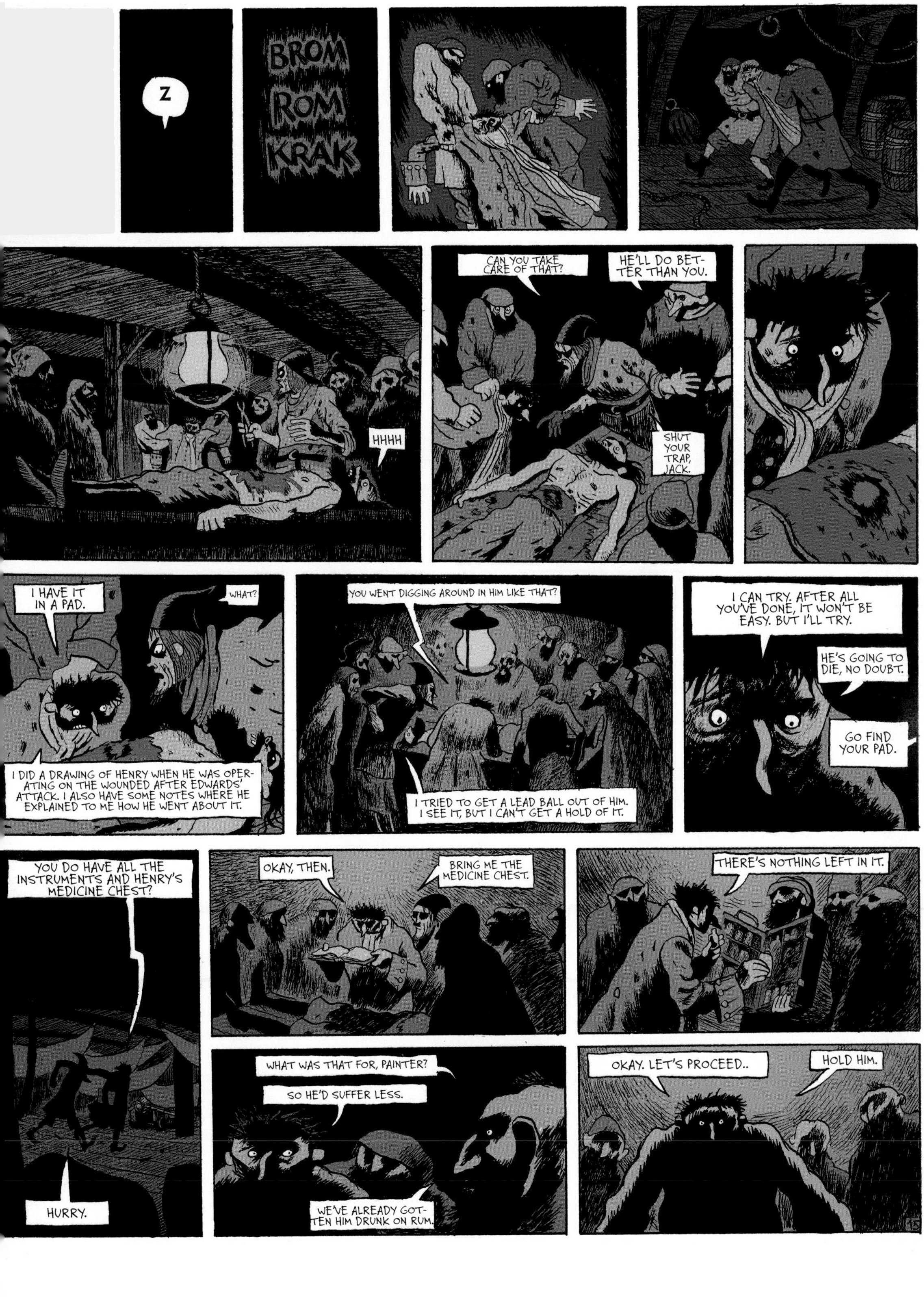

Z
BROM
ROM
KRAK
HHHH
CAN YOU TAKE CARE OF THAT?
HE'LL DO BETTER THAN YOU.
SHUT YOUR TRAP, JACK.
I HAVE IT IN A PAD.
WHAT?
I DID A DRAWING OF HENRY WHEN HE WAS OPERATING ON THE WOUNDED AFTER EDWARDS' ATTACK. I ALSO HAVE SOME NOTES WHERE HE EXPLAINED TO ME HOW HE WENT ABOUT IT.
YOU WENT DIGGING AROUND IN HIM LIKE THAT?
I TRIED TO GET A LEAD BALL OUT OF HIM. I SEE IT, BUT I CAN'T GET A HOLD OF IT.
I CAN TRY. AFTER ALL YOU'VE DONE, IT WON'T BE EASY. BUT I'LL TRY.
HE'S GOING TO DIE, NO DOUBT.
GO FIND YOUR PAD.
YOU DO HAVE ALL THE INSTRUMENTS AND HENRY'S MEDICINE CHEST?
HURRY.
OKAY, THEN.
BRING ME THE MEDICINE CHEST.
THERE'S NOTHING LEFT IN IT.
WHAT WAS THAT FOR, PAINTER?
SO HE'D SUFFER LESS.
WE'VE ALREADY GOTTEN HIM DRUNK ON RUM.
OKAY. LET'S PROCEED..
HOLD HIM.

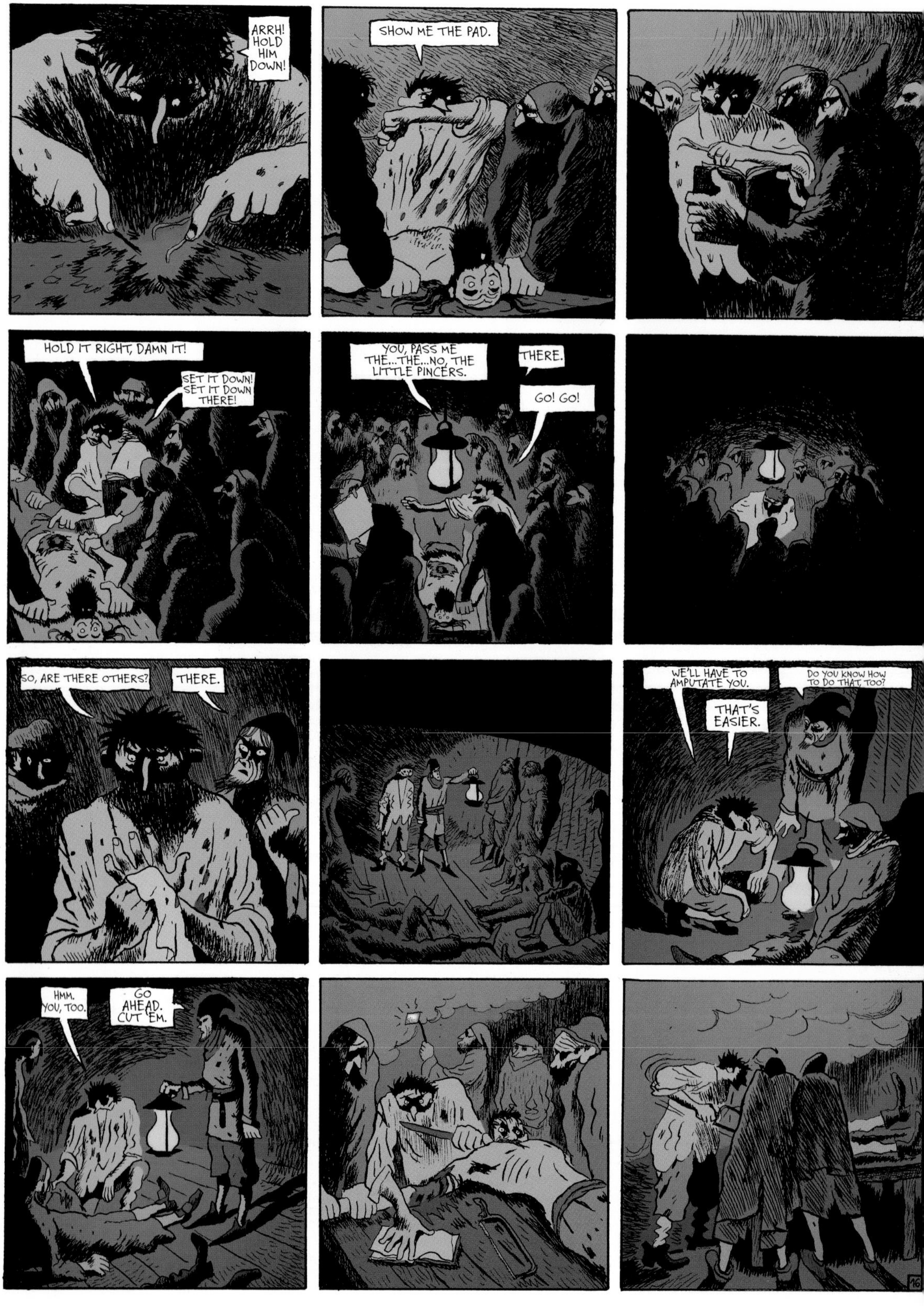

ARRH! HOLD HIM DOWN!
SHOW ME THE PAD.
HOLD IT RIGHT, DAMN IT!
SET IT DOWN! SET IT DOWN THERE!
YOU, PASS ME THE... THE... NO, THE LITTLE PINCERS.
THERE.
GO! GO!
SO, ARE THERE OTHERS?
THERE.
WE'LL HAVE TO AMPUTATE YOU.
THAT'S EASIER.
DO YOU KNOW HOW TO DO THAT, TOO?
HMM. YOU, TOO.
GO AHEAD. CUT 'EM.

WAAAAAHAAHA

TCHHH!

WHO'S IN CHARGE NOW?

LE FER.

LE FER.

LE FER.

LE FER.

LE FER.

WHAT DO YOU WE DO WITH THE ONES YOU FIXED UP?

GIVE THEM A DOUBLE RATIO TONIGHT, EXCEPT FOR THOSE WOUNDED IN THEIR BELLY.

GET BACK TO YOUR HOLE.

DOUBLE RATION FOR THE PAINTER.

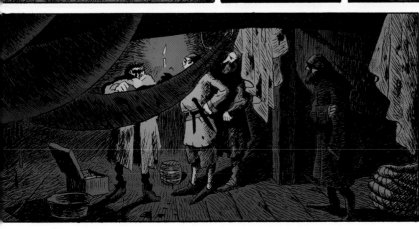

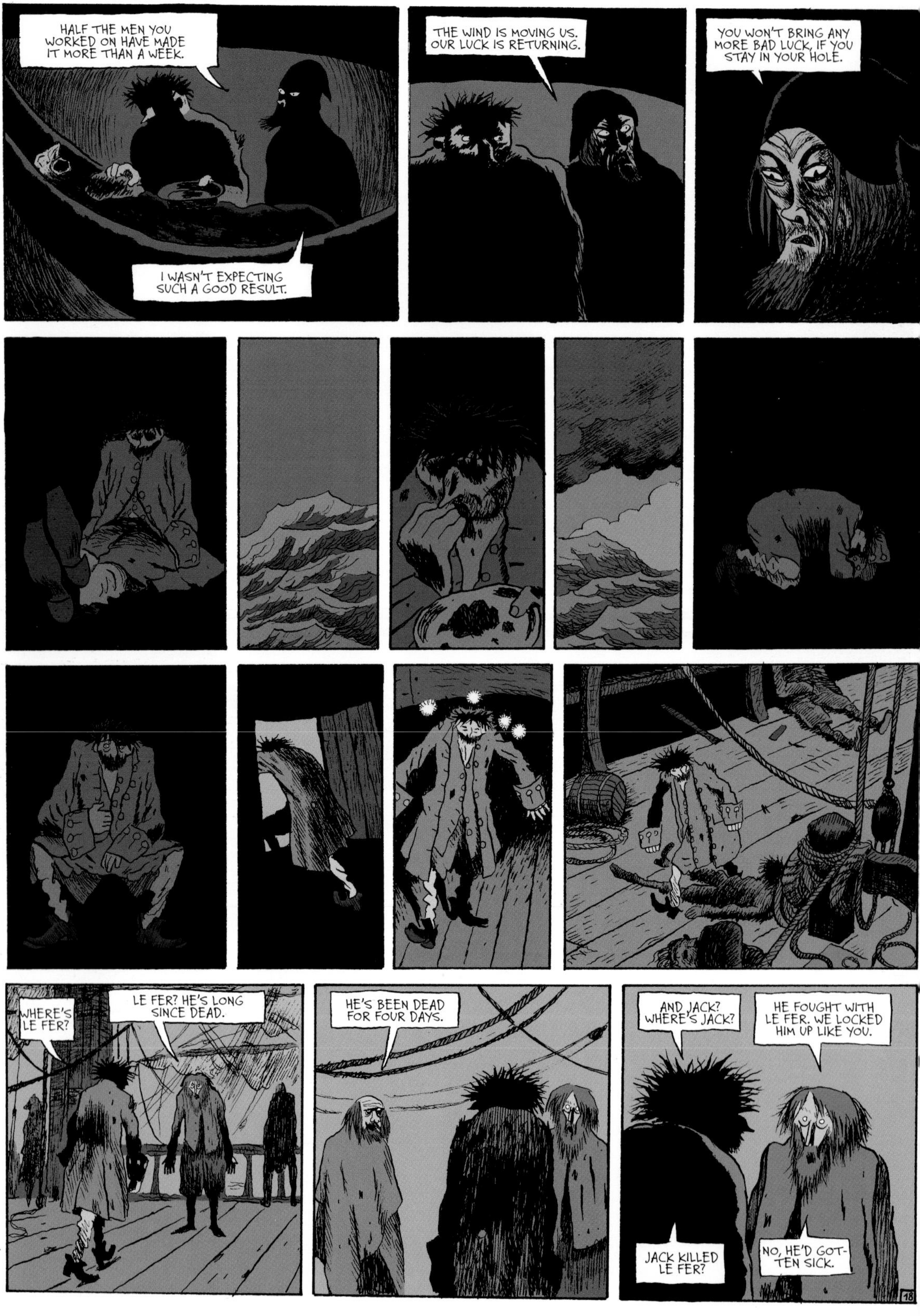
HALF THE MEN YOU WORKED ON HAVE MADE IT MORE THAN A WEEK.
I WASN'T EXPECTING SUCH A GOOD RESULT.
THE WIND IS MOVING US. OUR LUCK IS RETURNING.
YOU WON'T BRING ANY MORE BAD LUCK, IF YOU STAY IN YOUR HOLE.
WHERE'S LE FER?
LE FER? HE'S LONG SINCE DEAD.
HE'S BEEN DEAD FOR FOUR DAYS.
AND JACK? WHERE'S JACK?
HE FOUGHT WITH LE FER. WE LOCKED HIM UP LIKE YOU.
JACK KILLED LE FER?
NO, HE'D GOT-TEN SICK.

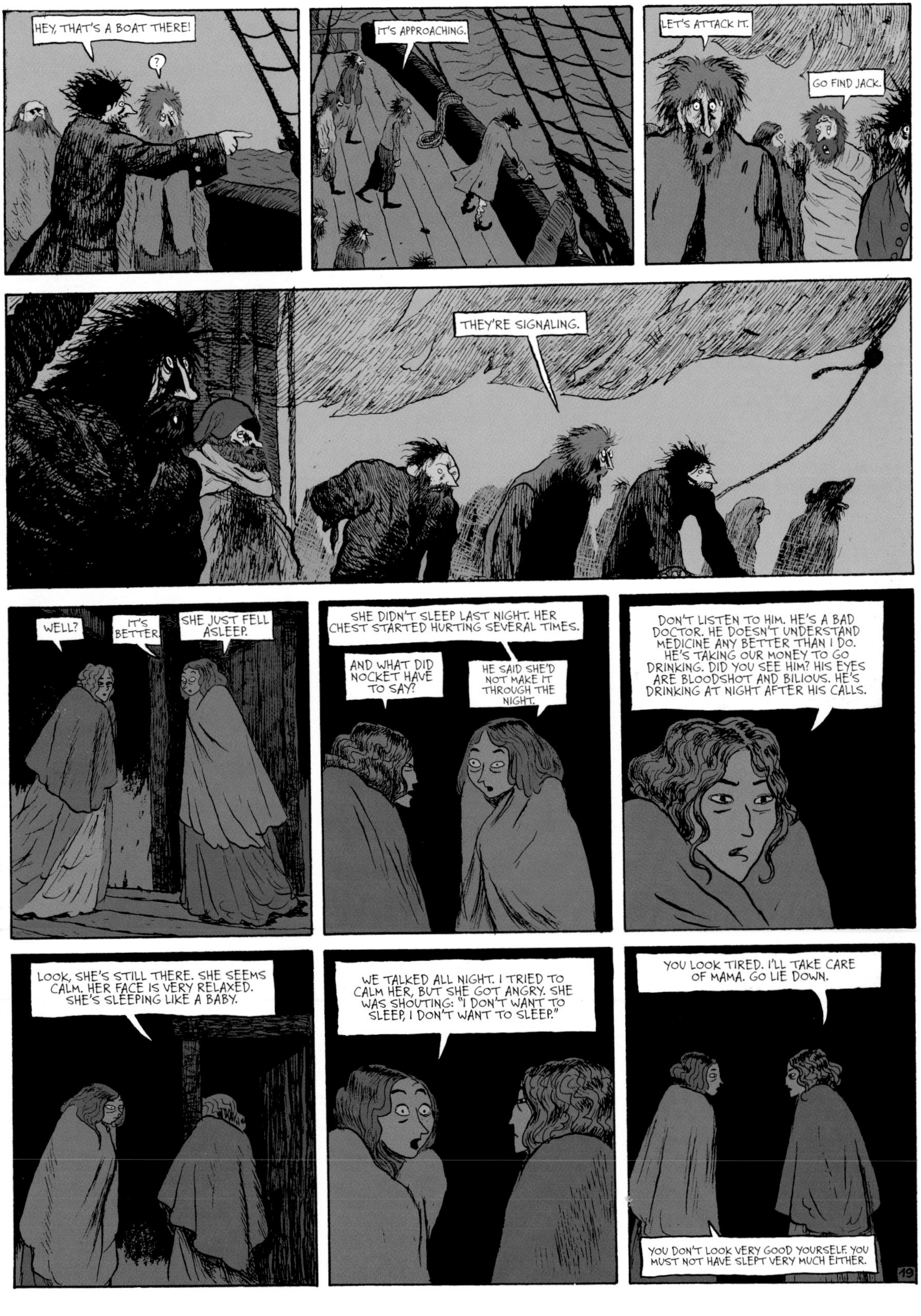
HEY, THAT'S A BOAT THERE!
?
IT'S APPROACHING.
LET'S ATTACK IT.
GO FIND JACK.
THEY'RE SIGNALING.
WELL?
IT'S BETTER.
SHE JUST FELL ASLEEP.
SHE DIDN'T SLEEP LAST NIGHT. HER CHEST STARTED HURTING SEVERAL TIMES.
AND WHAT DID NOCKET HAVE TO SAY?
HE SAID SHE'D NOT MAKE IT THROUGH THE NIGHT.
DON'T LISTEN TO HIM. HE'S A BAD DOCTOR. HE DOESN'T UNDERSTAND MEDICINE ANY BETTER THAN I DO. HE'S TAKING OUR MONEY TO GO DRINKING. DID YOU SEE HIM? HIS EYES ARE BLOODSHOT AND BILIOUS. HE'S DRINKING AT NIGHT AFTER HIS CALLS.
LOOK, SHE'S STILL THERE. SHE SEEMS CALM. HER FACE IS VERY RELAXED. SHE'S SLEEPING LIKE A BABY.
WE TALKED ALL NIGHT. I TRIED TO CALM HER, BUT SHE GOT ANGRY. SHE WAS SHOUTING: "I DON'T WANT TO SLEEP, I DON'T WANT TO SLEEP."
YOU LOOK TIRED. I'LL TAKE CARE OF MAMA. GO LIE DOWN.
YOU DON'T LOOK VERY GOOD YOURSELF. YOU MUST NOT HAVE SLEPT VERY MUCH EITHER.

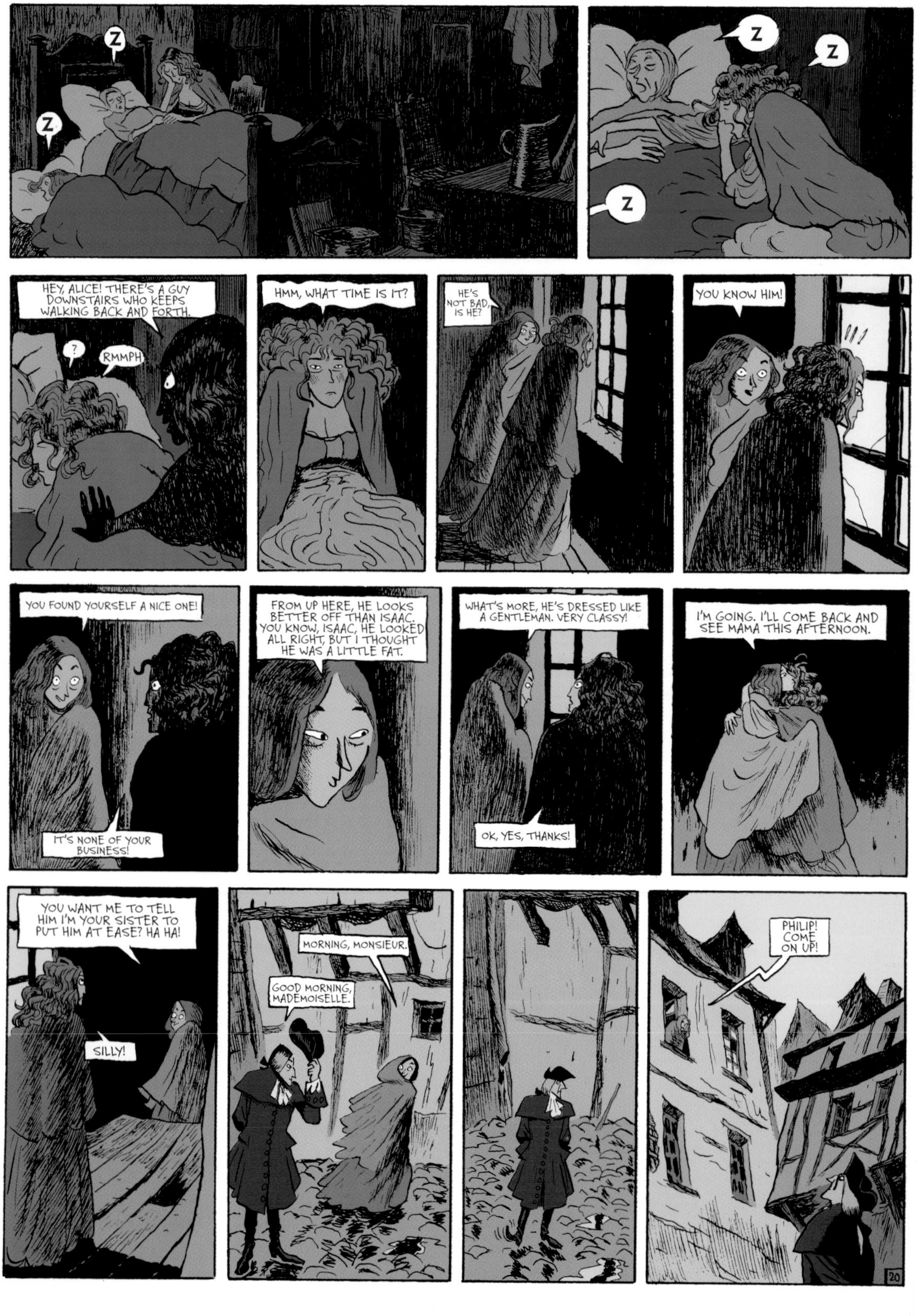
Z
Z
Z
Z
Z
HEY, ALICE! THERE'S A GUY DOWNSTAIRS WHO KEEPS WALKING BACK AND FORTH.
?
RMMPH
HMM, WHAT TIME IS IT?
HE'S NOT BAD, IS HE?
YOU KNOW HIM!
YOU FOUND YOURSELF A NICE ONE!
IT'S NONE OF YOUR BUSINESS!
FROM UP HERE, HE LOOKS BETTER OFF THAN ISAAC. YOU KNOW, ISAAC, HE LOOKED ALL RIGHT, BUT I THOUGHT HE WAS A LITTLE FAT.
WHAT'S MORE, HE'S DRESSED LIKE A GENTLEMAN. VERY CLASSY!
OK, YES, THANKS!
I'M GOING. I'LL COME BACK AND SEE MAMA THIS AFTERNOON.
YOU WANT ME TO TELL HIM I'M YOUR SISTER TO PUT HIM AT EASE? HA HA!
SILLY!
MORNING, MONSIEUR.
GOOD MORNING, MADEMOISELLE.
PHILIP! COME ON UP!

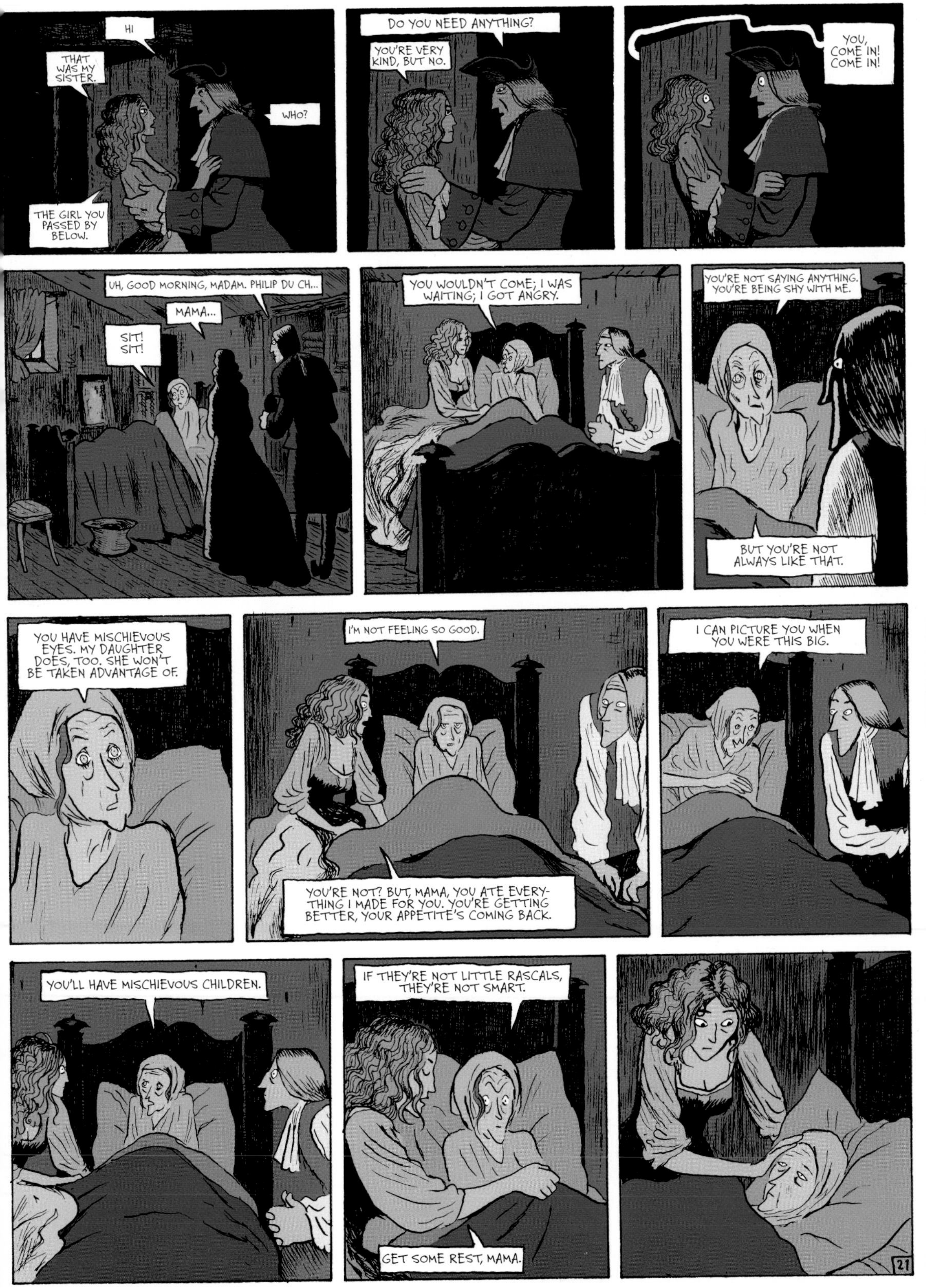
HI
THAT WAS MY SISTER.
WHO?
THE GIRL YOU PASSED BY BELOW.
DO YOU NEED ANYTHING?
YOU'RE VERY KIND, BUT NO.
YOU, COME IN! COME IN!
UH, GOOD MORNING, MADAM. PHILIP DU CH...
MAMA...
SIT! SIT!
YOU WOULDN'T COME; I WAS WAITING; I GOT ANGRY.
YOU'RE NOT SAYING ANYTHING. YOU'RE BEING SHY WITH ME.
BUT YOU'RE NOT ALWAYS LIKE THAT.
YOU HAVE MISCHIEVOUS EYES. MY DAUGHTER DOES, TOO. SHE WON'T BE TAKEN ADVANTAGE OF.
I'M NOT FEELING SO GOOD.
YOU'RE NOT? BUT, MAMA, YOU ATE EVERY-THING I MADE FOR YOU. YOU'RE GETTING BETTER, YOUR APPETITE'S COMING BACK.
I CAN PICTURE YOU WHEN YOU WERE THIS BIG.
YOU'LL HAVE MISCHIEVOUS CHILDREN.
IF THEY'RE NOT LITTLE RASCALS, THEY'RE NOT SMART.
GET SOME REST, MAMA.
21

HEY!

WE'RE HERE TO WASH YOU.

HERE. EAT UP.

BROUNCH BROMF MNURF

YOU'RE LOOKING ROSIER THAN YOUR MATES, YOU ARE. YOU SLEPT FOR TWO DAYS, YOU OLD BASTARD.

BOM

WAHAHAHA!

I'M DALLOUS, AND YOU'RE ON MY SHIP.

YOUR NAME IS I-SAAC SO-FER. IT'S WRITTEN HERE.

SHOFERR, ZHATCH IT.

A FELLOW WITH BIG EARS REFUSED TO BE PARTED FROM IT. HE TOLD ME IT WAS YOURS.

JACK?

I DON'T KNOW HIS NAME, AND I DON'T GIVE A DAMN! HAHAHAHOHOHO!

BUT THERE WERE LOTS OF OTHER PADS.

THIS IS ALL HE HAD.

YOU WERE DAMNED LUCKY TO STUMBLE UPON ME, MISTER SOFER.

I SAW THAT YOU WERE DOING RATHER POORLY. MY PHYSICIAN DIDN'T WANT ME TO BRING YOU ABOARD.

HE THOUGHT YOU'D ALL SPREAD YOUR SICKNESS TO US. I HAD A GREAT DEAL OF TROUBLE FINDING VOLUNTEERS TO BOARD YOUR SHIP.

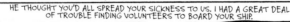

YOU'D SCARCELY SET FOOT ON THE LIFEBOAT WHEN YOU FELL DEAD ASLEEP.

AND THE OTHERS?

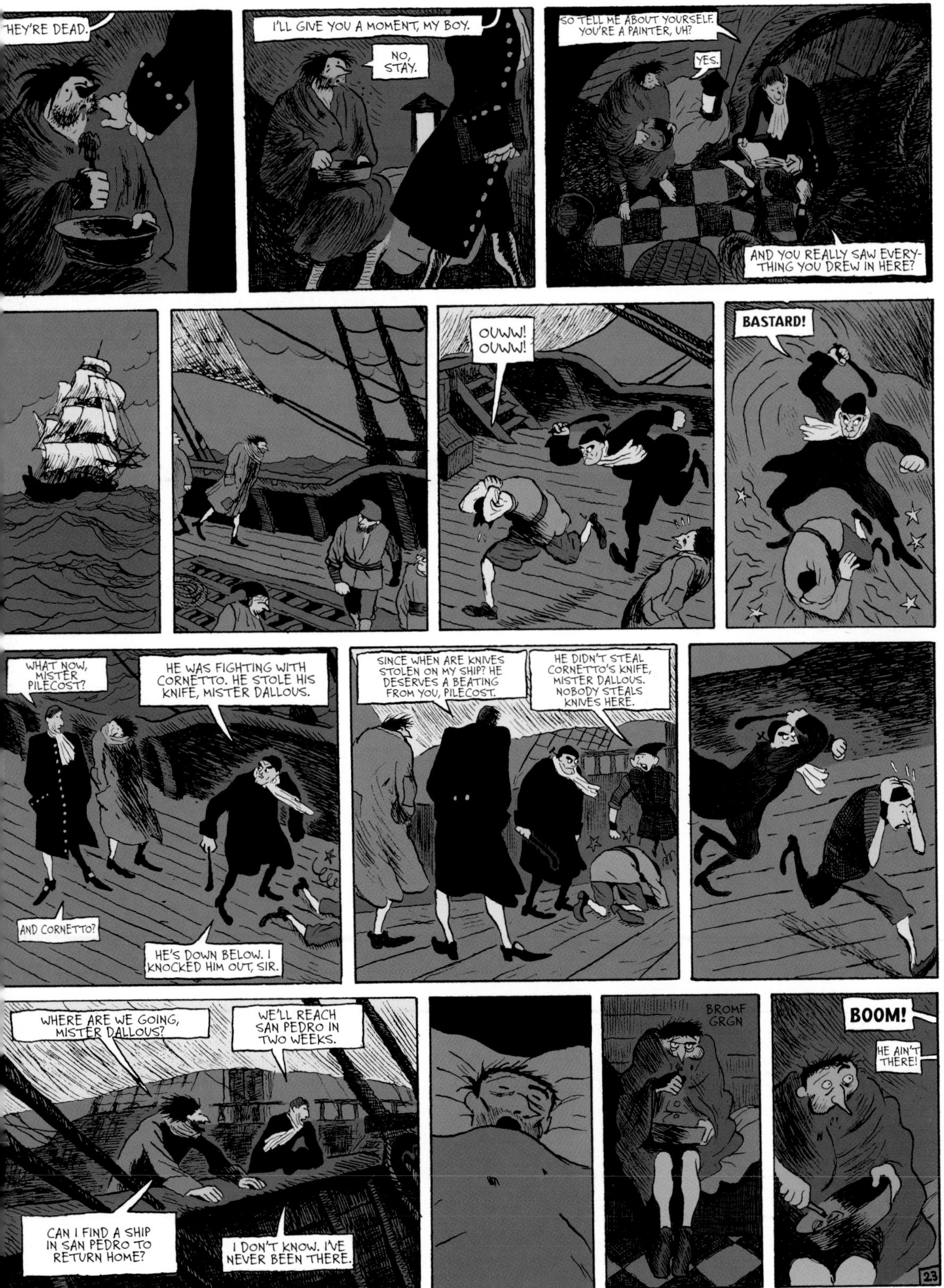

THEY'RE DEAD.
I'LL GIVE YOU A MOMENT, MY BOY.
NO, STAY.
SO TELL ME ABOUT YOURSELF. YOU'RE A PAINTER, UH?
YES.
AND YOU REALLY SAW EVERYTHING YOU DREW IN HERE?
OUWW! OUWW!
BASTARD!
WHAT NOW, MISTER PILECOST?
HE WAS FIGHTING WITH CORNETTO. HE STOLE HIS KNIFE, MISTER DALLOUS.
AND CORNETTO?
HE'S DOWN BELOW. I KNOCKED HIM OUT, SIR.
SINCE WHEN ARE KNIVES STOLEN ON MY SHIP? HE DESERVES A BEATING FROM YOU, PILECOST.
HE DIDN'T STEAL CORNETTO'S KNIFE, MISTER DALLOUS. NOBODY STEALS KNIVES HERE.
WHERE ARE WE GOING, MISTER DALLOUS?
WE'LL REACH SAN PEDRO IN TWO WEEKS.
CAN I FIND A SHIP IN SAN PEDRO TO RETURN HOME?
I DON'T KNOW. I'VE NEVER BEEN THERE.
BROMF GRGN
BOOM!
HE AIN'T THERE!
23

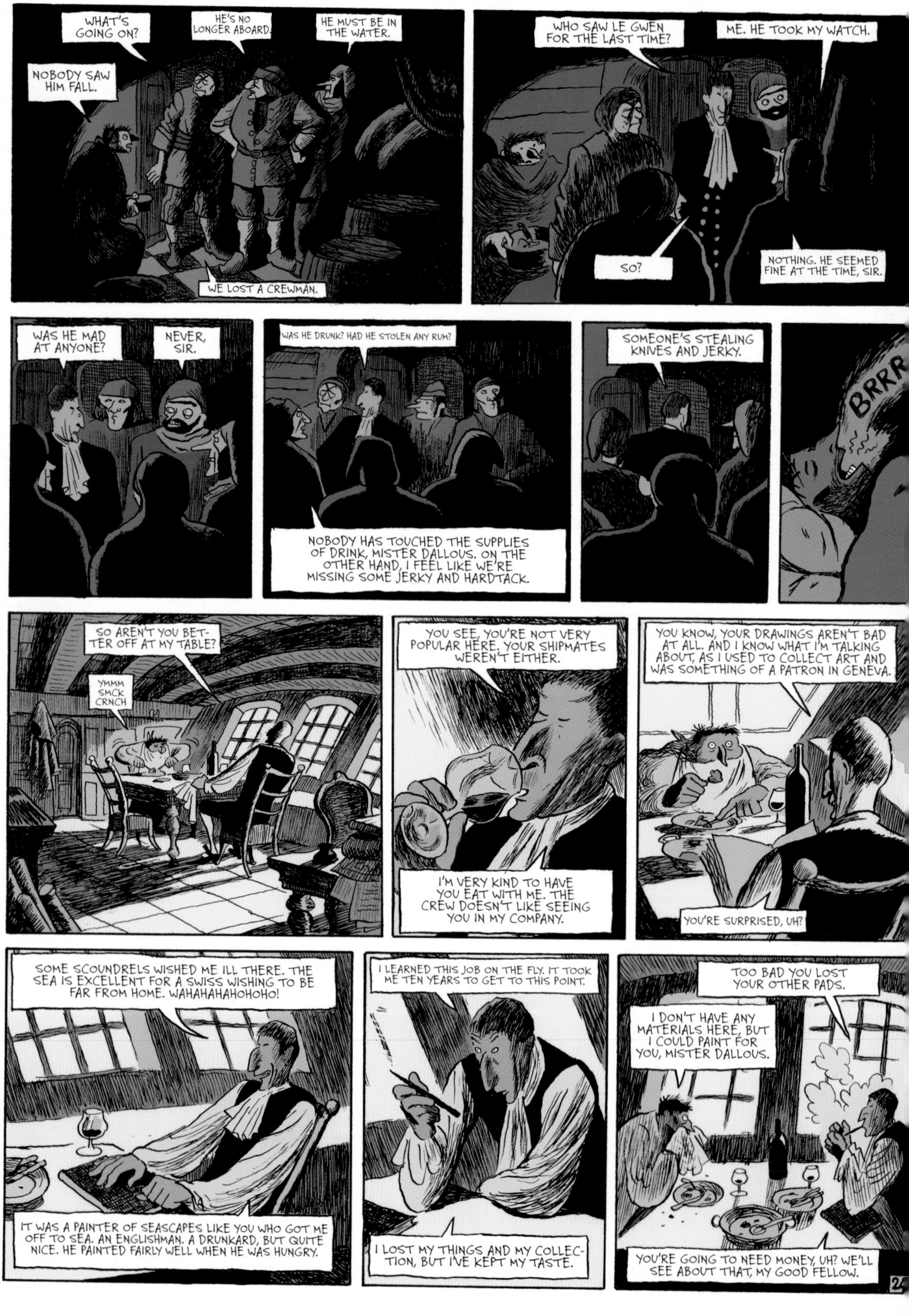

WHAT'S GOING ON?
HE'S NO LONGER ABOARD.
HE MUST BE IN THE WATER.
NOBODY SAW HIM FALL.
WE LOST A CREWMAN.
WHO SAW LE GWEN FOR THE LAST TIME?
ME. HE TOOK MY WATCH.
SO?
NOTHING. HE SEEMED FINE AT THE TIME, SIR.
WAS HE MAD AT ANYONE?
NEVER, SIR.
WAS HE DRUNK? HAD HE STOLEN ANY RUM?
NOBODY HAS TOUCHED THE SUPPLIES OF DRINK, MISTER DALLOUS. ON THE OTHER HAND, I FEEL LIKE WE'RE MISSING SOME JERKY AND HARDTACK.
SOMEONE'S STEALING KNIVES AND JERKY.
BRRR
SO AREN'T YOU BETTER OFF AT MY TABLE?
YMMM SMCK CRNCH
YOU SEE, YOU'RE NOT VERY POPULAR HERE. YOUR SHIPMATES WEREN'T EITHER.
I'M VERY KIND TO HAVE YOU EAT WITH ME. THE CREW DOESN'T LIKE SEEING YOU IN MY COMPANY.
YOU KNOW, YOUR DRAWINGS AREN'T BAD AT ALL. AND I KNOW WHAT I'M TALKING ABOUT, AS I USED TO COLLECT ART AND WAS SOMETHING OF A PATRON IN GENEVA.
YOU'RE SURPRISED, UH?
SOME SCOUNDRELS WISHED ME ILL THERE. THE SEA IS EXCELLENT FOR A SWISS WISHING TO BE FAR FROM HOME. WAHAHAHAHOHOHO!
IT WAS A PAINTER OF SEASCAPES LIKE YOU WHO GOT ME OFF TO SEA. AN ENGLISHMAN. A DRUNKARD, BUT QUITE NICE. HE PAINTED FAIRLY WELL WHEN HE WAS HUNGRY.
I LEARNED THIS JOB ON THE FLY. IT TOOK ME TEN YEARS TO GET TO THIS POINT.
I LOST MY THINGS AND MY COLLECTION, BUT I'VE KEPT MY TASTE.
TOO BAD YOU LOST YOUR OTHER PADS.
I DON'T HAVE ANY MATERIALS HERE, BUT I COULD PAINT FOR YOU, MISTER DALLOUS.
YOU'RE GOING TO NEED MONEY, UH? WE'LL SEE ABOUT THAT, MY GOOD FELLOW.

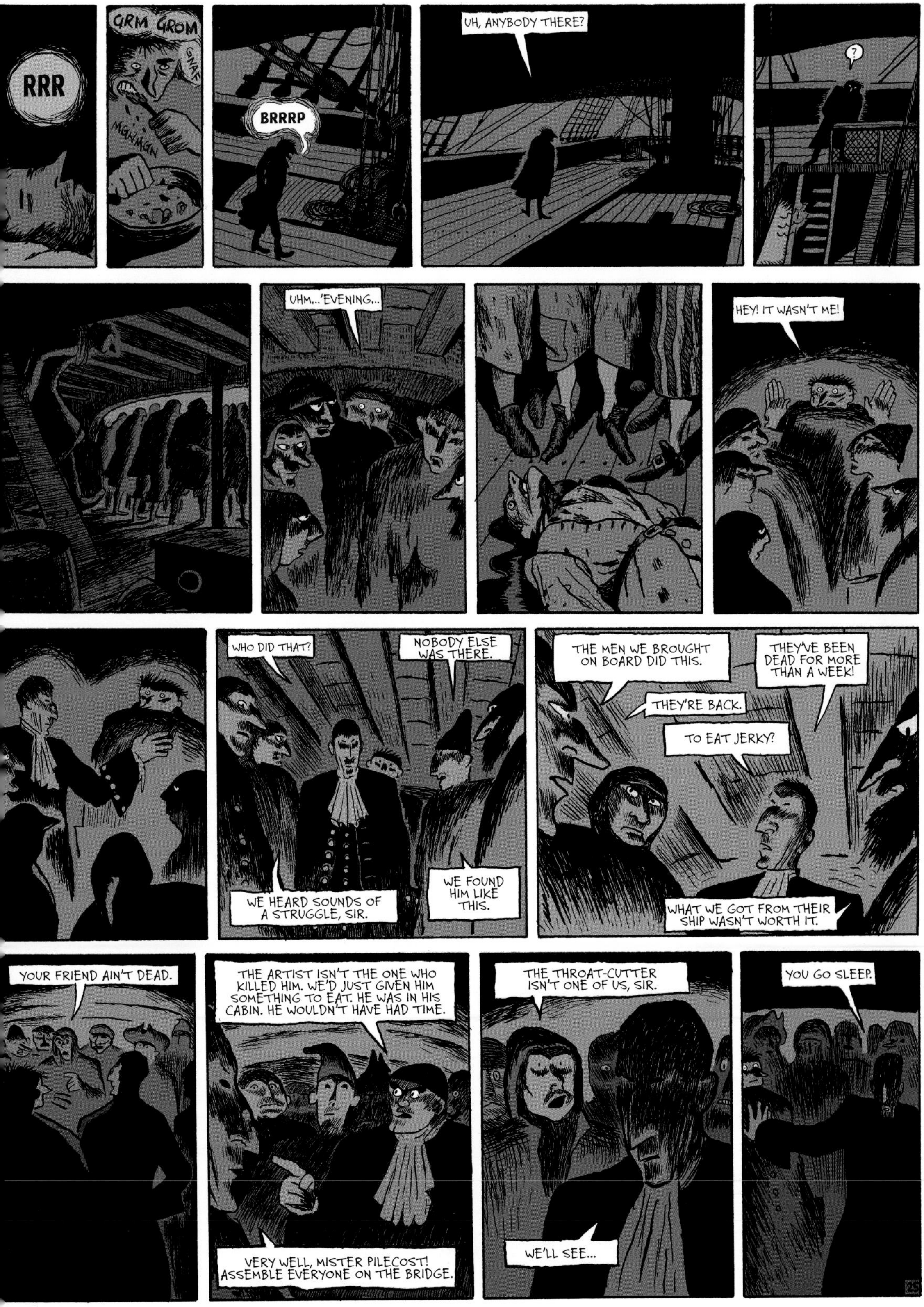
RRR
GRM GROM
GNAF
MGNMGN
BRRRP
UH, ANYBODY THERE?
?
UHM...'EVENING...
HEY! IT WASN'T ME!
WHO DID THAT?
NOBODY ELSE WAS THERE.
WE HEARD SOUNDS OF A STRUGGLE, SIR.
WE FOUND HIM LIKE THIS.
THE MEN WE BROUGHT ON BOARD DID THIS.
THEY'VE BEEN DEAD FOR MORE THAN A WEEK!
THEY'RE BACK.
TO EAT JERKY?
WHAT WE GOT FROM THEIR SHIP WASN'T WORTH IT.
YOUR FRIEND AIN'T DEAD.
THE ARTIST ISN'T THE ONE WHO KILLED HIM. WE'D JUST GIVEN HIM SOMETHING TO EAT. HE WAS IN HIS CABIN. HE WOULDN'T HAVE HAD TIME.
VERY WELL, MISTER PILECOST! ASSEMBLE EVERYONE ON THE BRIDGE.
THE THROAT-CUTTER ISN'T ONE OF US, SIR.
WE'LL SEE...
YOU GO SLEEP.

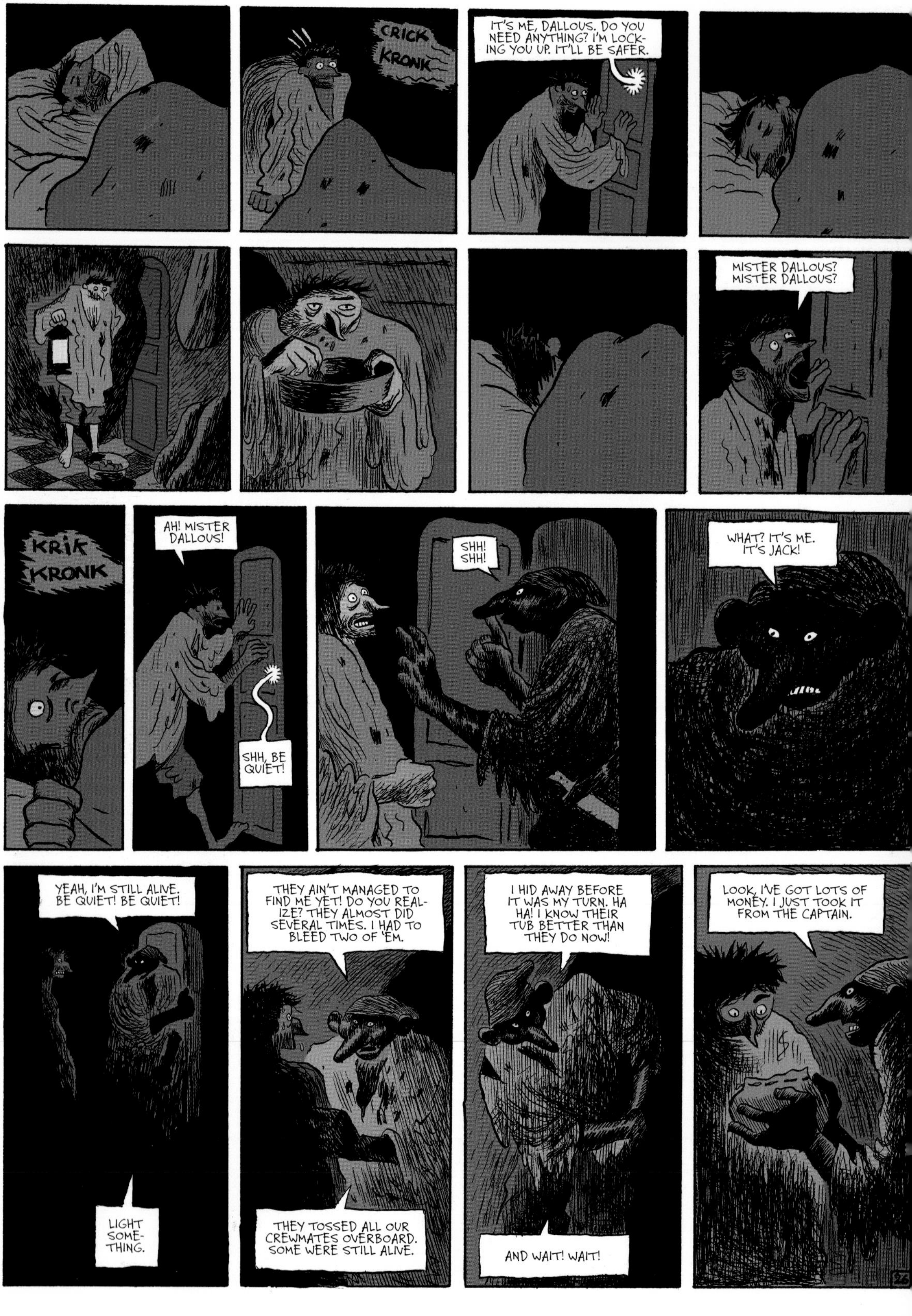
CRICK
KRONK
IT'S ME, DALLOUS. DO YOU NEED ANYTHING? I'M LOCKING YOU UP. IT'LL BE SAFER.
MISTER DALLOUS? MISTER DALLOUS?
KRIK
KRONK
AH! MISTER DALLOUS!
SHH, BE QUIET!
SHH! SHH!
WHAT? IT'S ME. IT'S JACK!
YEAH, I'M STILL ALIVE. BE QUIET! BE QUIET!
LIGHT SOMETHING.
THEY AIN'T MANAGED TO FIND ME YET! DO YOU REALIZE? THEY ALMOST DID SEVERAL TIMES. I HAD TO BLEED TWO OF 'EM.
THEY TOSSED ALL OUR CREWMATES OVERBOARD. SOME WERE STILL ALIVE.
I HID AWAY BEFORE IT WAS MY TURN. HA HA! I KNOW THEIR TUB BETTER THAN THEY DO NOW!
AND WAIT! WAIT!
LOOK, I'VE GOT LOTS OF MONEY. I JUST TOOK IT FROM THE CAPTAIN.

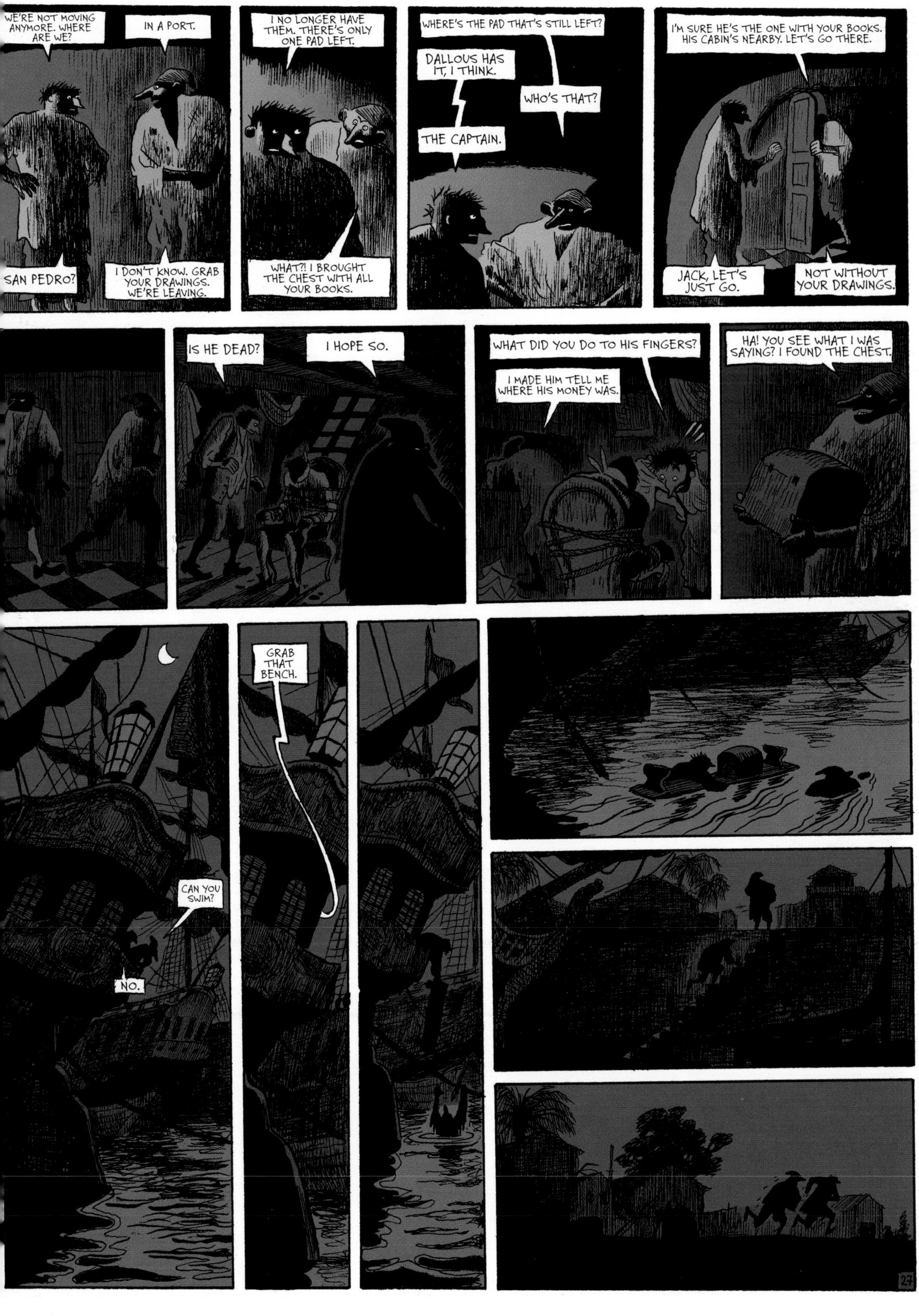
WE'RE NOT MOVING ANYMORE. WHERE ARE WE?
IN A PORT.
SAN PEDRO?
I DON'T KNOW. GRAB YOUR DRAWINGS. WE'RE LEAVING.
I NO LONGER HAVE THEM. THERE'S ONLY ONE PAD LEFT.
WHAT?! I BROUGHT THE CHEST WITH ALL YOUR BOOKS.
WHERE'S THE PAD THAT'S STILL LEFT?
DALLOUS HAS IT, I THINK.
WHO'S THAT?
THE CAPTAIN.
I'M SURE HE'S THE ONE WITH YOUR BOOKS. HIS CABIN'S NEARBY. LET'S GO THERE.
JACK, LET'S JUST GO.
NOT WITHOUT YOUR DRAWINGS.
IS HE DEAD?
I HOPE SO.
WHAT DID YOU DO TO HIS FINGERS?
I MADE HIM TELL ME WHERE HIS MONEY WAS.
HA! YOU SEE WHAT I WAS SAYING? I FOUND THE CHEST.
CAN YOU SWIM?
NO.
GRAB THAT BENCH.

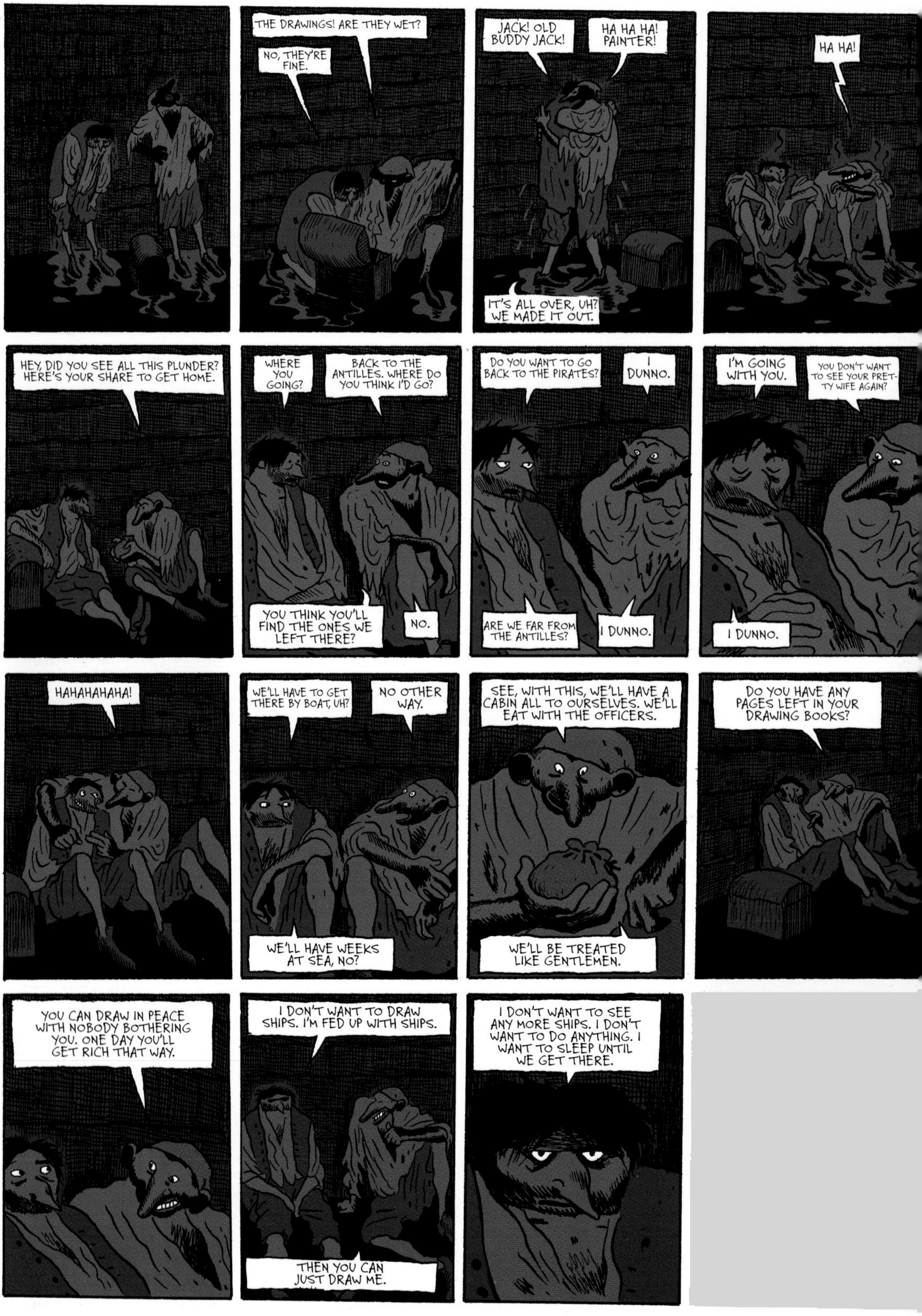
THE DRAWINGS! ARE THEY WET?
NO, THEY'RE FINE.
JACK! OLD BUDDY JACK!
HA HA HA! PAINTER!
IT'S ALL OVER, UH? WE MADE IT OUT.
HA HA!
HEY, DID YOU SEE ALL THIS PLUNDER? HERE'S YOUR SHARE TO GET HOME.
WHERE YOU GOING?
BACK TO THE ANTILLES. WHERE DO YOU THINK I'D GO?
YOU THINK YOU'LL FIND THE ONES WE LEFT THERE?
NO.
DO YOU WANT TO GO BACK TO THE PIRATES?
I DUNNO.
ARE WE FAR FROM THE ANTILLES?
I DUNNO.
I'M GOING WITH YOU.
YOU DON'T WANT TO SEE YOUR PRETTY WIFE AGAIN?
I DUNNO.
HAHAHAHAHA!
WE'LL HAVE TO GET THERE BY BOAT, UH?
NO OTHER WAY.
WE'LL HAVE WEEKS AT SEA, NO?
SEE, WITH THIS, WE'LL HAVE A CABIN ALL TO OURSELVES. WE'LL EAT WITH THE OFFICERS.
WE'LL BE TREATED LIKE GENTLEMEN.
DO YOU HAVE ANY PAGES LEFT IN YOUR DRAWING BOOKS?
YOU CAN DRAW IN PEACE WITH NOBODY BOTHERING YOU. ONE DAY YOU'LL GET RICH THAT WAY.
I DON'T WANT TO DRAW SHIPS. I'M FED UP WITH SHIPS.
THEN YOU CAN JUST DRAW ME.
I DON'T WANT TO SEE ANY MORE SHIPS. I DON'T WANT TO DO ANYTHING. I WANT TO SLEEP UNTIL WE GET THERE.

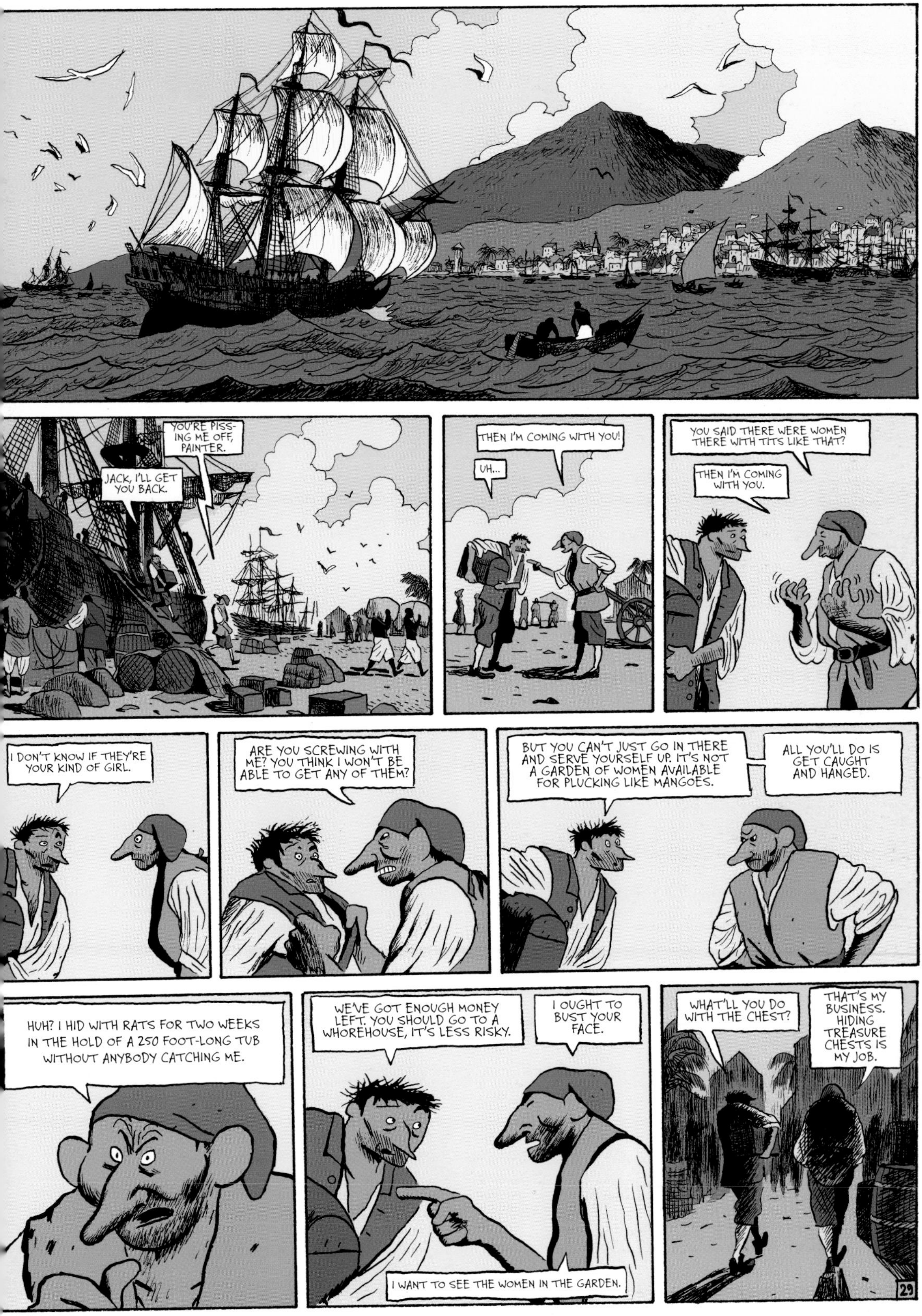
JACK, I'LL GET YOU BACK.
YOU'RE PISSING ME OFF, PAINTER.
THEN I'M COMING WITH YOU!
UH...
YOU SAID THERE WERE WOMEN THERE WITH TITS LIKE THAT?
THEN I'M COMING WITH YOU.
I DON'T KNOW IF THEY'RE YOUR KIND OF GIRL.
ARE YOU SCREWING WITH ME? YOU THINK I WON'T BE ABLE TO GET ANY OF THEM?
BUT YOU CAN'T JUST GO IN THERE AND SERVE YOURSELF UP. IT'S NOT A GARDEN OF WOMEN AVAILABLE FOR PLUCKING LIKE MANGOES.
ALL YOU'LL DO IS GET CAUGHT AND HANGED.
HUH? I HID WITH RATS FOR TWO WEEKS IN THE HOLD OF A 250 FOOT-LONG TUB WITHOUT ANYBODY CATCHING ME.
WE'VE GOT ENOUGH MONEY LEFT. YOU SHOULD GO TO A WHOREHOUSE, IT'S LESS RISKY.
I OUGHT TO BUST YOUR FACE.
I WANT TO SEE THE WOMEN IN THE GARDEN.
WHAT'LL YOU DO WITH THE CHEST?
THAT'S MY BUSINESS. HIDING TREASURE CHESTS IS MY JOB.

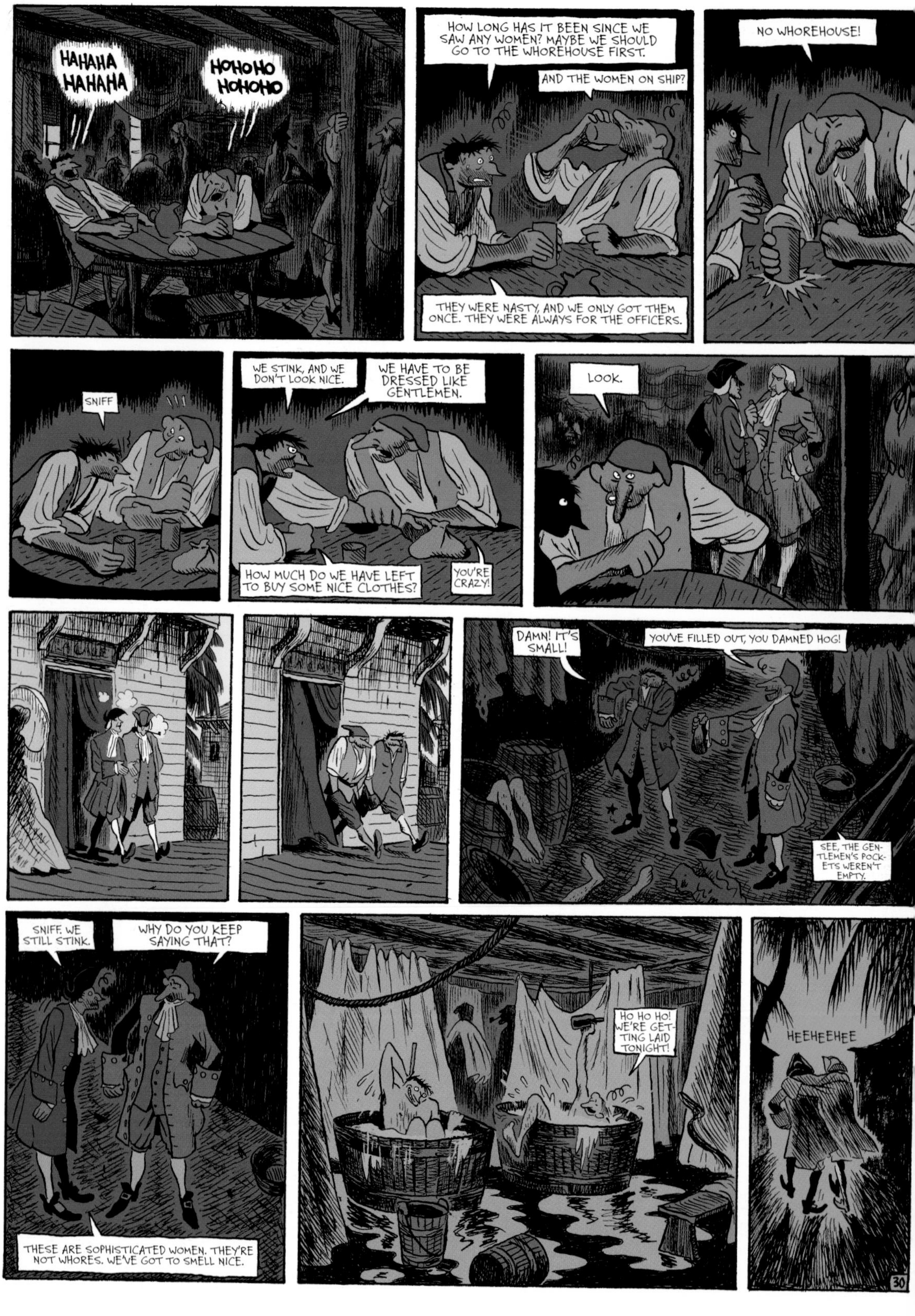
HAHAHA HAHAHA
HOHOHO HOHOHO
HOW LONG HAS IT BEEN SINCE WE SAW ANY WOMEN? MAYBE WE SHOULD GO TO THE WHOREHOUSE FIRST.
AND THE WOMEN ON SHIP?
THEY WERE NASTY, AND WE ONLY GOT THEM ONCE. THEY WERE ALWAYS FOR THE OFFICERS.
NO WHOREHOUSE!
SNIFF
WE STINK, AND WE DON'T LOOK NICE.
WE HAVE TO BE DRESSED LIKE GENTLEMEN.
HOW MUCH DO WE HAVE LEFT TO BUY SOME NICE CLOTHES?
YOU'RE CRAZY!
LOOK.
DAMN! IT'S SMALL!
YOU'VE FILLED OUT, YOU DAMNED HOG!
SEE, THE GENTLEMEN'S POCKETS WEREN'T EMPTY.
SNIFF. WE STILL STINK.
WHY DO YOU KEEP SAYING THAT?
THESE ARE SOPHISTICATED WOMEN. THEY'RE NOT WHORES. WE'VE GOT TO SMELL NICE.
HO HO HO! WE'RE GETTING LAID TONIGHT!
HEEHEEHEE

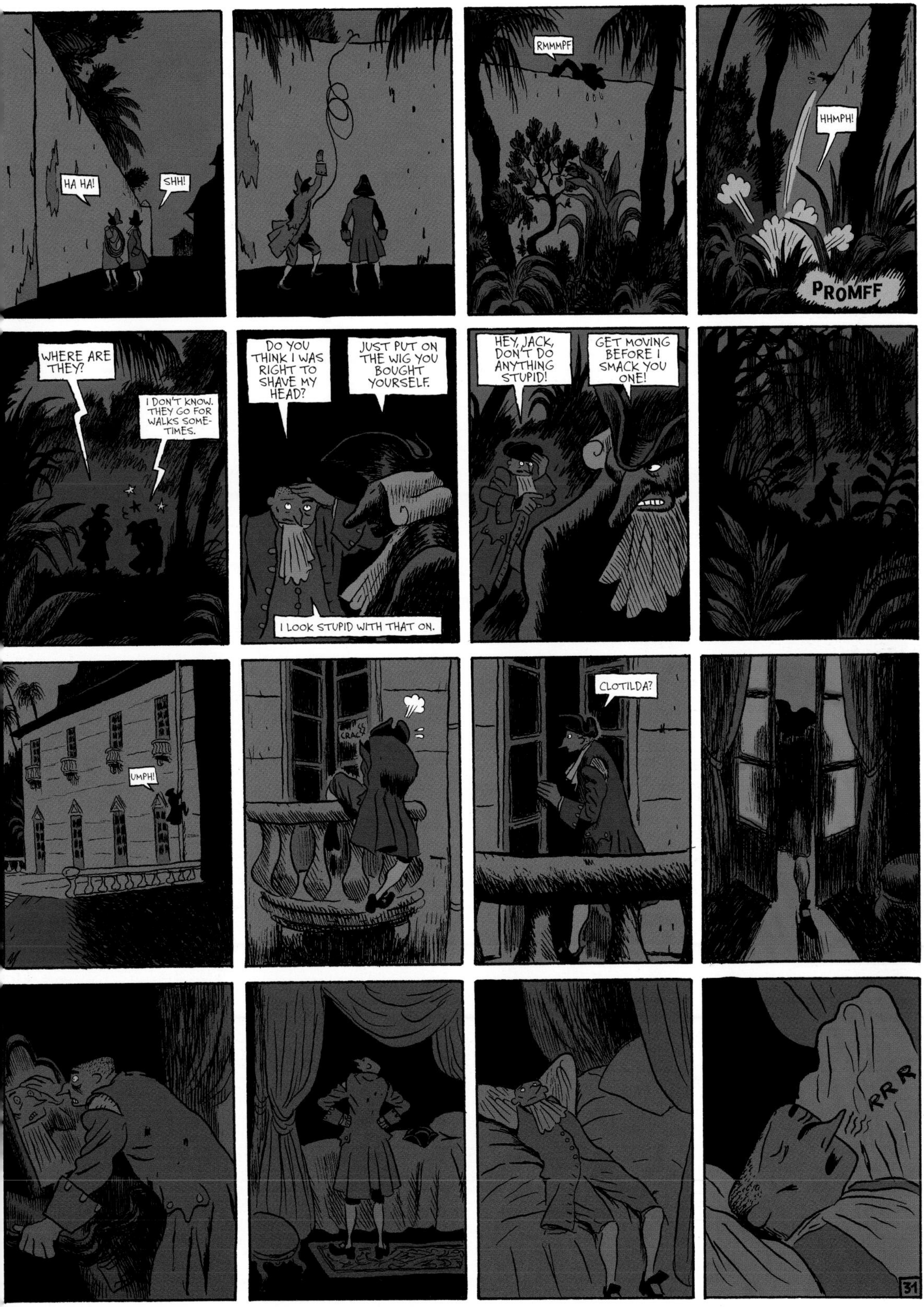
HA HA!
SHH!
RMMMPF
HHMPH!
PROMFF
WHERE ARE THEY?
I DON'T KNOW. THEY GO FOR WALKS SOME-TIMES.
DO YOU THINK I WAS RIGHT TO SHAVE MY HEAD?
JUST PUT ON THE WIG YOU BOUGHT YOURSELF.
I LOOK STUPID WITH THAT ON.
HEY, JACK, DON'T DO ANYTHING STUPID!
GET MOVING BEFORE I SMACK YOU ONE!
UMPH!
CRACK
CLOTILDA?
RRR

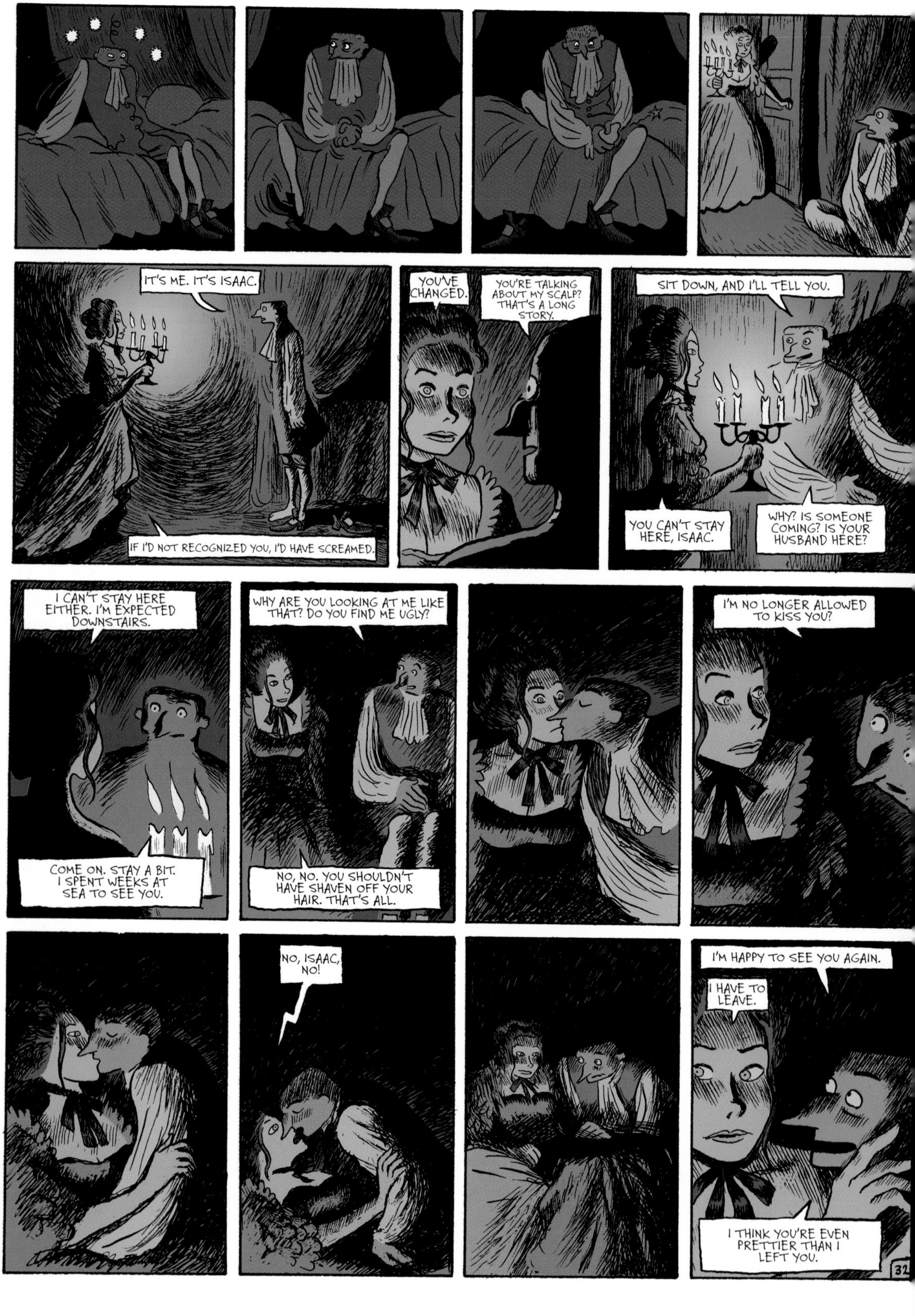
IT'S ME. IT'S ISAAC.
IF I'D NOT RECOGNIZED YOU, I'D HAVE SCREAMED.
YOU'VE CHANGED.
YOU'RE TALKING ABOUT MY SCALP? THAT'S A LONG STORY.
SIT DOWN, AND I'LL TELL YOU.
YOU CAN'T STAY HERE, ISAAC.
WHY? IS SOMEONE COMING? IS YOUR HUSBAND HERE?
I CAN'T STAY HERE EITHER. I'M EXPECTED DOWNSTAIRS.
COME ON. STAY A BIT. I SPENT WEEKS AT SEA TO SEE YOU.
WHY ARE YOU LOOKING AT ME LIKE THAT? DO YOU FIND ME UGLY?
NO, NO. YOU SHOULDN'T HAVE SHAVEN OFF YOUR HAIR. THAT'S ALL.
I'M NO LONGER ALLOWED TO KISS YOU?
NO, ISAAC, NO!
I'M HAPPY TO SEE YOU AGAIN.
I HAVE TO LEAVE.
I THINK YOU'RE EVEN PRETTIER THAN I LEFT YOU.

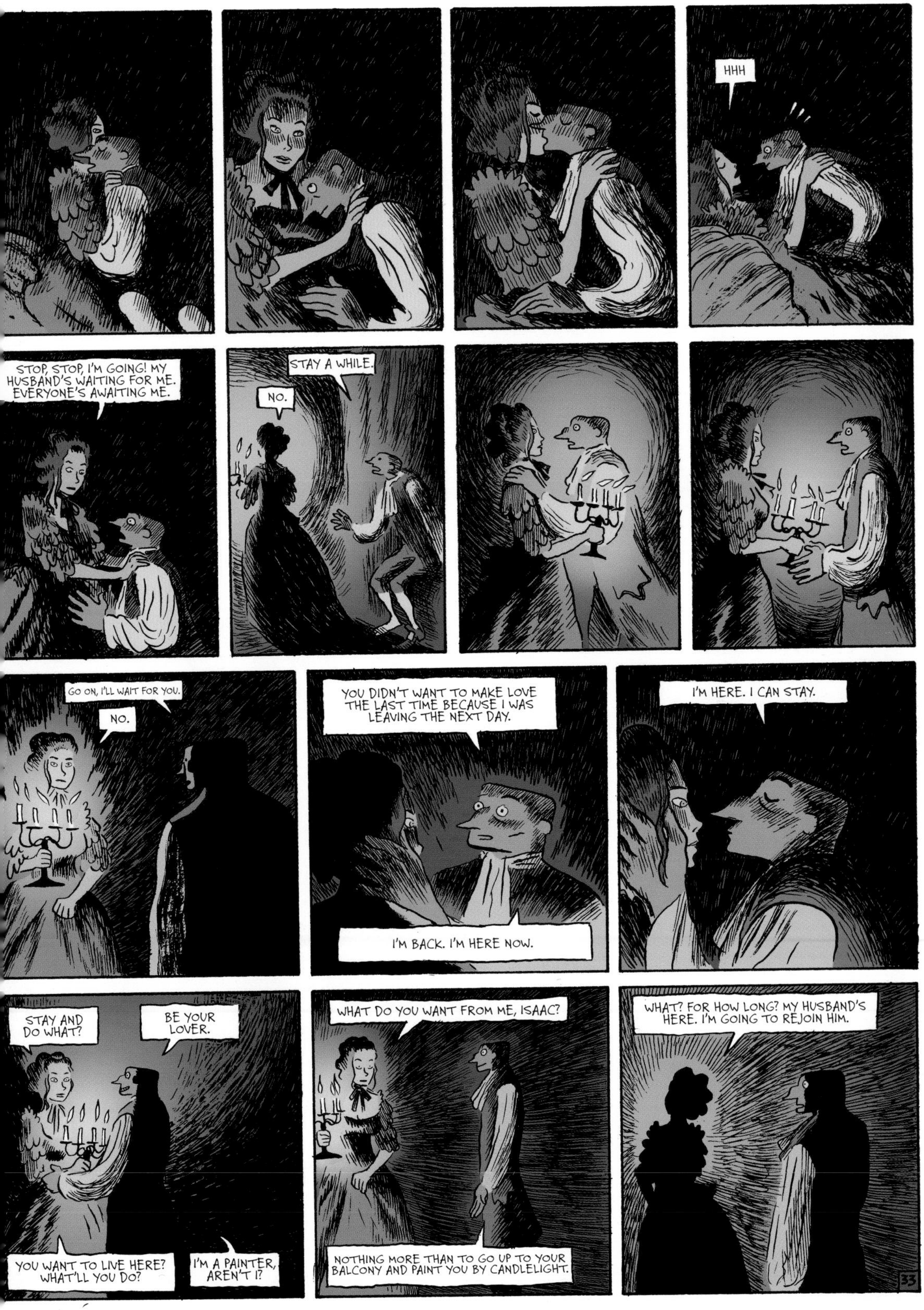
HHH
STOP, STOP, I'M GOING! MY HUSBAND'S WAITING FOR ME. EVERYONE'S AWAITING ME.
STAY A WHILE.
NO.
GO ON, I'LL WAIT FOR YOU.
NO.
YOU DIDN'T WANT TO MAKE LOVE THE LAST TIME BECAUSE I WAS LEAVING THE NEXT DAY.
I'M BACK. I'M HERE NOW.
I'M HERE. I CAN STAY.
STAY AND DO WHAT?
BE YOUR LOVER.
YOU WANT TO LIVE HERE? WHAT'LL YOU DO?
I'M A PAINTER, AREN'T I?
WHAT DO YOU WANT FROM ME, ISAAC?
NOTHING MORE THAN TO GO UP TO YOUR BALCONY AND PAINT YOU BY CANDLELIGHT.
WHAT? FOR HOW LONG? MY HUSBAND'S HERE. I'M GOING TO REJOIN HIM.

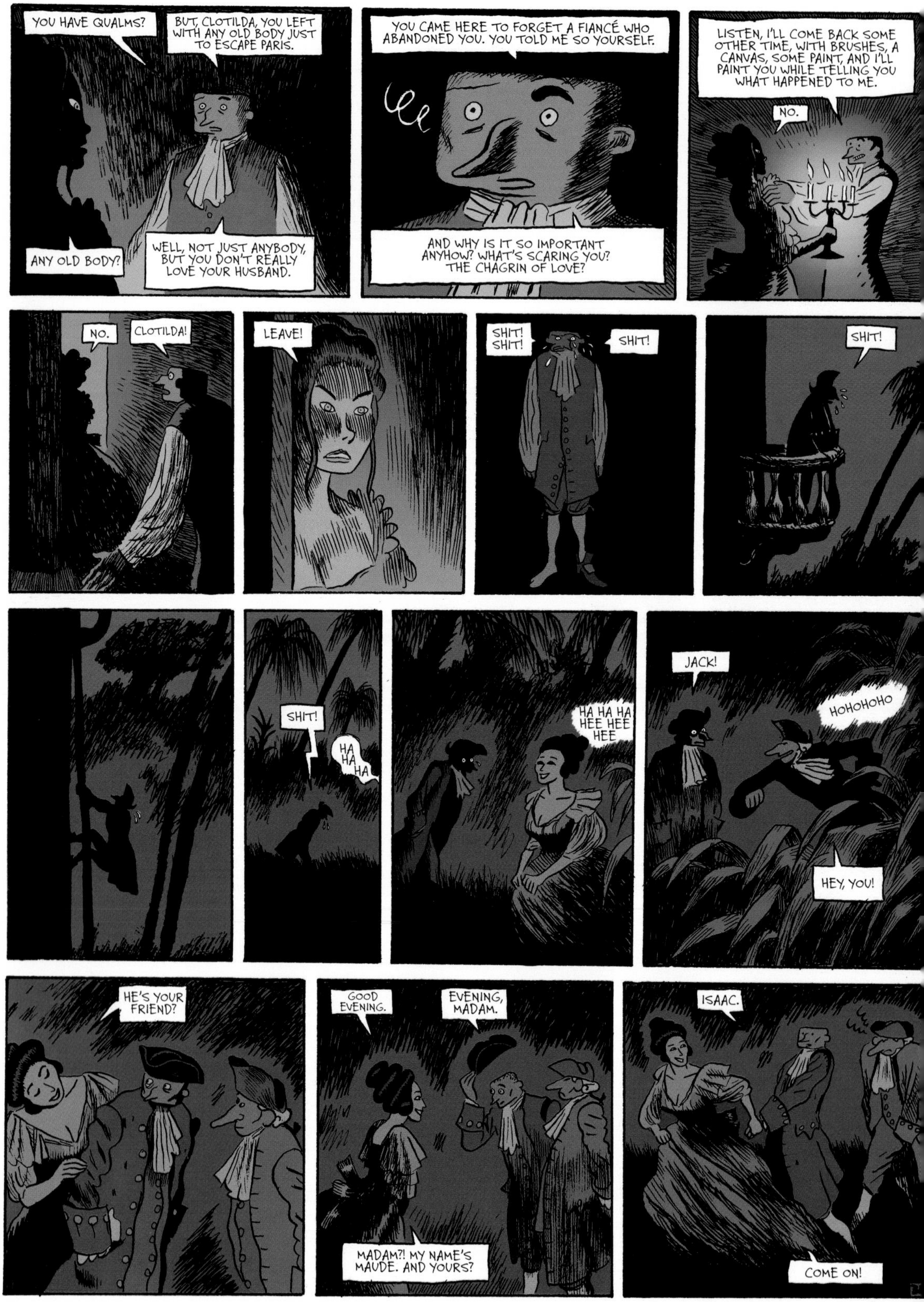
YOU HAVE QUALMS?
BUT, CLOTILDA, YOU LEFT WITH ANY OLD BODY JUST TO ESCAPE PARIS.
ANY OLD BODY?
WELL, NOT JUST ANYBODY, BUT YOU DON'T REALLY LOVE YOUR HUSBAND.
YOU CAME HERE TO FORGET A FIANCÉ WHO ABANDONED YOU. YOU TOLD ME SO YOURSELF.
AND WHY IS IT SO IMPORTANT ANYHOW? WHAT'S SCARING YOU? THE CHAGRIN OF LOVE?
LISTEN, I'LL COME BACK SOME OTHER TIME, WITH BRUSHES, A CANVAS, SOME PAINT, AND I'LL PAINT YOU WHILE TELLING YOU WHAT HAPPENED TO ME.
NO.
NO.
CLOTILDA!
LEAVE!
SHIT! SHIT!
SHIT!
SHIT!
SHIT!
HA HA HA
HA HA HA HEE HEE HEE
JACK!
HOHOHOHO
HEY, YOU!
HE'S YOUR FRIEND?
GOOD EVENING.
EVENING, MADAM.
MADAM?! MY NAME'S MAUDE. AND YOURS?
ISAAC.
COME ON!

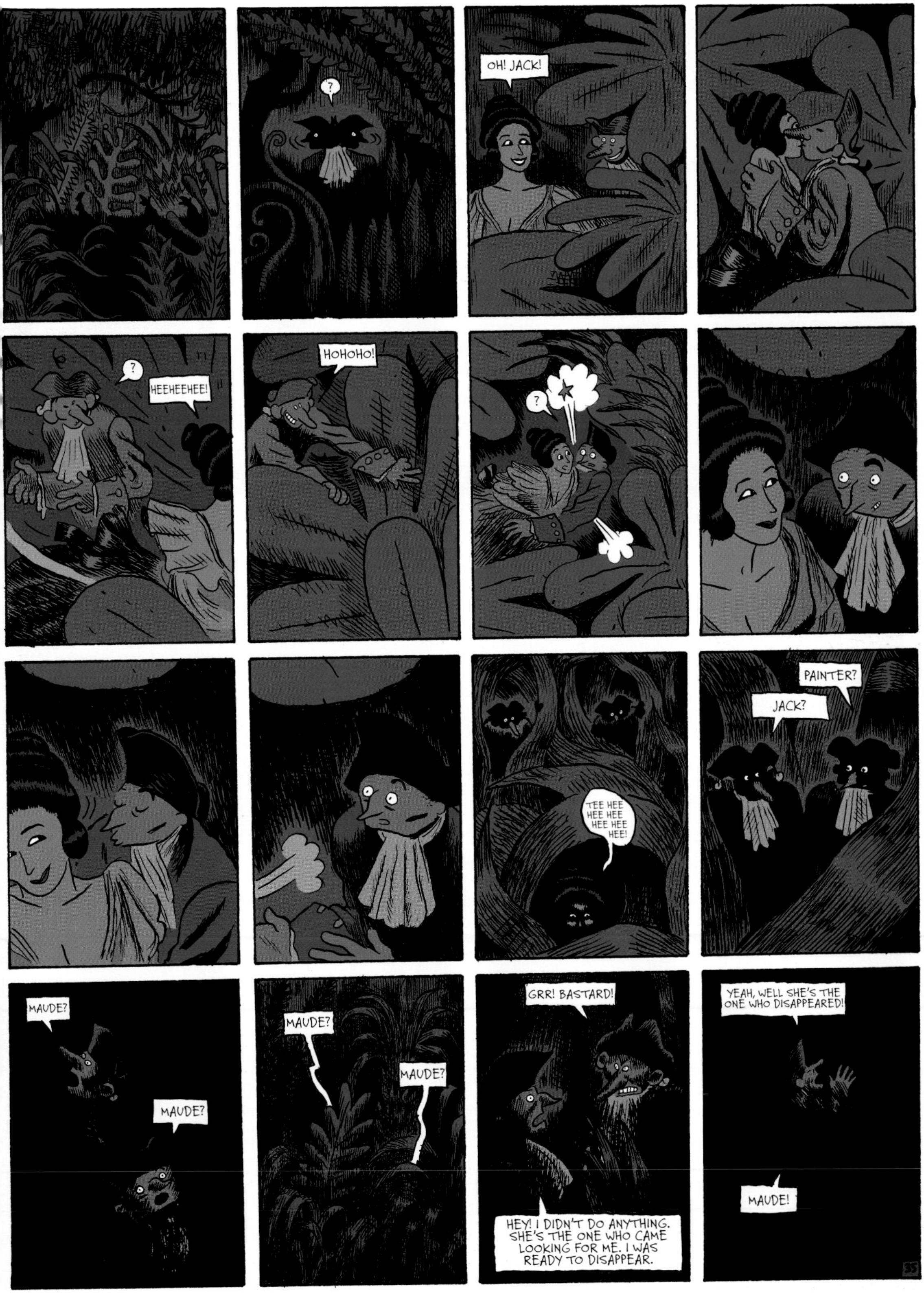
?
OH! JACK!
?
HEEHEEHEE!
HOHOHO!
?
TEE HEE HEE HEE HEE HEE HEE!
PAINTER?
JACK?
MAUDE?
MAUDE?
MAUDE?
MAUDE?
GRR! BASTARD!
HEY! I DIDN'T DO ANYTHING. SHE'S THE ONE WHO CAME LOOKING FOR ME. I WAS READY TO DISAPPEAR.
YEAH, WELL SHE'S THE ONE WHO DISAPPEARED!
MAUDE!

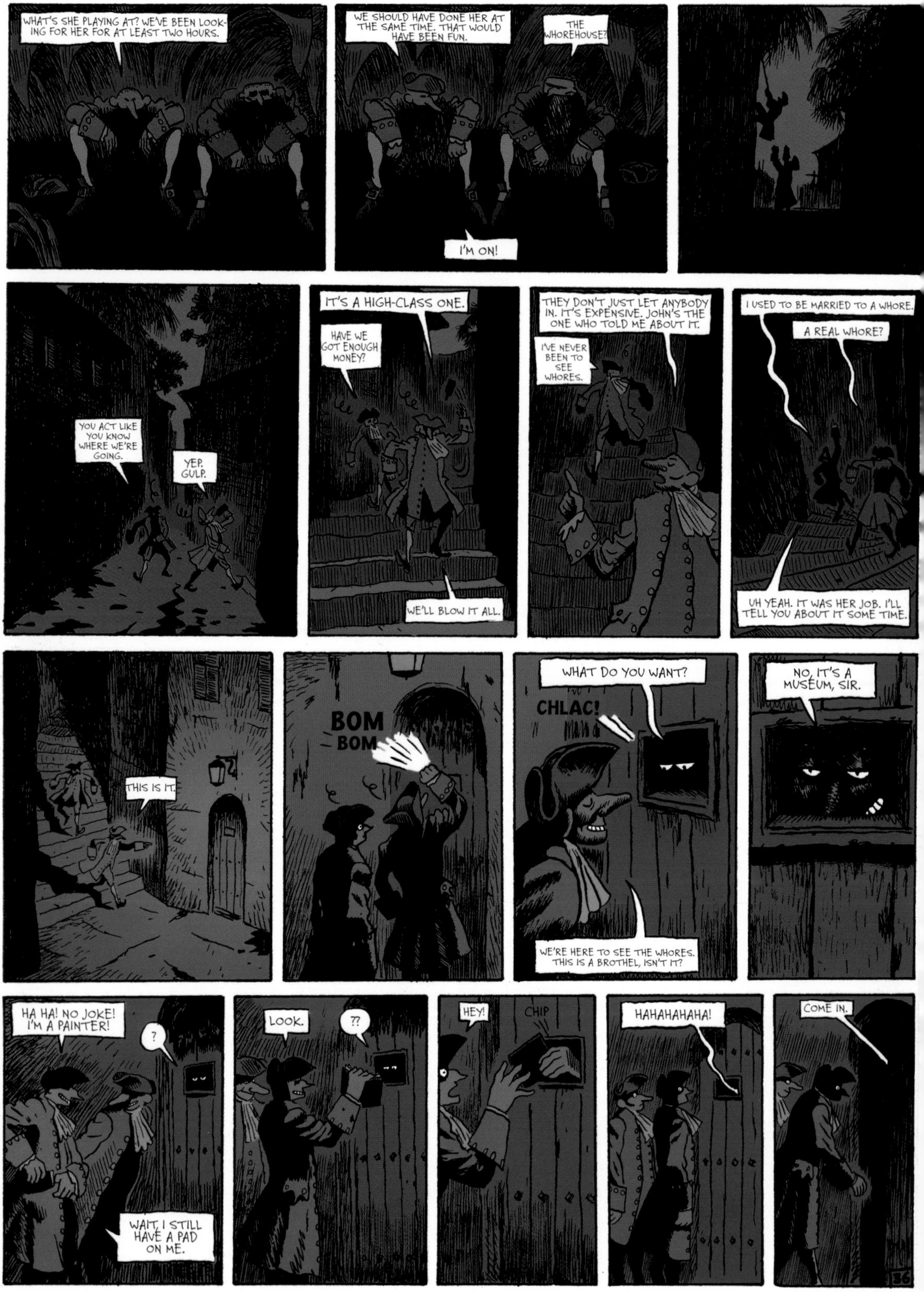
WHAT'S SHE PLAYING AT? WE'VE BEEN LOOKING FOR HER FOR AT LEAST TWO HOURS.
WE SHOULD HAVE DONE HER AT THE SAME TIME. THAT WOULD HAVE BEEN FUN.
THE WHOREHOUSE?
I'M ON!
YOU ACT LIKE YOU KNOW WHERE WE'RE GOING.
YEP. GULP.
IT'S A HIGH-CLASS ONE.
HAVE WE GOT ENOUGH MONEY?
WE'LL BLOW IT ALL.
THEY DON'T JUST LET ANYBODY IN. IT'S EXPENSIVE. JOHN'S THE ONE WHO TOLD ME ABOUT IT.
I'VE NEVER BEEN TO SEE WHORES.
I USED TO BE MARRIED TO A WHORE.
A REAL WHORE?
UH YEAH. IT WAS HER JOB. I'LL TELL YOU ABOUT IT SOME TIME.
THIS IS IT.
BOM
BOM
WHAT DO YOU WANT?
CHLAC!
WE'RE HERE TO SEE THE WHORES. THIS IS A BROTHEL, ISN'T IT?
NO, IT'S A MUSEUM, SIR.
HA HA! NO JOKE! I'M A PAINTER!
?
WAIT, I STILL HAVE A PAD ON ME.
LOOK.
??
HEY!
CHIP
HAHAHAHAHA!
COME IN.
36

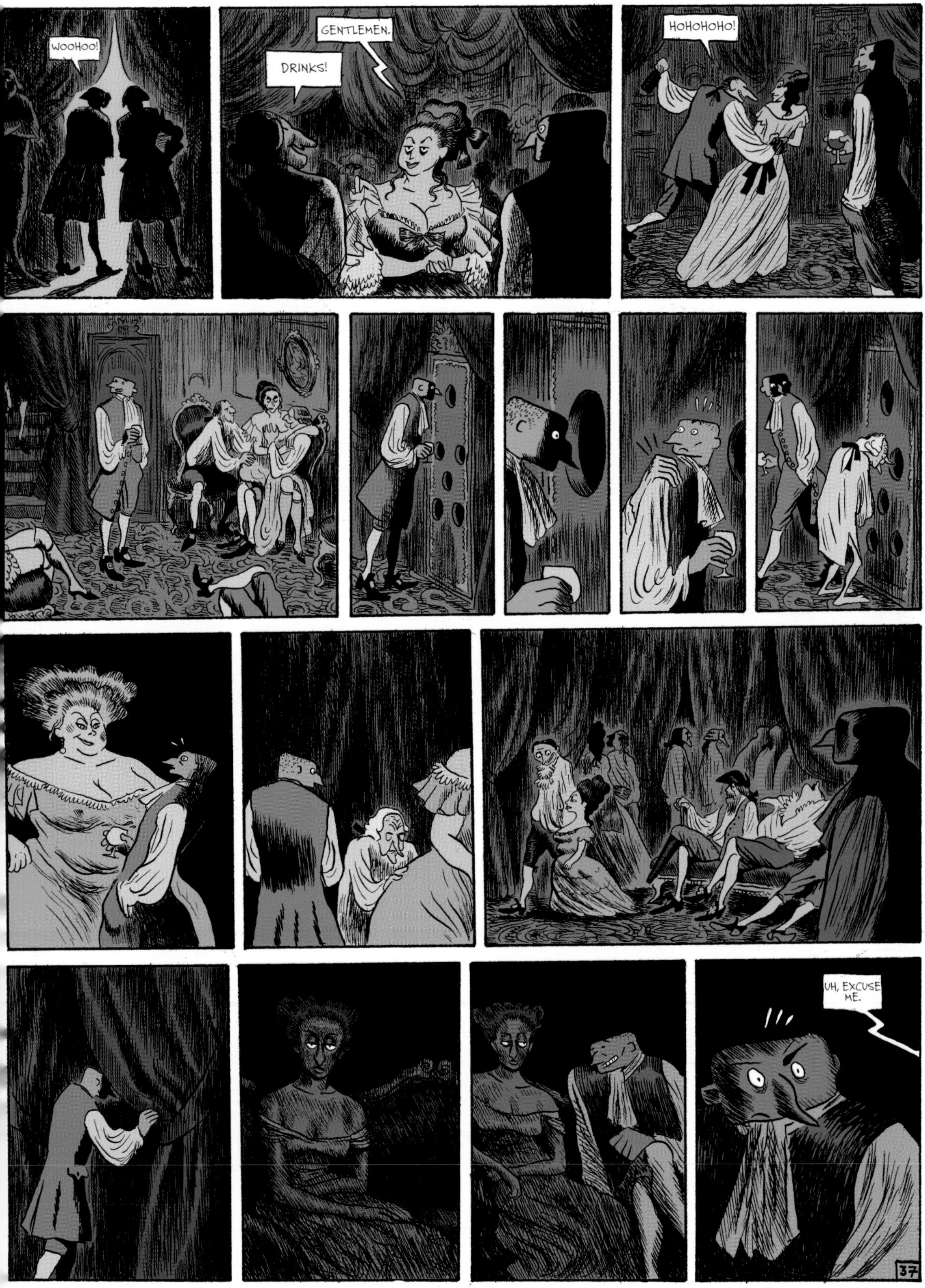
WOOHOO!
DRINKS!
GENTLEMEN.
HOHOHOHO!
UH, EXCUSE ME.

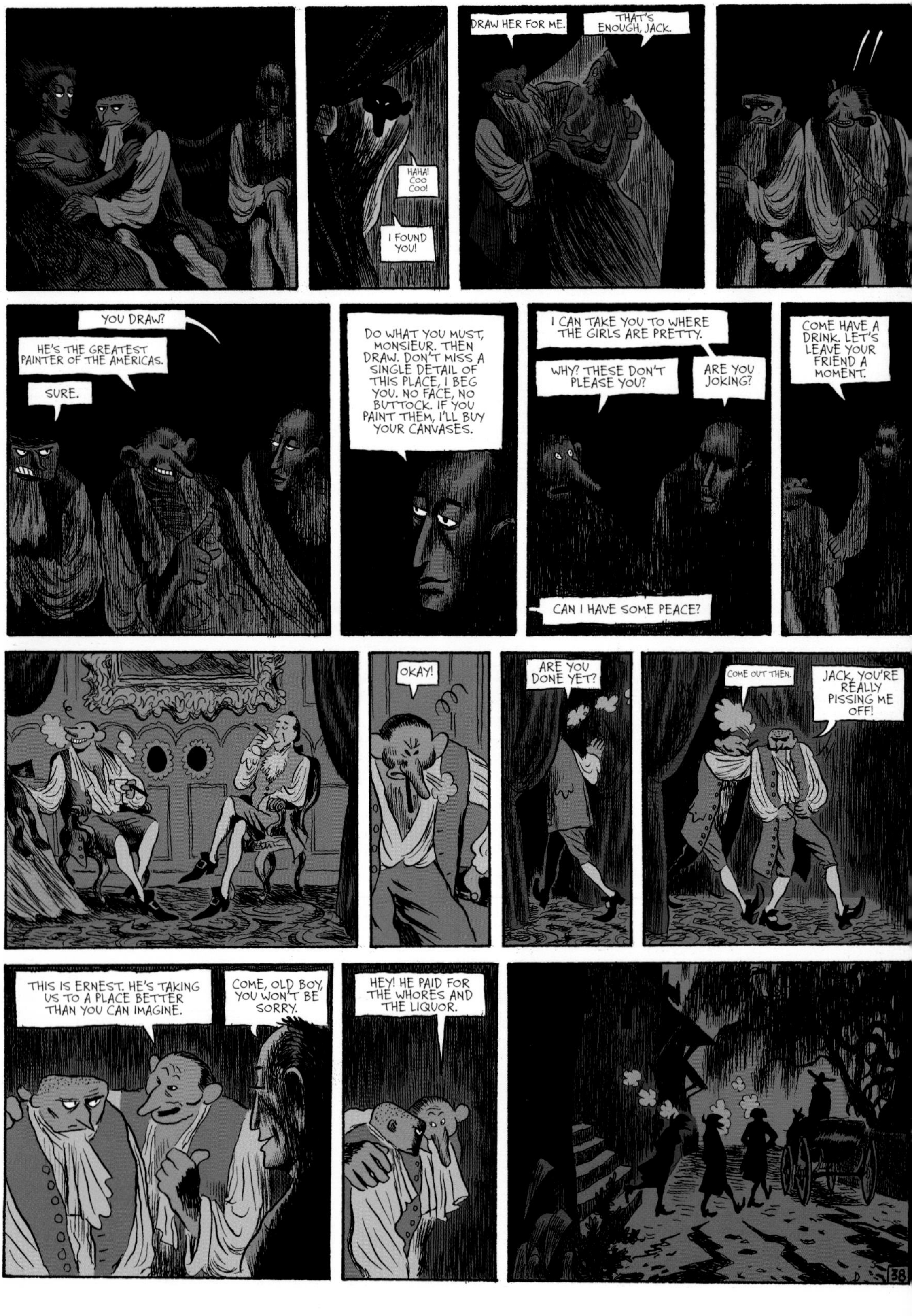
HAHA! COO COO!
I FOUND YOU!
DRAW HER FOR ME.
THAT'S ENOUGH, JACK.
YOU DRAW?
HE'S THE GREATEST PAINTER OF THE AMERICAS.
SURE.
DO WHAT YOU MUST, MONSIEUR. THEN DRAW. DON'T MISS A SINGLE DETAIL OF THIS PLACE, I BEG YOU. NO FACE, NO BUTTOCK. IF YOU PAINT THEM, I'LL BUY YOUR CANVASES.
I CAN TAKE YOU TO WHERE THE GIRLS ARE PRETTY.
WHY? THESE DON'T PLEASE YOU?
ARE YOU JOKING?
CAN I HAVE SOME PEACE?
COME HAVE A DRINK. LET'S LEAVE YOUR FRIEND A MOMENT.
OKAY!
ARE YOU DONE YET?
COME OUT THEN.
JACK, YOU'RE REALLY PISSING ME OFF!
THIS IS ERNEST. HE'S TAKING US TO A PLACE BETTER THAN YOU CAN IMAGINE.
COME, OLD BOY, YOU WON'T BE SORRY.
HEY! HE PAID FOR THE WHORES AND THE LIQUOR.

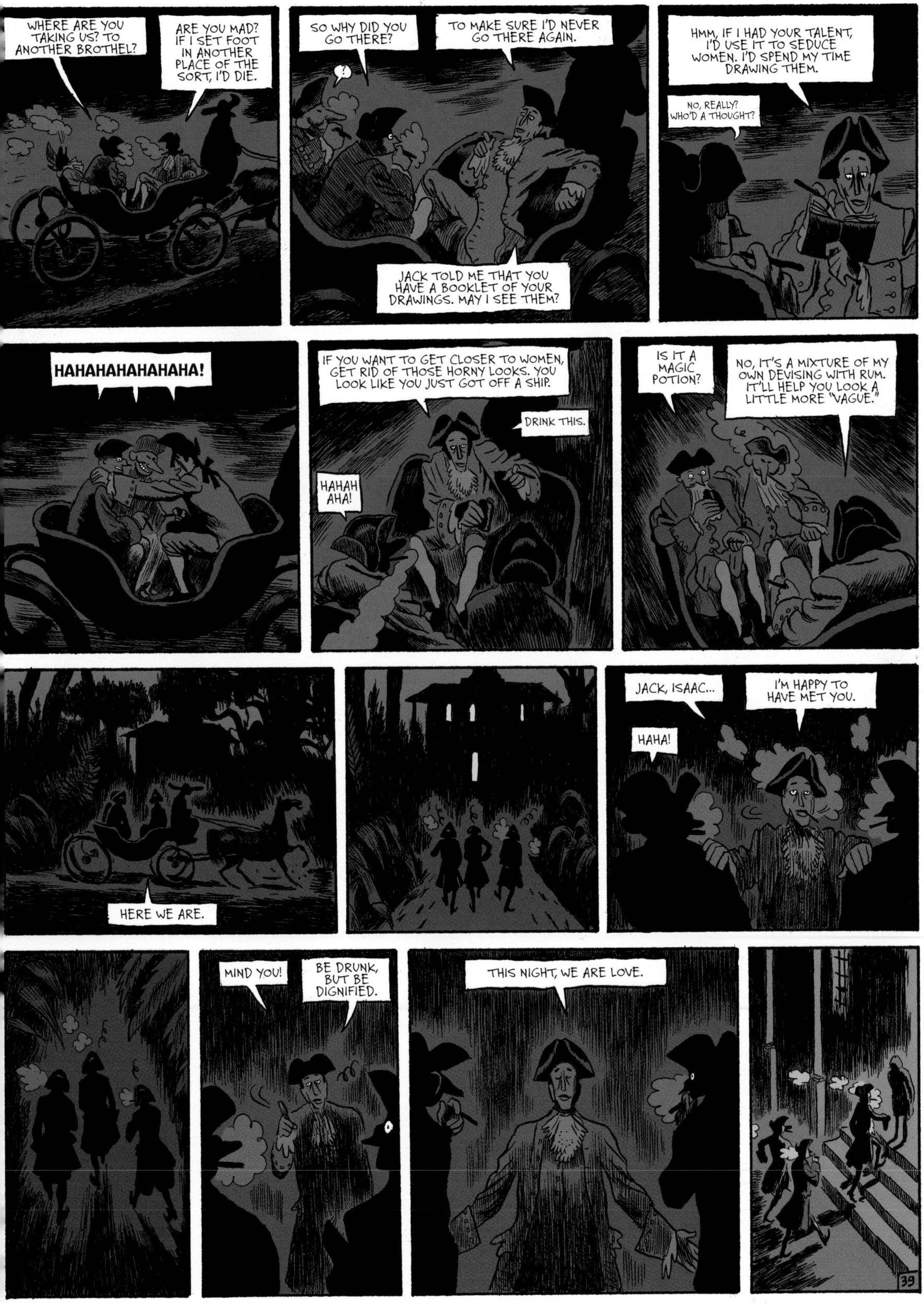
WHERE ARE YOU TAKING US? TO ANOTHER BROTHEL?
ARE YOU MAD? IF I SET FOOT IN ANOTHER PLACE OF THE SORT, I'D DIE.
SO WHY DID YOU GO THERE?
?
TO MAKE SURE I'D NEVER GO THERE AGAIN.
JACK TOLD ME THAT YOU HAVE A BOOKLET OF YOUR DRAWINGS. MAY I SEE THEM?
HMM, IF I HAD YOUR TALENT, I'D USE IT TO SEDUCE WOMEN. I'D SPEND MY TIME DRAWING THEM.
NO, REALLY? WHO'D A THOUGHT?
HAHAHAHAHAHAHA!
IF YOU WANT TO GET CLOSER TO WOMEN, GET RID OF THOSE HORNY LOOKS. YOU LOOK LIKE YOU JUST GOT OFF A SHIP.
DRINK THIS.
HAHAH AHA!
IS IT A MAGIC POTION?
NO, IT'S A MIXTURE OF MY OWN DEVISING WITH RUM. IT'LL HELP YOU LOOK A LITTLE MORE "VAGUE."
HERE WE ARE.
JACK, ISAAC...
I'M HAPPY TO HAVE MET YOU.
HAHA!
MIND YOU!
BE DRUNK, BUT BE DIGNIFIED.
THIS NIGHT, WE ARE LOVE.

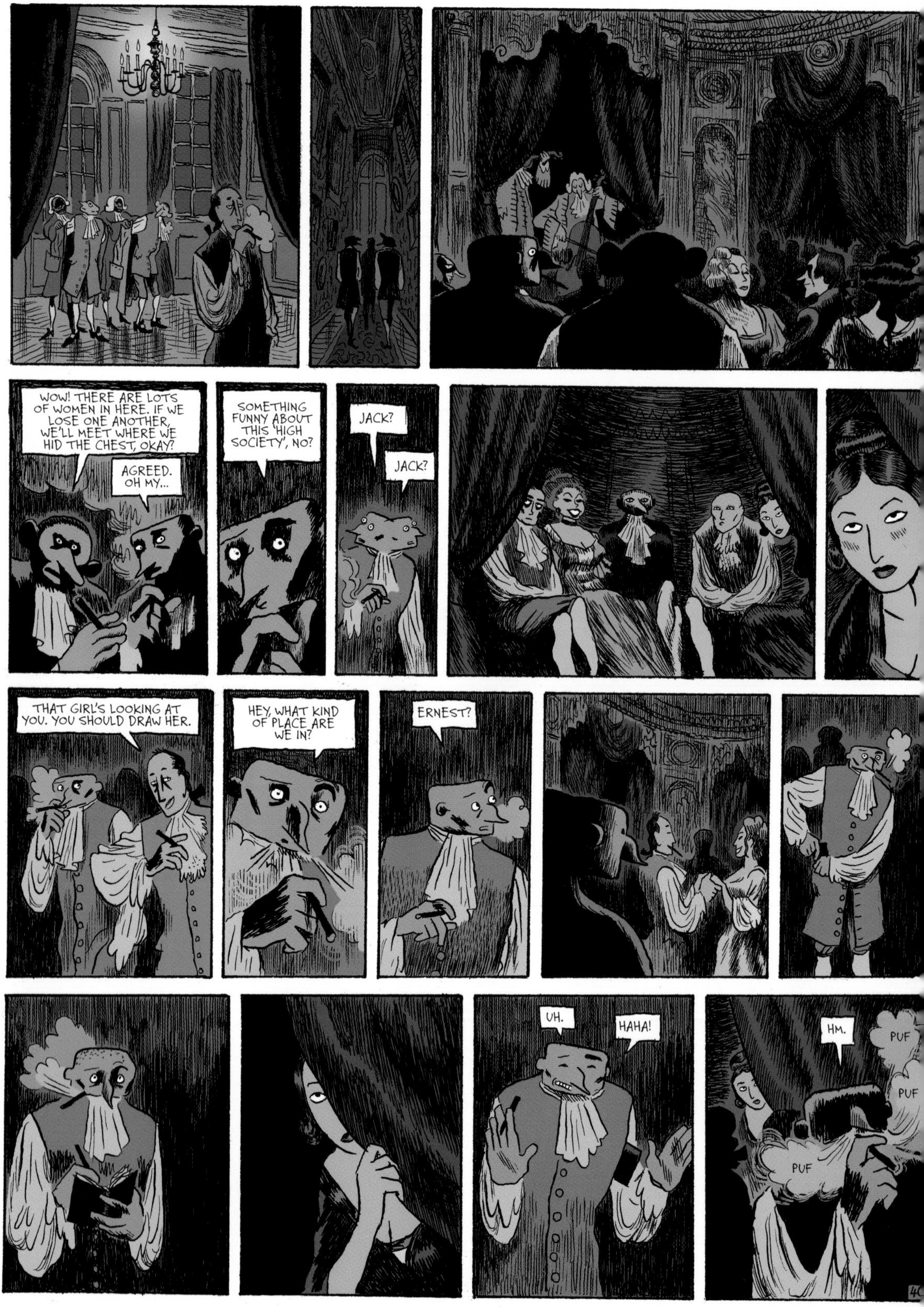
WOW! THERE ARE LOTS OF WOMEN IN HERE. IF WE LOSE ONE ANOTHER, WE'LL MEET WHERE WE HID THE CHEST, OKAY?
AGREED. OH MY...
SOMETHING FUNNY ABOUT THIS 'HIGH SOCIETY', NO?
JACK?
JACK?
THAT GIRL'S LOOKING AT YOU. YOU SHOULD DRAW HER.
HEY, WHAT KIND OF PLACE ARE WE IN?
ERNEST?
UH.
HAHA!
HM.
PUF
PUF
PUF

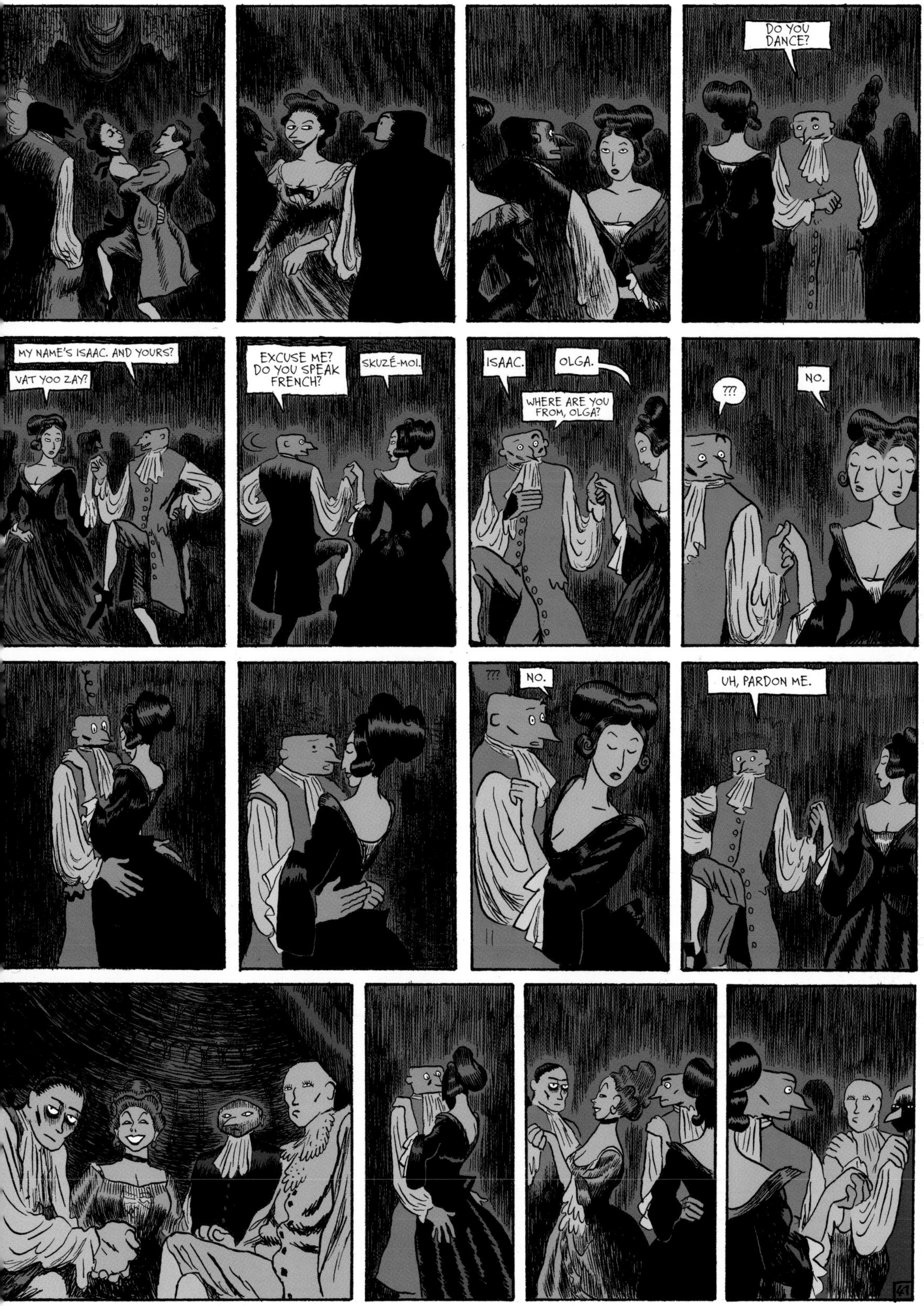
DO YOU DANCE?
MY NAME'S ISAAC. AND YOURS?
VAT YOO ZAY?
EXCUSE ME? DO YOU SPEAK FRENCH?
SKUZÉ-MOI.
ISAAC.
OLGA.
WHERE ARE YOU FROM, OLGA?
???
NO.
???
NO.
UH, PARDON ME.

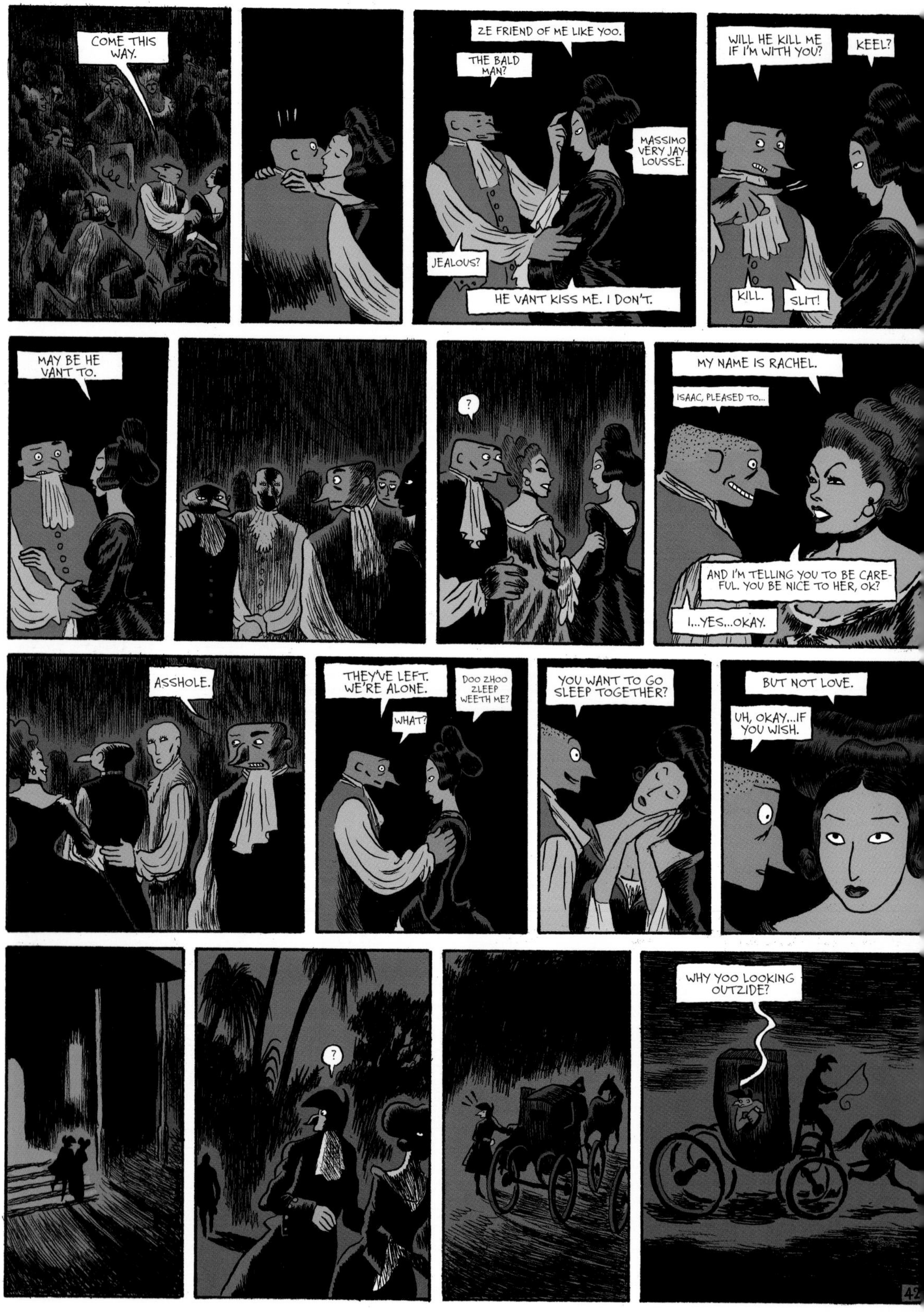
COME THIS WAY.
ZE FRIEND OF ME LIKE YOO.
THE BALD MAN?
MASSIMO VERY JAY-LOUSSE.
JEALOUS?
HE VANT KISS ME. I DON'T.
WILL HE KILL ME IF I'M WITH YOU?
KEEL?
KILL.
SLIT!
MAY BE HE VANT TO.
?
MY NAME IS RACHEL.
ISAAC, PLEASED TO...
AND I'M TELLING YOU TO BE CARE-FUL. YOU BE NICE TO HER, OK?
I...YES...OKAY.
ASSHOLE.
THEY'VE LEFT. WE'RE ALONE.
DOO ZHOO ZLEEP WEETH ME?
WHAT?
YOU WANT TO GO SLEEP TOGETHER?
BUT NOT LOVE.
UH, OKAY...IF YOU WISH.
?
WHY YOO LOOKING OUTZIDE?

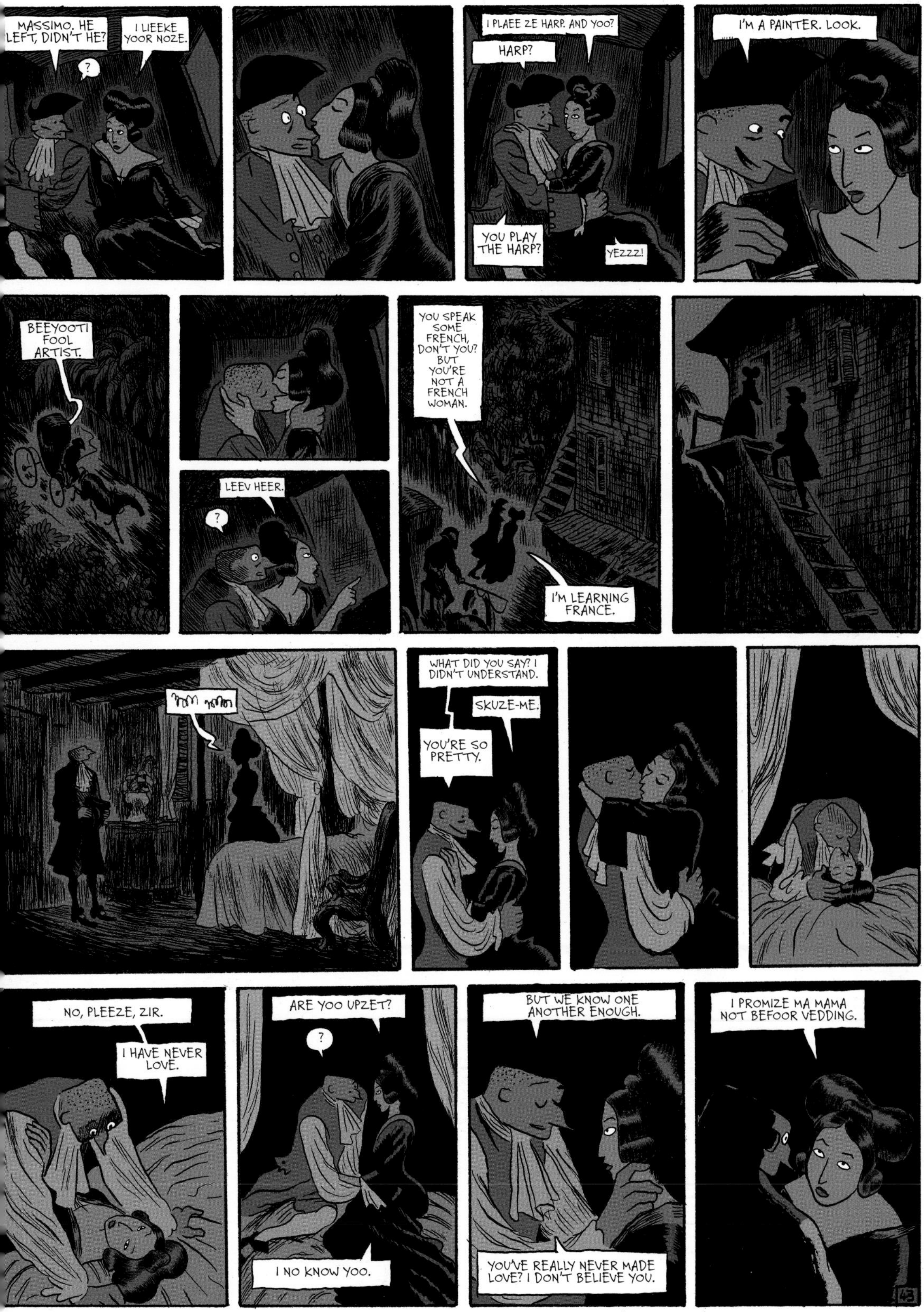
MASSIMO. HE LEFT, DIDN'T HE?
I LIEEKE YOOR NOZE.
?
I PLAEE ZE HARP. AND YOO?
HARP?
YOU PLAY THE HARP?
YEZZZ!
I'M A PAINTER. LOOK.
BEEYOOTI FOOL ARTIST.
LEEV HEER.
?
YOU SPEAK SOME FRENCH, DON'T YOU? BUT YOU'RE NOT A FRENCH WOMAN.
I'M LEARNING FRANCE.
WHAT DID YOU SAY? I DIDN'T UNDERSTAND.
SKUZE-ME.
YOU'RE SO PRETTY.
NO, PLEEZE, ZIR.
I HAVE NEVER LOVE.
ARE YOO UPZET?
?
I NO KNOW YOO.
BUT WE KNOW ONE ANOTHER ENOUGH.
YOU'VE REALLY NEVER MADE LOVE? I DON'T BELIEVE YOU.
I PROMIZE MA MAMA NOT BEFOOR VEDDING.

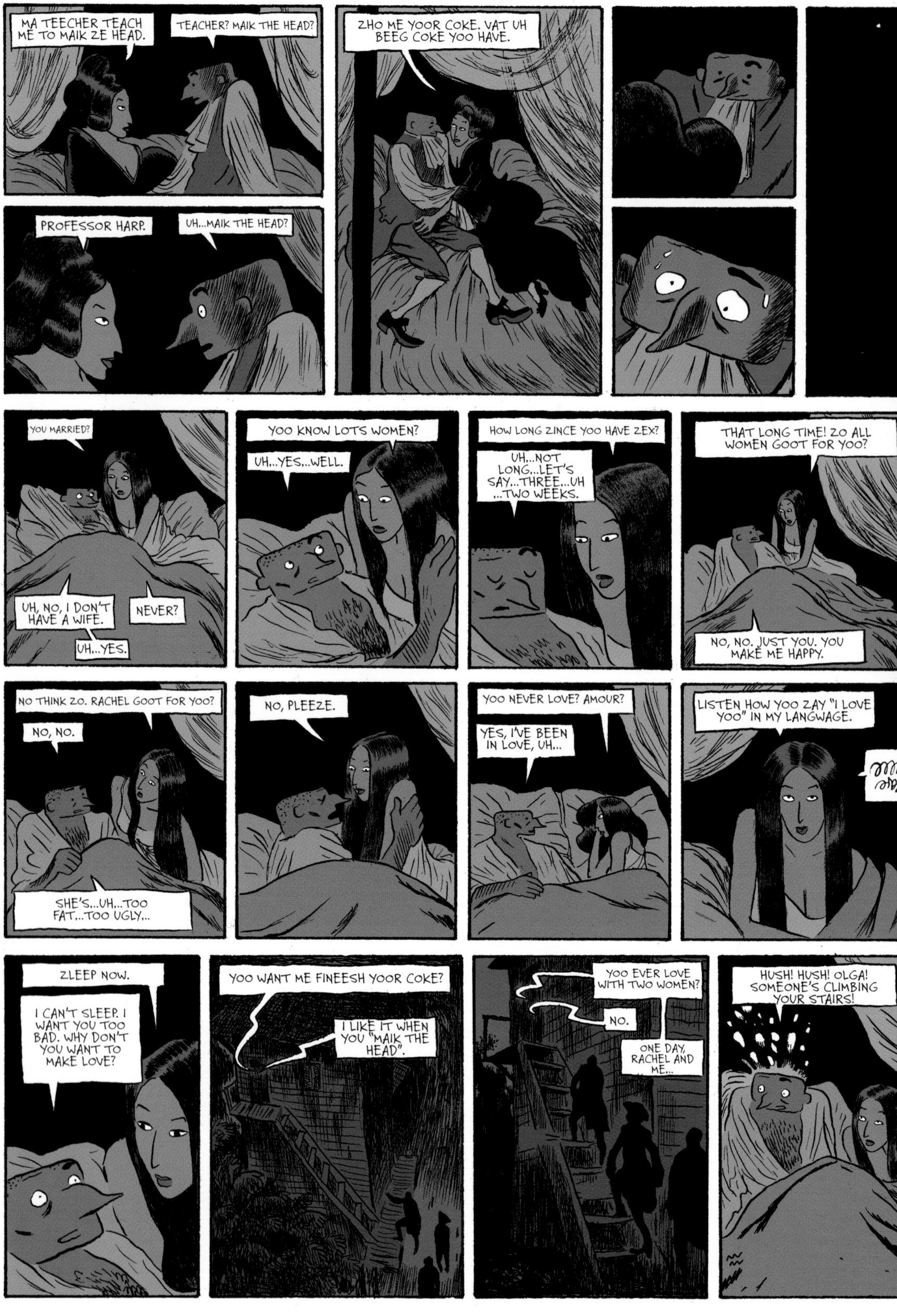
MA TEECHER TEACH ME TO MAIK ZE HEAD.
TEACHER? MAIK THE HEAD?
PROFESSOR HARP.
UH...MAIK THE HEAD?
ZHO ME YOOR COKE. VAT UH BEEG COKE YOO HAVE.
YOU MARRIED?
UH, NO, I DON'T HAVE A WIFE.
NEVER?
UH...YES.
YOO KNOW LOTS WOMEN?
UH...YES...WELL.
HOW LONG ZINCE YOO HAVE ZEX?
UH...NOT LONG...LET'S SAY...THREE...UH ...TWO WEEKS.
THAT LONG TIME! ZO ALL WOMEN GOOT FOR YOO?
NO, NO. JUST YOU. YOU MAKE ME HAPPY.
NO THINK ZO. RACHEL GOOT FOR YOO?
NO, NO.
SHE'S...UH...TOO FAT...TOO UGLY...
NO, PLEEZE.
YOO NEVER LOVE? AMOUR?
YES, I'VE BEEN IN LOVE, UH...
LISTEN HOW YOO ZAY "I LOVE YOO" IN MY LANGWAGE.
ZLEEP NOW.
I CAN'T SLEEP. I WANT YOU TOO BAD. WHY DON'T YOU WANT TO MAKE LOVE?
YOO WANT ME FINEESH YOOR COKE?
I LIKE IT WHEN YOU "MAIK THE HEAD".
YOO EVER LOVE WITH TWO WOMEN?
NO.
ONE DAY, RACHEL AND ME...
HUSH! HUSH! OLGA! SOMEONE'S CLIMBING YOUR STAIRS!

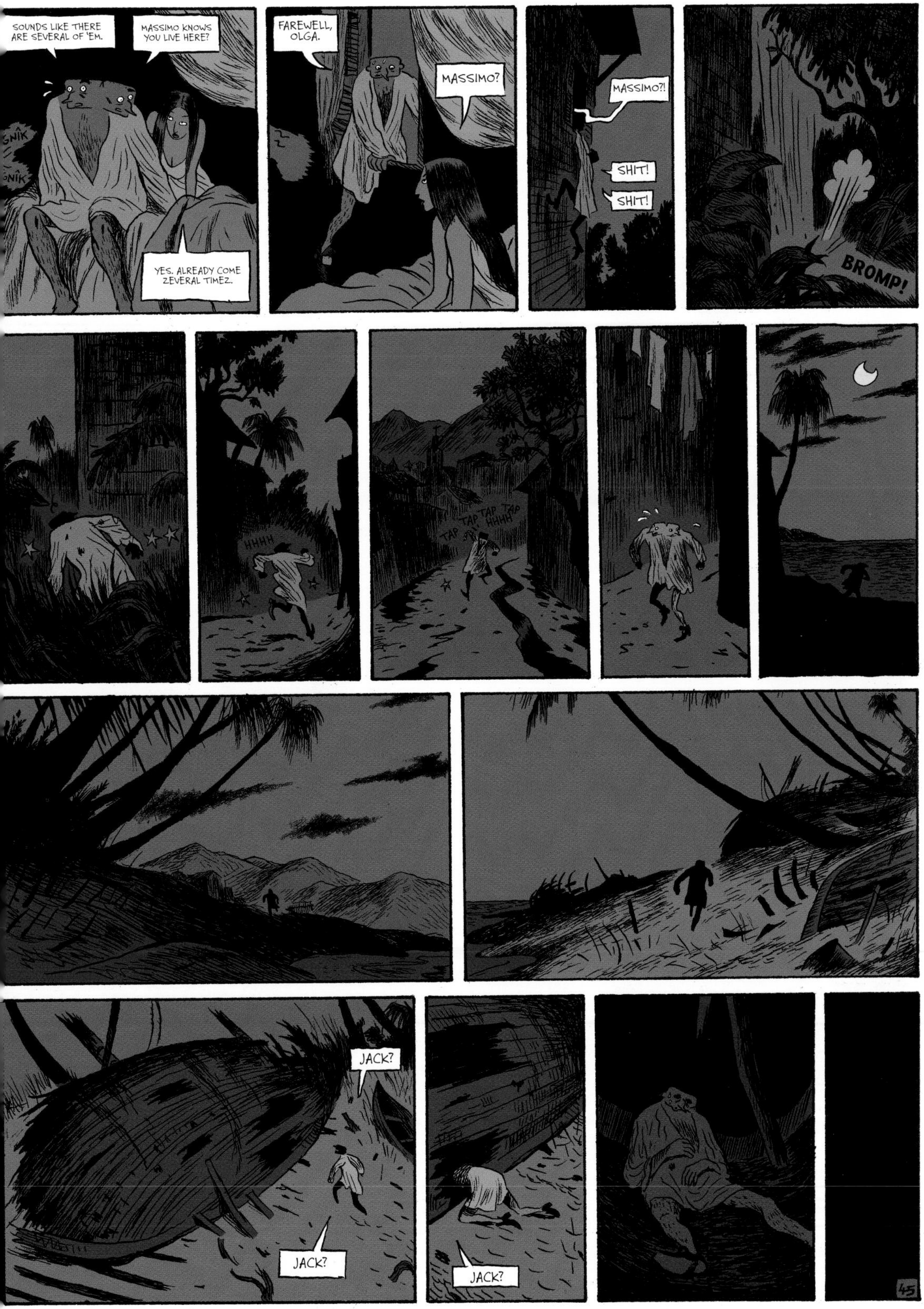
SOUNDS LIKE THERE ARE SEVERAL OF 'EM.
MASSIMO KNOWS YOU LIVE HERE?
GNIK
GNIK
YES. ALREADY COME ZEVERAL TIMEZ.
FAREWELL, OLGA.
MASSIMO?
MASSIMO?!
SHIT!
SHIT!
BROMP!
HHHH
TAP TAP TAP TAP
HHHH
JACK?
JACK?
JACK?

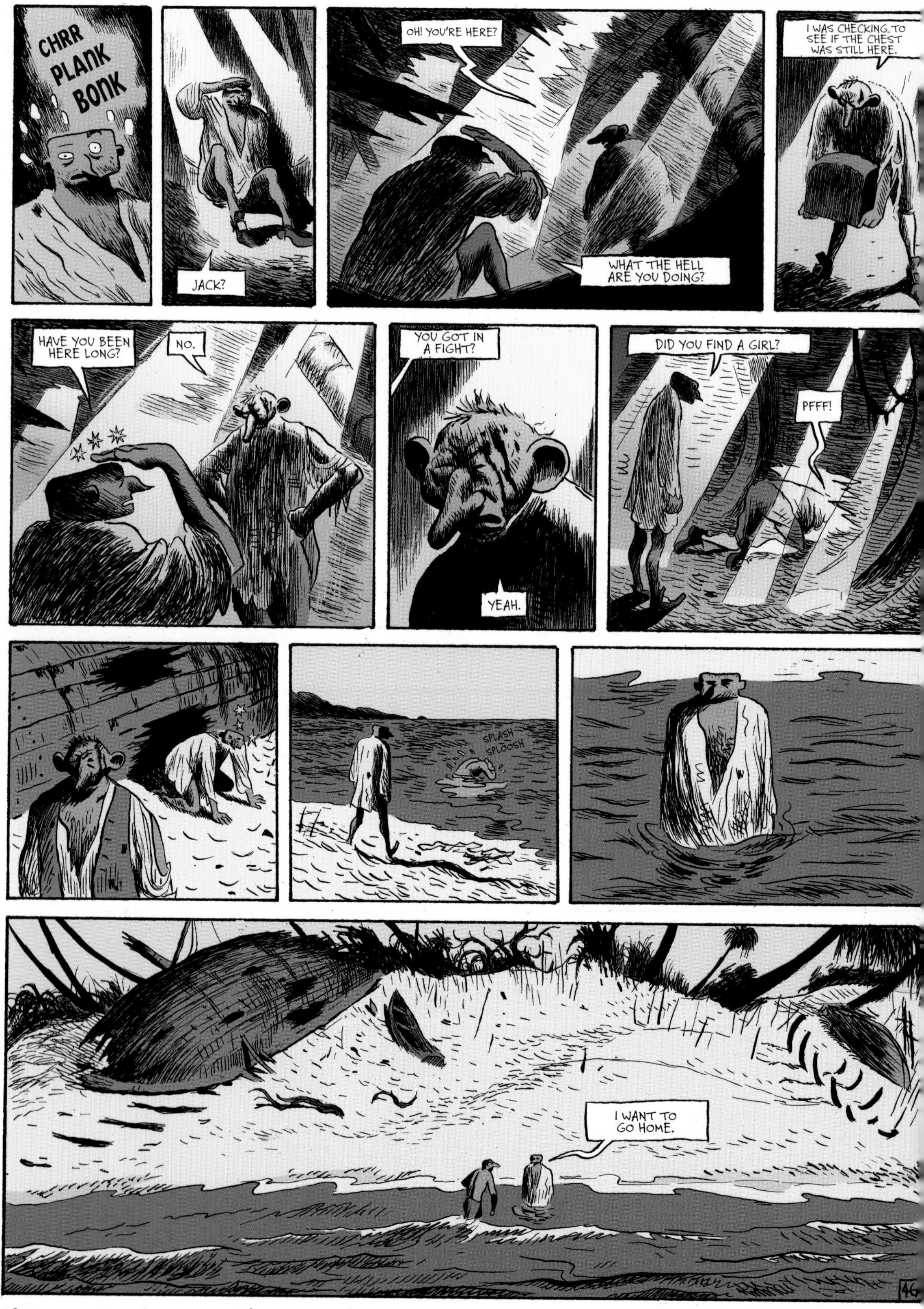
CHRR
PLANK
BONK
JACK?
OH! YOU'RE HERE?
WHAT THE HELL ARE YOU DOING?
I WAS CHECKING TO SEE IF THE CHEST WAS STILL HERE.
HAVE YOU BEEN HERE LONG?
NO.
YOU GOT IN A FIGHT?
YEAH.
DID YOU FIND A GIRL?
PFFF!
SPLASH
SPLOOSH
I WANT TO GO HOME.

Christopheblain juillet 2002

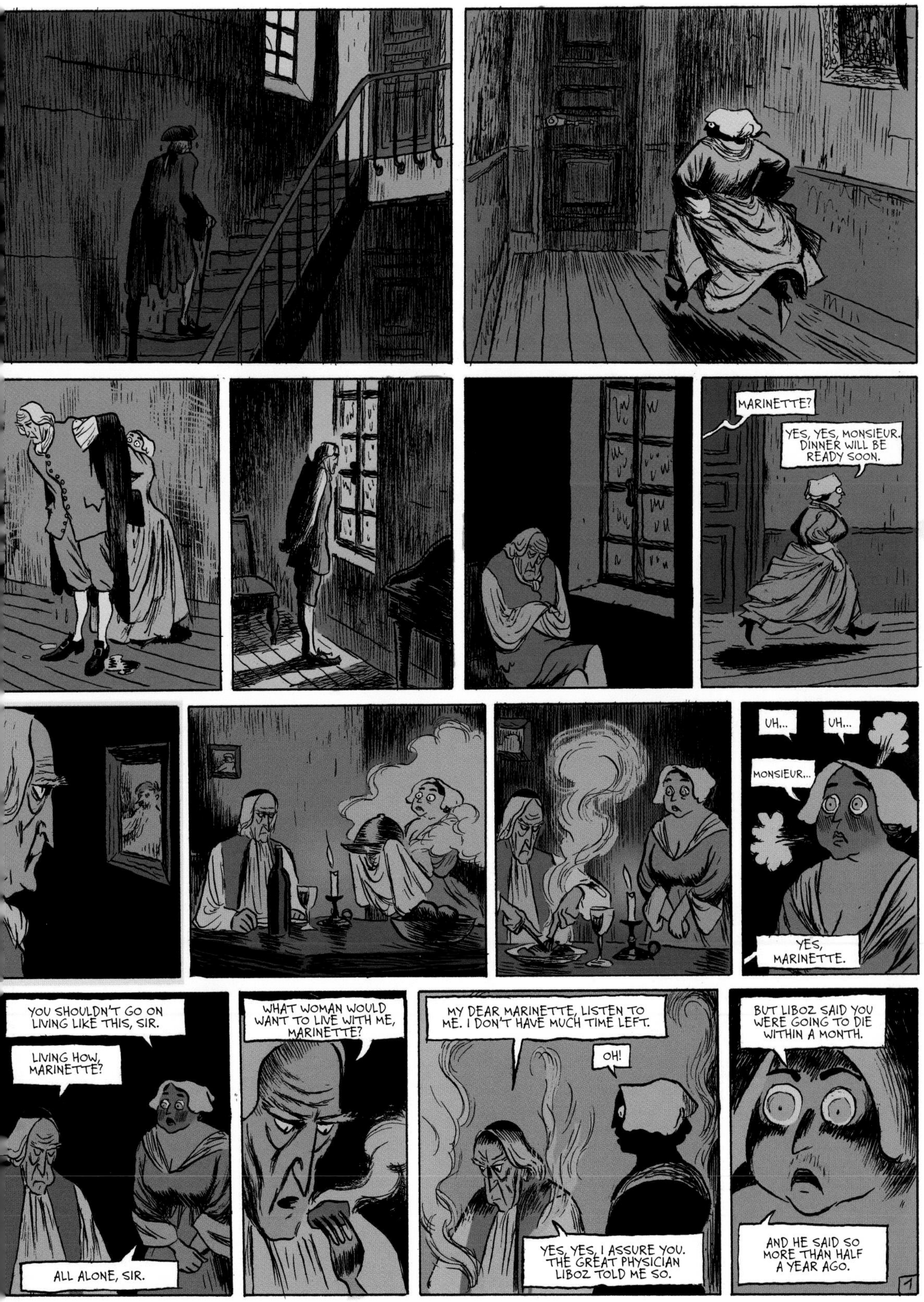
MARINETTE?
YES, YES, MONSIEUR. DINNER WILL BE READY SOON.
UH...
UH...
MONSIEUR...
YES, MARINETTE.
YOU SHOULDN'T GO ON LIVING LIKE THIS, SIR.
LIVING HOW, MARINETTE?
ALL ALONE, SIR.
WHAT WOMAN WOULD WANT TO LIVE WITH ME, MARINETTE?
MY DEAR MARINETTE, LISTEN TO ME. I DON'T HAVE MUCH TIME LEFT.
OH!
YES, YES, I ASSURE YOU. THE GREAT PHYSICIAN LIBOZ TOLD ME SO.
BUT LIBOZ SAID YOU WERE GOING TO DIE WITHIN A MONTH.
AND HE SAID SO MORE THAN HALF A YEAR AGO.
1

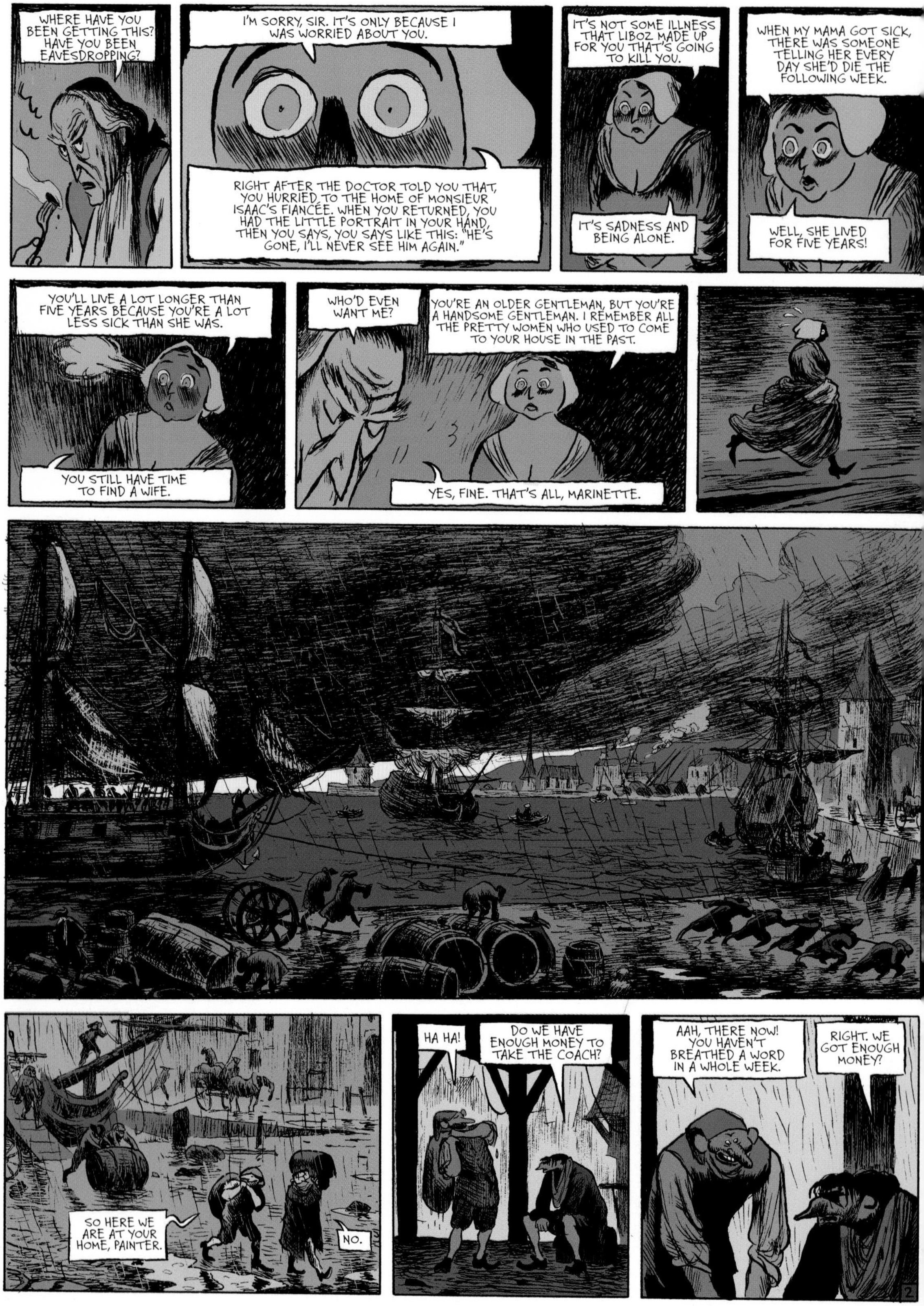
WHERE HAVE YOU BEEN GETTING THIS? HAVE YOU BEEN EAVESDROPPING?
I'M SORRY, SIR. IT'S ONLY BECAUSE I WAS WORRIED ABOUT YOU.
RIGHT AFTER THE DOCTOR TOLD YOU THAT, YOU HURRIED TO THE HOME OF MONSIEUR ISAAC'S FIANCÉE. WHEN YOU RETURNED, YOU HAD THE LITTLE PORTRAIT IN YOUR HAND, THEN YOU SAYS, YOU SAYS LIKE THIS: "HE'S GONE, I'LL NEVER SEE HIM AGAIN."
IT'S NOT SOME ILLNESS THAT LIBOZ MADE UP FOR YOU THAT'S GOING TO KILL YOU.
IT'S SADNESS AND BEING ALONE.
WHEN MY MAMA GOT SICK, THERE WAS SOMEONE TELLING HER EVERY DAY SHE'D DIE THE FOLLOWING WEEK.
WELL, SHE LIVED FOR FIVE YEARS!
YOU'LL LIVE A LOT LONGER THAN FIVE YEARS BECAUSE YOU'RE A LOT LESS SICK THAN SHE WAS.
YOU STILL HAVE TIME TO FIND A WIFE.
WHO'D EVEN WANT ME?
YOU'RE AN OLDER GENTLEMAN, BUT YOU'RE A HANDSOME GENTLEMAN. I REMEMBER ALL THE PRETTY WOMEN WHO USED TO COME TO YOUR HOUSE IN THE PAST.
YES, FINE. THAT'S ALL, MARINETTE.
SO HERE WE ARE AT YOUR HOME, PAINTER.
NO.
HA HA!
DO WE HAVE ENOUGH MONEY TO TAKE THE COACH?
AAH, THERE NOW! YOU HAVEN'T BREATHED A WORD IN A WHOLE WEEK.
RIGHT. WE GOT ENOUGH MONEY?

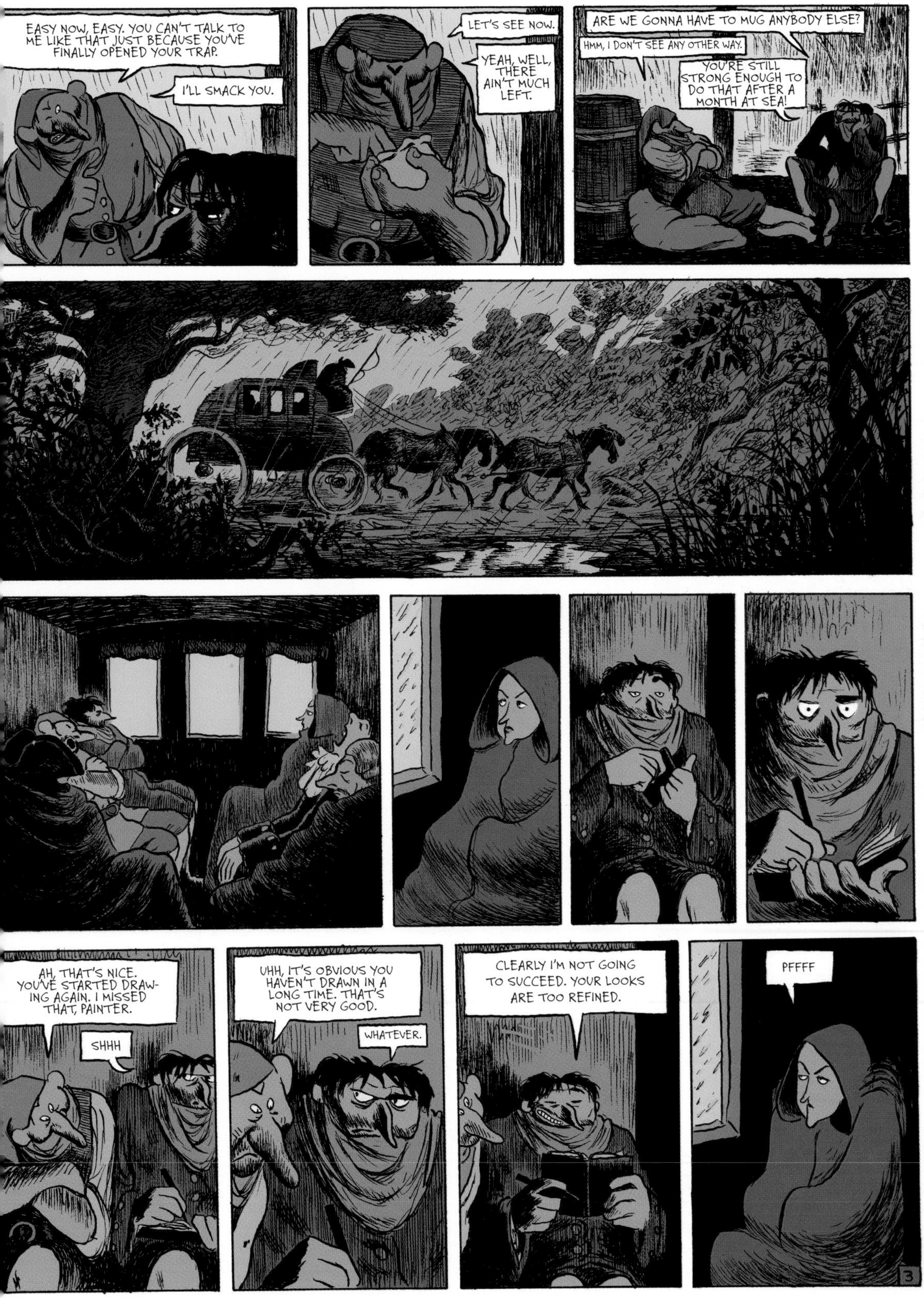
EASY NOW, EASY. YOU CAN'T TALK TO ME LIKE THAT JUST BECAUSE YOU'VE FINALLY OPENED YOUR TRAP.
I'LL SMACK YOU.
LET'S SEE NOW.
YEAH, WELL, THERE AIN'T MUCH LEFT.
ARE WE GONNA HAVE TO MUG ANYBODY ELSE?
HMM, I DON'T SEE ANY OTHER WAY.
YOU'RE STILL STRONG ENOUGH TO DO THAT AFTER A MONTH AT SEA!
AH, THAT'S NICE. YOU'VE STARTED DRAWING AGAIN. I MISSED THAT, PAINTER.
SHHH
UHH, IT'S OBVIOUS YOU HAVEN'T DRAWN IN A LONG TIME. THAT'S NOT VERY GOOD.
WHATEVER.
CLEARLY I'M NOT GOING TO SUCCEED. YOUR LOOKS ARE TOO REFINED.
PFFFF

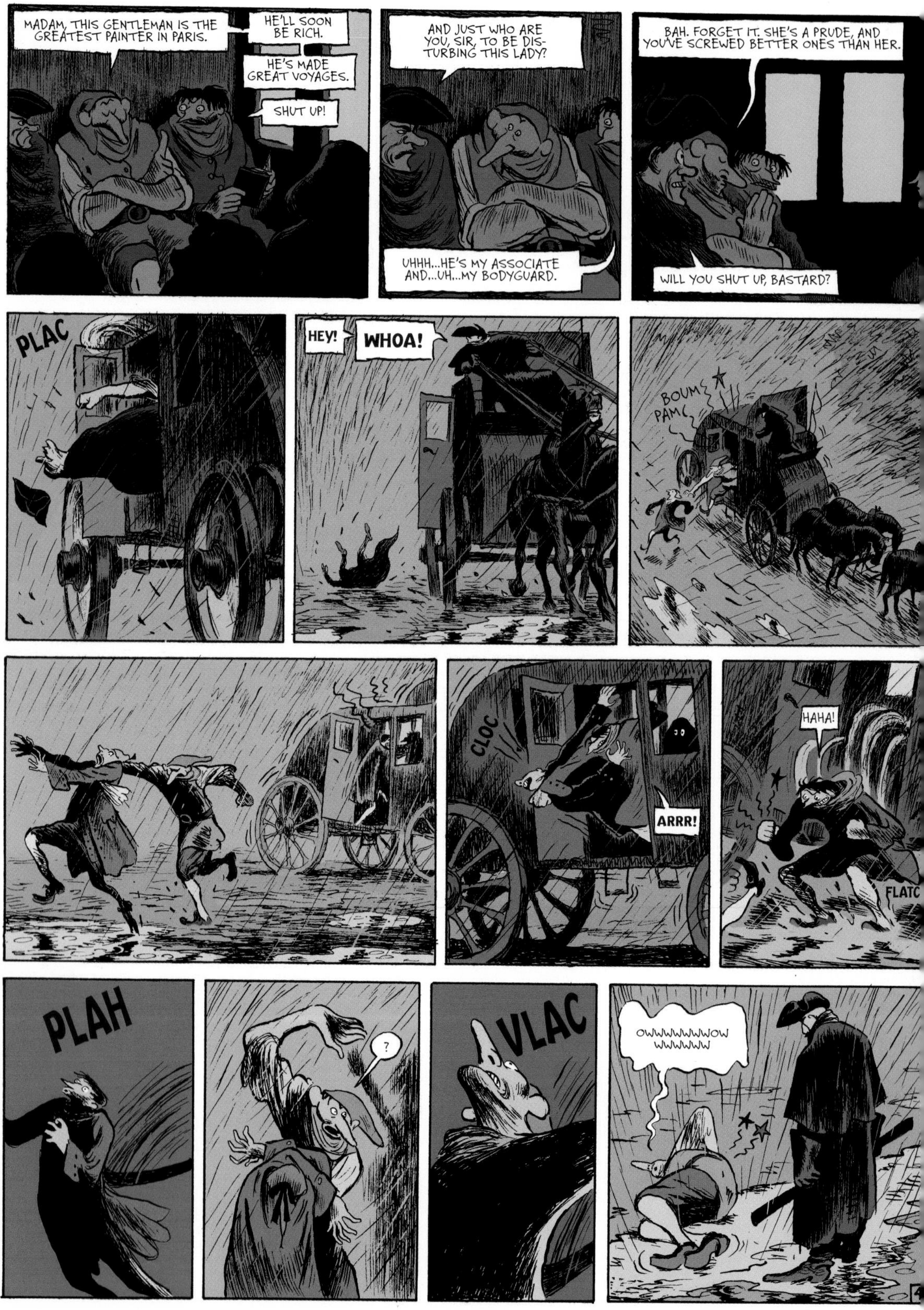
MADAM, THIS GENTLEMAN IS THE GREATEST PAINTER IN PARIS.
HE'LL SOON BE RICH.
HE'S MADE GREAT VOYAGES.
SHUT UP!
AND JUST WHO ARE YOU, SIR, TO BE DISTURBING THIS LADY?
UHHH...HE'S MY ASSOCIATE AND...UH...MY BODYGUARD.
BAH. FORGET IT. SHE'S A PRUDE, AND YOU'VE SCREWED BETTER ONES THAN HER.
WILL YOU SHUT UP, BASTARD?
PLAC
HEY!
WHOA!
BOUM
PAM
CLOC
ARRR!
HAHA!
FLATC
PLAH
?
VLAC
OWWWWWWWOW WWWWWW

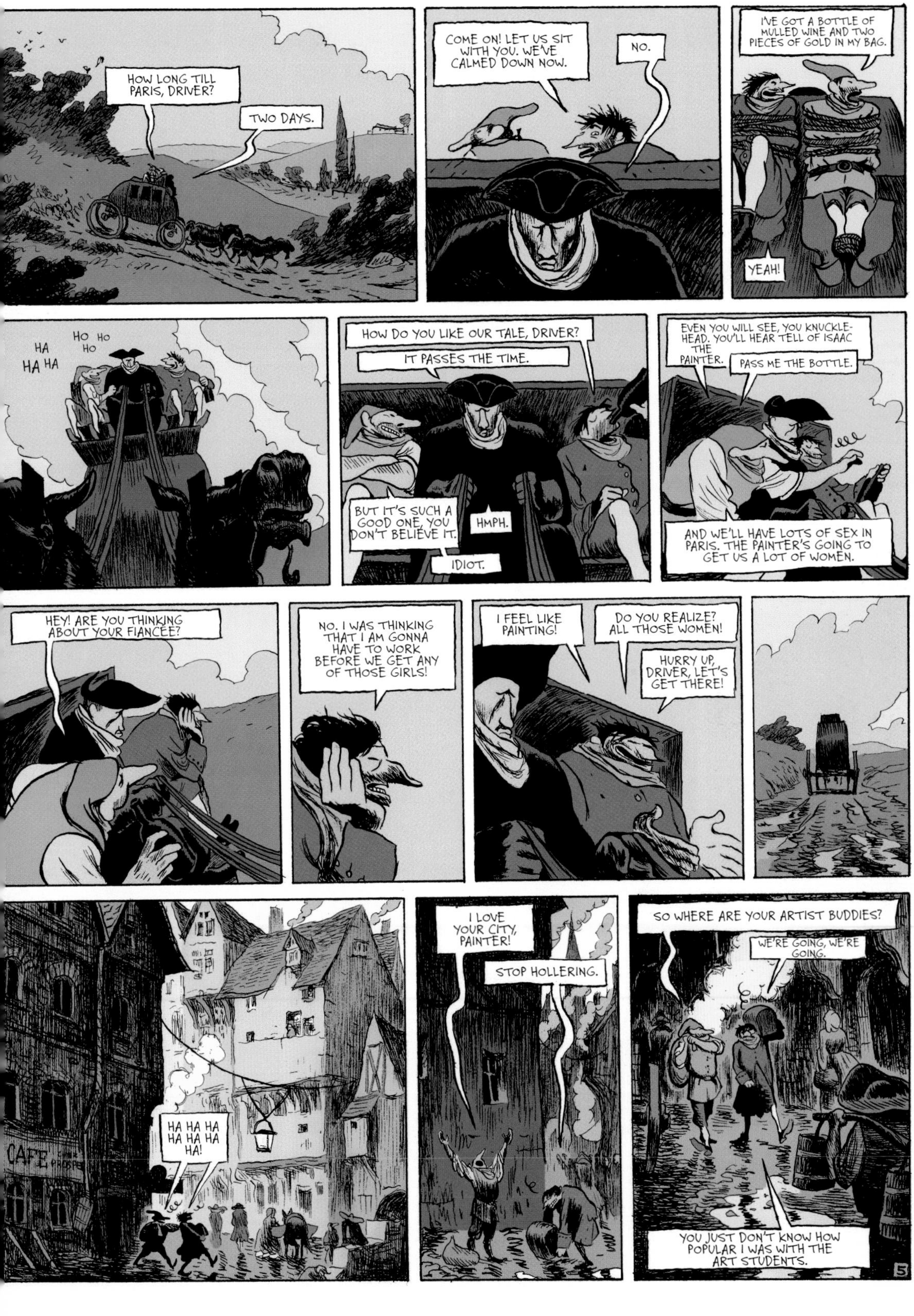
HOW LONG TILL PARIS, DRIVER?
TWO DAYS.
COME ON! LET US SIT WITH YOU. WE'VE CALMED DOWN NOW.
NO.
I'VE GOT A BOTTLE OF MULLED WINE AND TWO PIECES OF GOLD IN MY BAG.
YEAH!
HA HA HA
HO HO HO
HOW DO YOU LIKE OUR TALE, DRIVER?
IT PASSES THE TIME.
BUT IT'S SUCH A GOOD ONE, YOU DON'T BELIEVE IT.
HMPH.
IDIOT.
EVEN YOU WILL SEE, YOU KNUCKLE-HEAD. YOU'LL HEAR TELL OF ISAAC THE PAINTER.
PASS ME THE BOTTLE.
AND WE'LL HAVE LOTS OF SEX IN PARIS. THE PAINTER'S GOING TO GET US A LOT OF WOMEN.
HEY! ARE YOU THINKING ABOUT YOUR FIANCÉE?
NO. I WAS THINKING THAT I AM GONNA HAVE TO WORK BEFORE WE GET ANY OF THOSE GIRLS!
I FEEL LIKE PAINTING!
DO YOU REALIZE? ALL THOSE WOMEN!
HURRY UP, DRIVER, LET'S GET THERE!
CAFE
HA HA HA HA HA HA HA!
I LOVE YOUR CITY, PAINTER!
STOP HOLLERING.
SO WHERE ARE YOUR ARTIST BUDDIES?
WE'RE GOING, WE'RE GOING.
YOU JUST DON'T KNOW HOW POPULAR I WAS WITH THE ART STUDENTS.

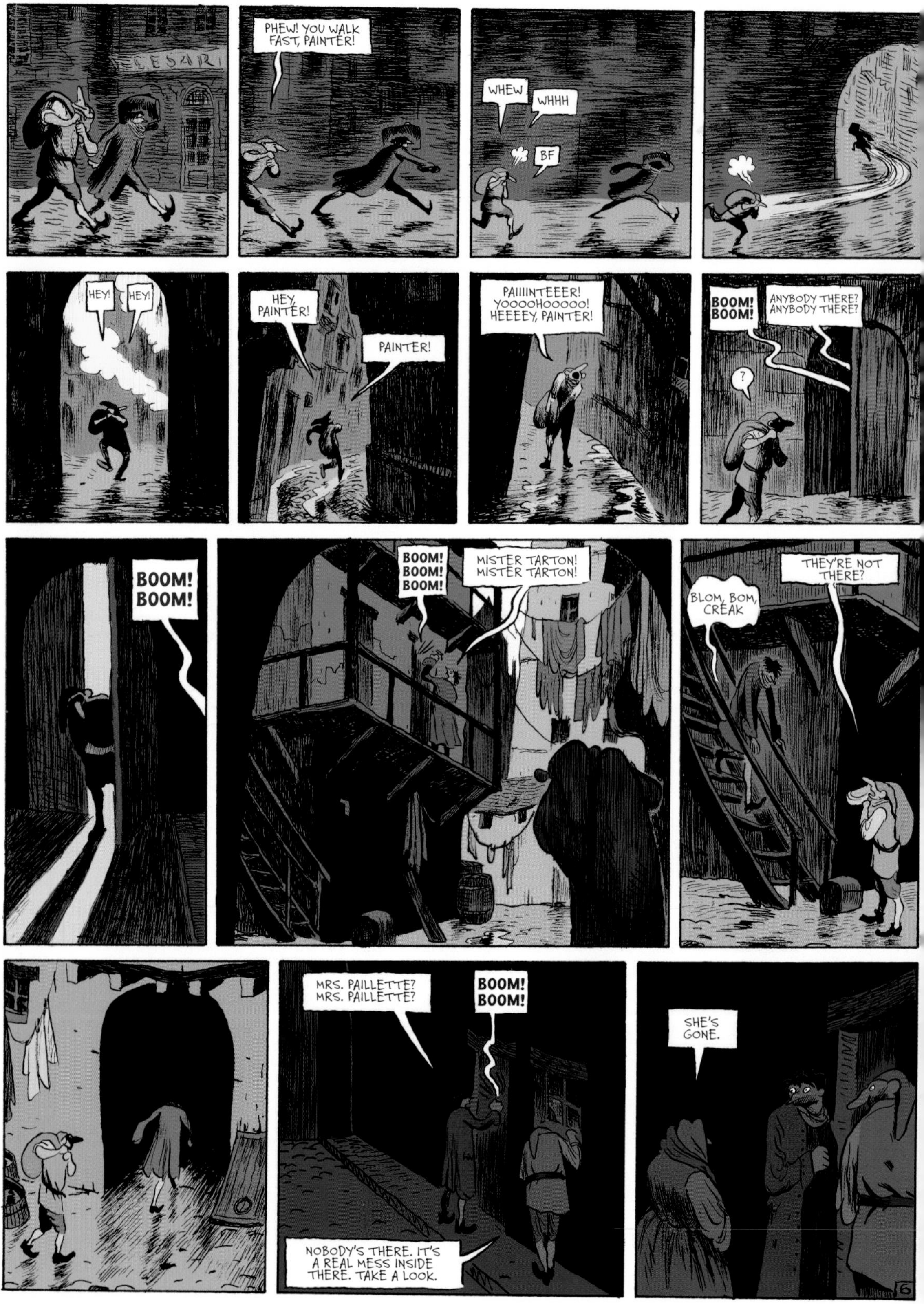
PHEW! YOU WALK FAST, PAINTER!
WHEW
WHHH
BF
HEY!
HEY!
HEY, PAINTER!
PAINTER!
PAIIIINTEEER! YOOOOHOOOOO! HEEEEY, PAINTER!
BOOM! BOOM!
ANYBODY THERE? ANYBODY THERE?
?
BOOM! BOOM!
BOOM! BOOM! BOOM!
MISTER TARTON! MISTER TARTON!
BLOM, BOM, CREAK
THEY'RE NOT THERE?
MRS. PAILLETTE? MRS. PAILLETTE?
BOOM! BOOM!
NOBODY'S THERE. IT'S A REAL MESS INSIDE THERE. TAKE A LOOK.
SHE'S GONE.

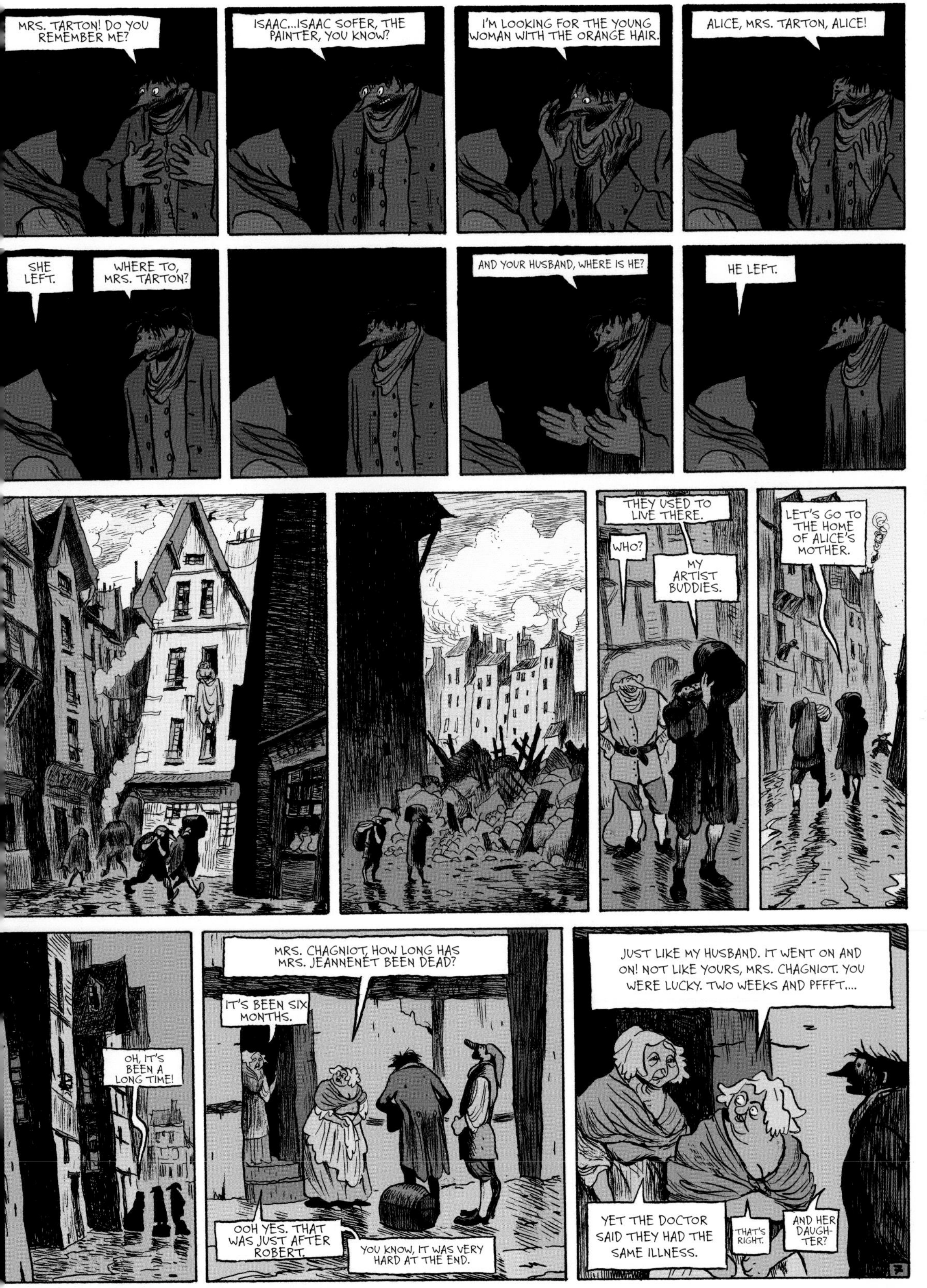
MRS. TARTON! DO YOU REMEMBER ME?
ISAAC...ISAAC SOFER, THE PAINTER, YOU KNOW?
I'M LOOKING FOR THE YOUNG WOMAN WITH THE ORANGE HAIR.
ALICE, MRS. TARTON, ALICE!
SHE LEFT.
WHERE TO, MRS. TARTON?
AND YOUR HUSBAND, WHERE IS HE?
HE LEFT.
THEY USED TO LIVE THERE.
WHO?
MY ARTIST BUDDIES.
LET'S GO TO THE HOME OF ALICE'S MOTHER.
OH, IT'S BEEN A LONG TIME!
MRS. CHAGNIOT, HOW LONG HAS MRS. JEANNENET BEEN DEAD?
IT'S BEEN SIX MONTHS.
OOH YES. THAT WAS JUST AFTER ROBERT.
YOU KNOW, IT WAS VERY HARD AT THE END.
JUST LIKE MY HUSBAND. IT WENT ON AND ON! NOT LIKE YOURS, MRS. CHAGNIOT. YOU WERE LUCKY. TWO WEEKS AND PFFFT....
YET THE DOCTOR SAID THEY HAD THE SAME ILLNESS.
THAT'S RIGHT.
AND HER DAUGHTER?

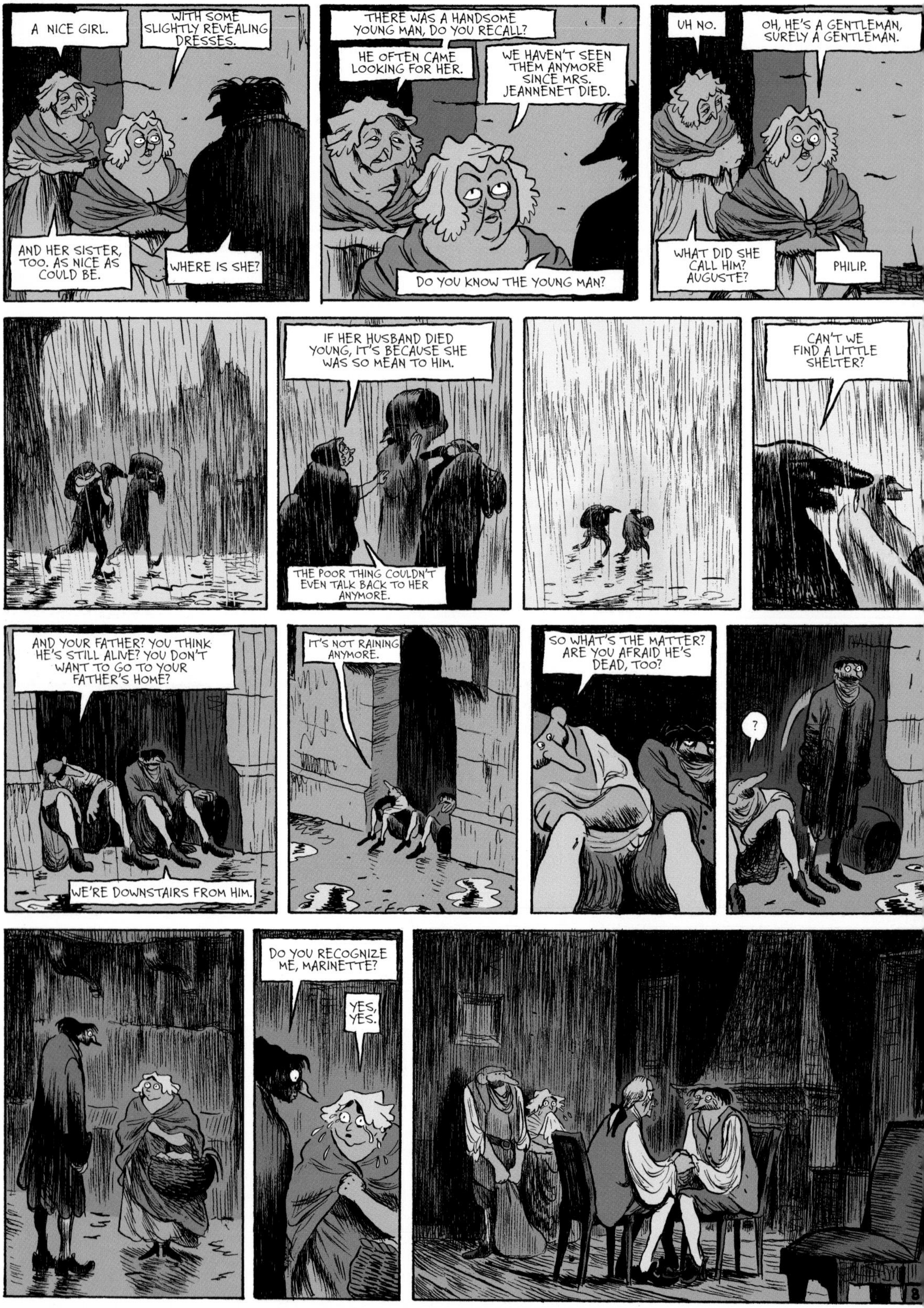

A NICE GIRL.
WITH SOME SLIGHTLY REVEALING DRESSES.
AND HER SISTER, TOO. AS NICE AS COULD BE.
WHERE IS SHE?
THERE WAS A HANDSOME YOUNG MAN, DO YOU RECALL?
HE OFTEN CAME LOOKING FOR HER.
WE HAVEN'T SEEN THEM ANYMORE SINCE MRS. JEANNENET DIED.
DO YOU KNOW THE YOUNG MAN?
UH NO.
OH, HE'S A GENTLEMAN, SURELY A GENTLEMAN.
WHAT DID SHE CALL HIM? AUGUSTE?
PHILIP.
IF HER HUSBAND DIED YOUNG, IT'S BECAUSE SHE WAS SO MEAN TO HIM.
THE POOR THING COULDN'T EVEN TALK BACK TO HER ANYMORE.
CAN'T WE FIND A LITTLE SHELTER?
AND YOUR FATHER? YOU THINK HE'S STILL ALIVE? YOU DON'T WANT TO GO TO YOUR FATHER'S HOME?
WE'RE DOWNSTAIRS FROM HIM.
IT'S NOT RAINING ANYMORE.
SO WHAT'S THE MATTER? ARE YOU AFRAID HE'S DEAD, TOO?
?
DO YOU RECOGNIZE ME, MARINETTE?
YES, YES.

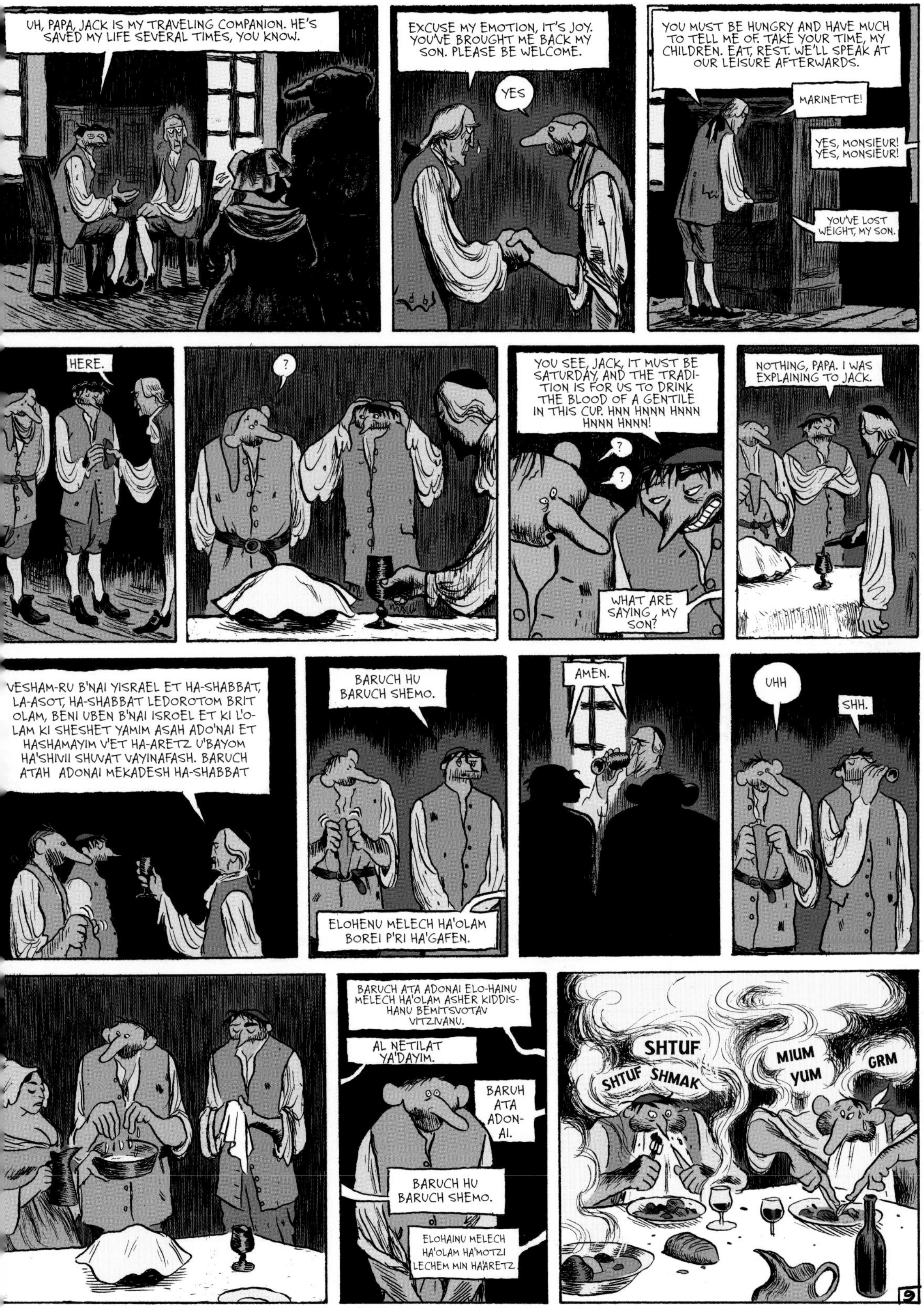
UH, PAPA, JACK IS MY TRAVELING COMPANION. HE'S SAVED MY LIFE SEVERAL TIMES, YOU KNOW.
EXCUSE MY EMOTION, IT'S JOY. YOU'VE BROUGHT ME BACK MY SON. PLEASE BE WELCOME.
YES
YOU MUST BE HUNGRY AND HAVE MUCH TO TELL ME OF. TAKE YOUR TIME, MY CHILDREN. EAT, REST. WE'LL SPEAK AT OUR LEISURE AFTERWARDS.
MARINETTE!
YES, MONSIEUR! YES, MONSIEUR!
YOU'VE LOST WEIGHT, MY SON.
HERE.
?
YOU SEE, JACK, IT MUST BE SATURDAY, AND THE TRADITION IS FOR US TO DRINK THE BLOOD OF A GENTILE IN THIS CUP. HNN HNNN HNNN HNNN HNNN!
?
?
WHAT ARE SAYING, MY SON?
NOTHING, PAPA. I WAS EXPLAINING TO JACK.
VESHAM-RU B'NAI YISRAEL ET HA-SHABBAT, LA-ASOT, HA-SHABBAT LEDOROTOM BRIT OLAM, BENI UBEN B'NAI ISROEL ET KI L'OLAM KI SHESHET YAMIM ASAH ADO'NAI ET HASHAMAYIM V'ET HA-ARETZ U'BAYOM HA'SHIVII SHUVAT VAYINAFASH. BARUCH ATAH ADONAI MEKADESH HA-SHABBAT
BARUCH HU BARUCH SHEMO.
ELOHENU MELECH HA'OLAM BOREI P'RI HA'GAFEN.
AMEN.
UHH
SHH.
BARUCH ATA ADONAI ELO-HAINU MELECH HA'OLAM ASHER KIDDISHANU BEMITSVOTAV VITZIVANU.
AL NETILAT YA'DAYIM.
BARUH ATA ADONAI.
BARUCH HU BARUCH SHEMO.
ELOHAINU MELECH HA'OLAM HA'MOTZI LECHEM MIN HA'ARETZ
SHTUF
SHTUF SHMAK
MIUM
YUM
GRM

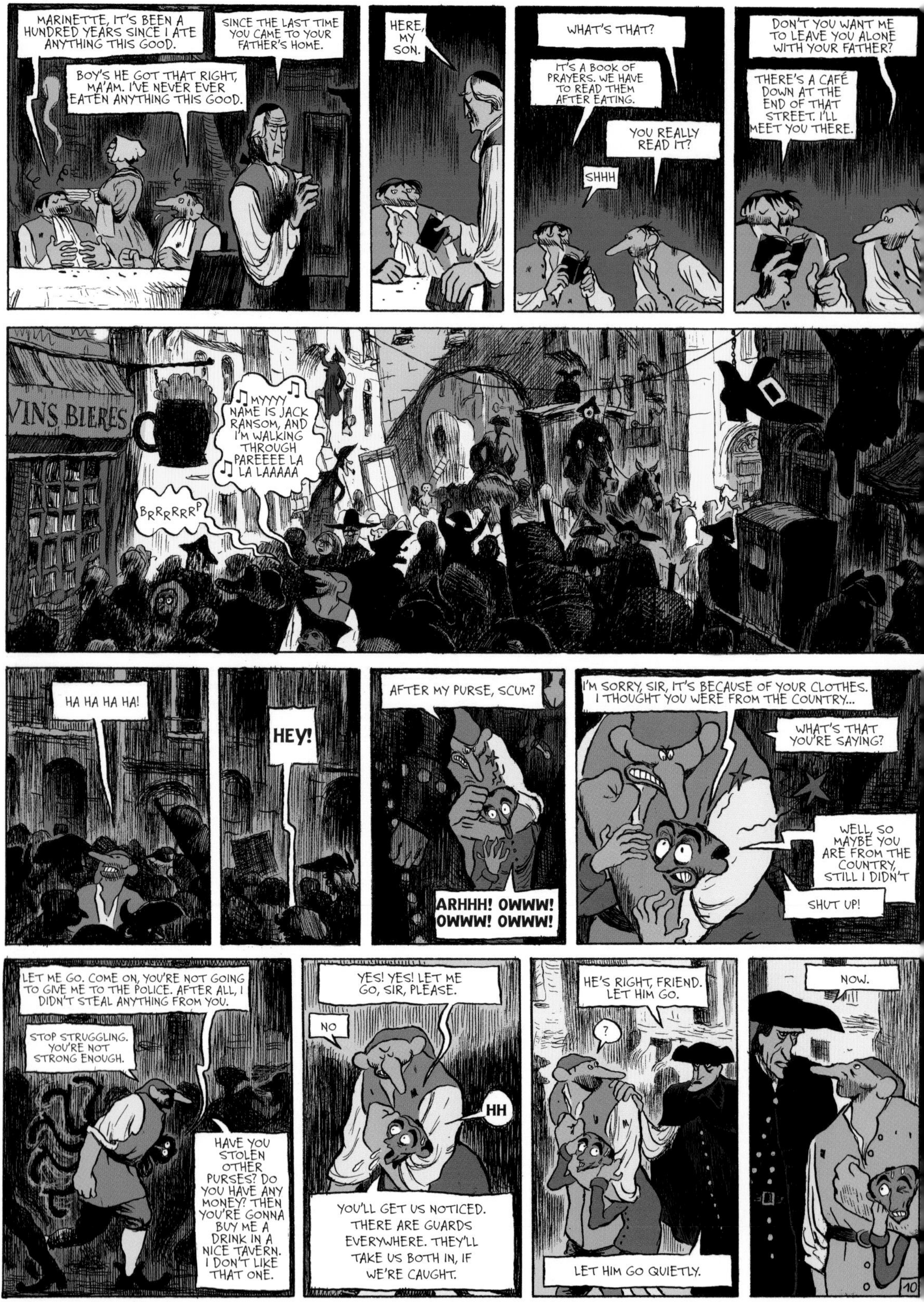
MARINETTE, IT'S BEEN A HUNDRED YEARS SINCE I ATE ANYTHING THIS GOOD.
SINCE THE LAST TIME YOU CAME TO YOUR FATHER'S HOME.
BOY'S HE GOT THAT RIGHT, MA'AM. I'VE NEVER EVER EATEN ANYTHING THIS GOOD.
HERE, MY SON.
WHAT'S THAT?
IT'S A BOOK OF PRAYERS. WE HAVE TO READ THEM AFTER EATING.
YOU REALLY READ IT?
SHHH
DON'T YOU WANT ME TO LEAVE YOU ALONE WITH YOUR FATHER?
THERE'S A CAFÉ DOWN AT THE END OF THAT STREET. I'LL MEET YOU THERE.
VINS BIERES
♫ MYYYY NAME IS JACK RANSOM, AND I'M WALKING THROUGH PAREEEE LA LA LAAAAA ♫
BRRRRRP
HA HA HA HA!
HEY!
AFTER MY PURSE, SCUM?
ARHHH! OWWW! OWWW! OWWW!
I'M SORRY, SIR, IT'S BECAUSE OF YOUR CLOTHES. I THOUGHT YOU WERE FROM THE COUNTRY...
WHAT'S THAT YOU'RE SAYING?
WELL, SO MAYBE YOU ARE FROM THE COUNTRY, STILL I DIDN'T
SHUT UP!
LET ME GO. COME ON, YOU'RE NOT GOING TO GIVE ME TO THE POLICE. AFTER ALL, I DIDN'T STEAL ANYTHING FROM YOU.
STOP STRUGGLING. YOU'RE NOT STRONG ENOUGH.
HAVE YOU STOLEN OTHER PURSES? DO YOU HAVE ANY MONEY? THEN YOU'RE GONNA BUY ME A DRINK IN A NICE TAVERN. I DON'T LIKE THAT ONE.
YES! YES! LET ME GO, SIR, PLEASE.
NO
HH
YOU'LL GET US NOTICED. THERE ARE GUARDS EVERYWHERE. THEY'LL TAKE US BOTH IN, IF WE'RE CAUGHT.
HE'S RIGHT, FRIEND. LET HIM GO.
?
LET HIM GO QUIETLY.
NOW.

YOU'RE PORTUGUESE. YOU TALK LIKE A PORTUGUESE.

SHOW ME A NICE TAVERN, PORTUGUESE.

HURRY UP, FOOL.

YOU HAVE A KNIFE?

ME, TOO.

A FELLOW WITH EARS LIKE THIS AND A NOSE LIKE THAT.

JACK!

JACK!

SHIT! SHIT! SHIT!

SHIT! SHIT!

HEY! I SAW A GUY WHO LOOKS LIKE WHAT YOU'RE SAYING. HE WAS WITH THREE WENCHES. HE LEFT A SHORT WHILE AGO. HE SEEMED IN A HURRY. THE OTHERS WERE CLOSE BEHIND. THEY DIDN'T LOOK TOO FRIENDLY.

JACK! JAAAAAACK!

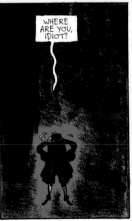

WHERE ARE YOU, IDIOT?

JA...

ENOUGH.

BRFMFGL

11

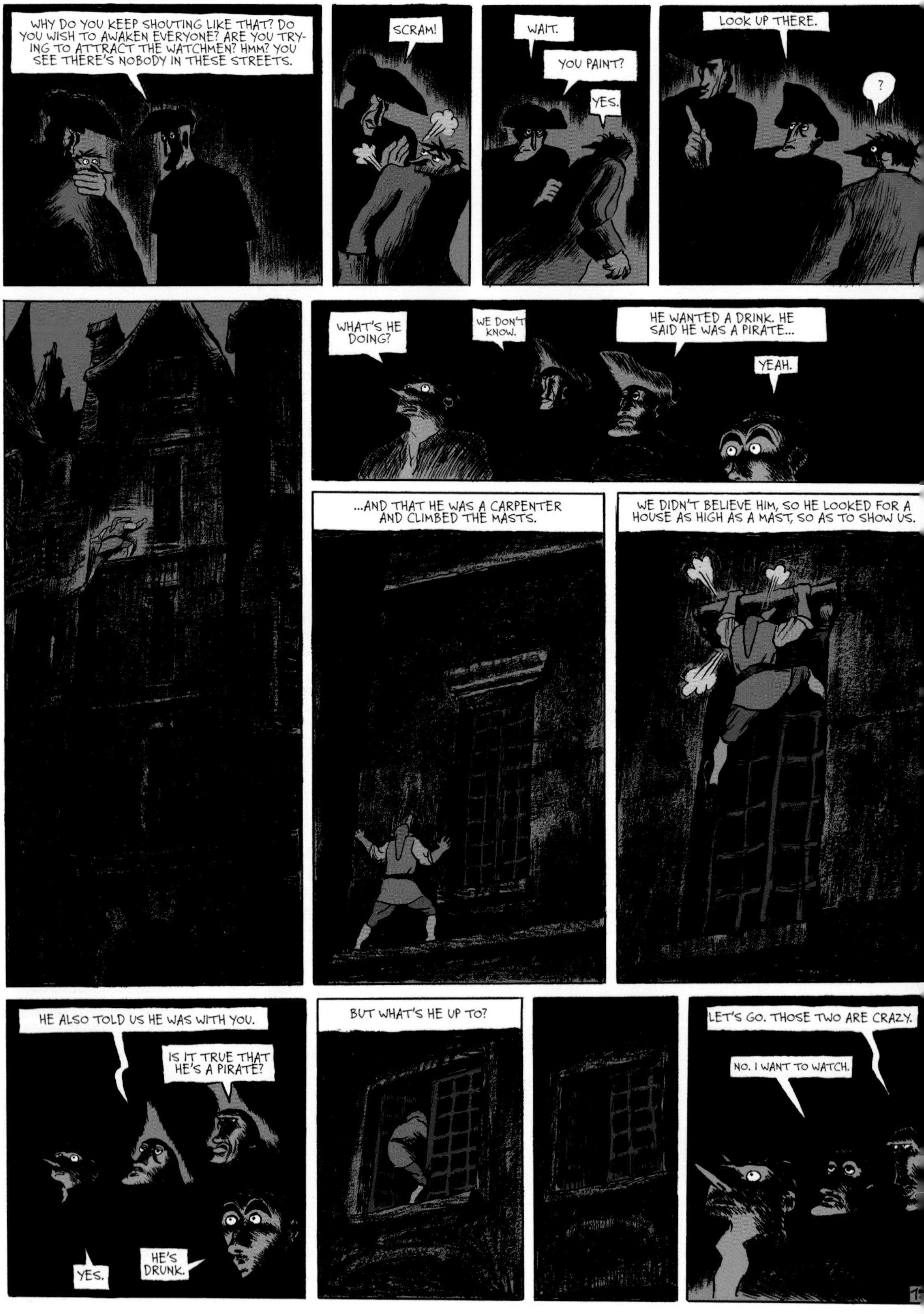
WHY DO YOU KEEP SHOUTING LIKE THAT? DO YOU WISH TO AWAKEN EVERYONE? ARE YOU TRYING TO ATTRACT THE WATCHMEN? HMM? YOU SEE THERE'S NOBODY IN THESE STREETS.
SCRAM!
WAIT.
YOU PAINT?
YES.
LOOK UP THERE.
?
WHAT'S HE DOING?
WE DON'T KNOW.
HE WANTED A DRINK. HE SAID HE WAS A PIRATE...
YEAH.
...AND THAT HE WAS A CARPENTER AND CLIMBED THE MASTS.
WE DIDN'T BELIEVE HIM, SO HE LOOKED FOR A HOUSE AS HIGH AS A MAST, SO AS TO SHOW US.
HE ALSO TOLD US HE WAS WITH YOU.
IS IT TRUE THAT HE'S A PIRATE?
YES.
HE'S DRUNK.
BUT WHAT'S HE UP TO?
LET'S GO. THOSE TWO ARE CRAZY.
NO. I WANT TO WATCH.

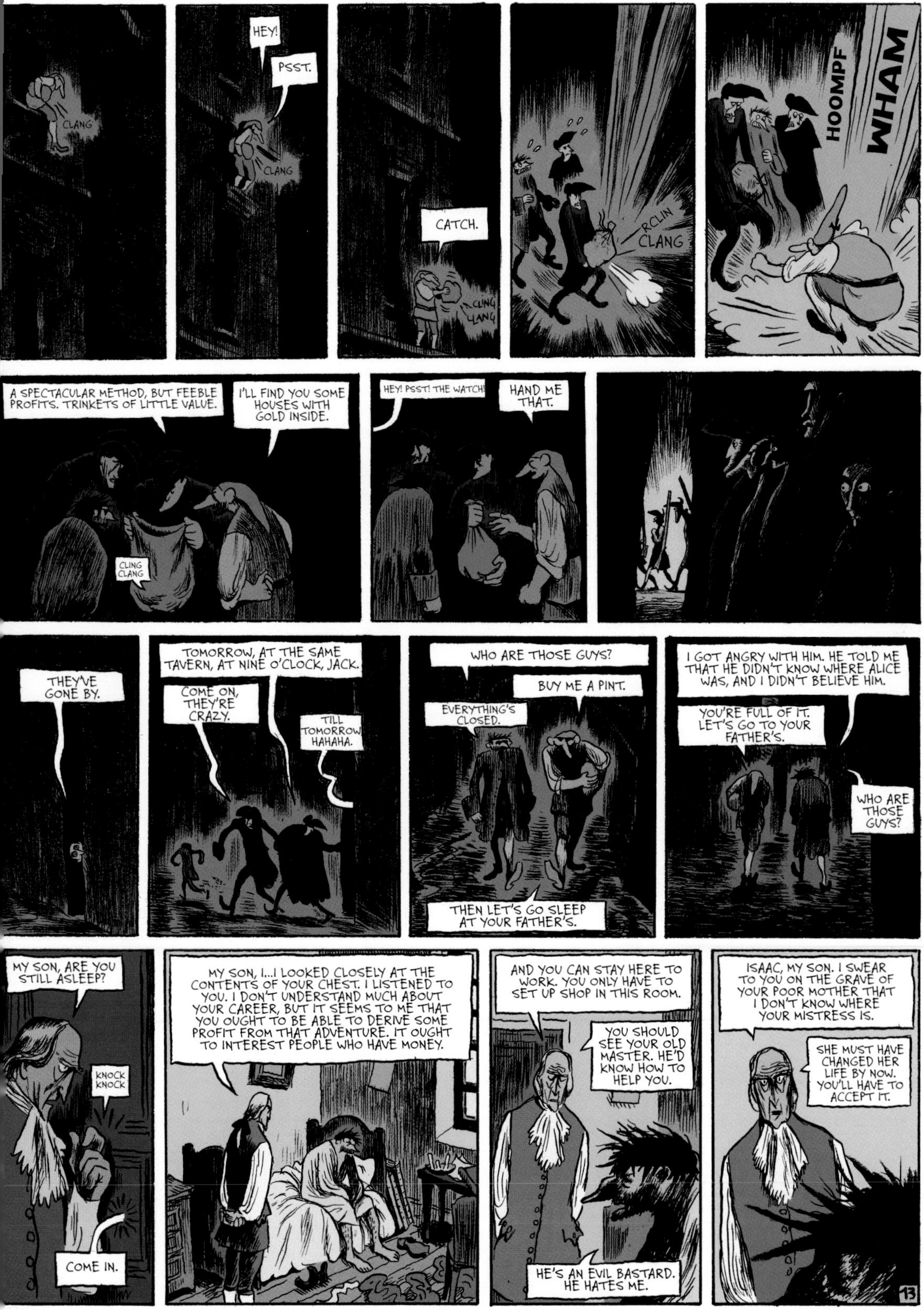
CLANG
HEY!
PSST.
CLANG
CATCH.
CLING CLANG
RCLIN CLANG
HOOMPF
WHAM
A SPECTACULAR METHOD, BUT FEEBLE PROFITS. TRINKETS OF LITTLE VALUE.
CLING CLANG
I'LL FIND YOU SOME HOUSES WITH GOLD INSIDE.
HEY! PSST! THE WATCH!
HAND ME THAT.
THEY'VE GONE BY.
TOMORROW, AT THE SAME TAVERN, AT NINE O'CLOCK, JACK.
COME ON, THEY'RE CRAZY.
TILL TOMORROW HAHAHA.
WHO ARE THOSE GUYS?
BUY ME A PINT.
EVERYTHING'S CLOSED.
THEN LET'S GO SLEEP AT YOUR FATHER'S.
I GOT ANGRY WITH HIM. HE TOLD ME THAT HE DIDN'T KNOW WHERE ALICE WAS, AND I DIDN'T BELIEVE HIM.
YOU'RE FULL OF IT. LET'S GO TO YOUR FATHER'S.
WHO ARE THOSE GUYS?
MY SON, ARE YOU STILL ASLEEP?
KNOCK KNOCK
COME IN.
MY SON, I...I LOOKED CLOSELY AT THE CONTENTS OF YOUR CHEST. I LISTENED TO YOU. I DON'T UNDERSTAND MUCH ABOUT YOUR CAREER, BUT IT SEEMS TO ME THAT YOU OUGHT TO BE ABLE TO DERIVE SOME PROFIT FROM THAT ADVENTURE. IT OUGHT TO INTEREST PEOPLE WHO HAVE MONEY.
AND YOU CAN STAY HERE TO WORK. YOU ONLY HAVE TO SET UP SHOP IN THIS ROOM.
YOU SHOULD SEE YOUR OLD MASTER. HE'D KNOW HOW TO HELP YOU.
HE'S AN EVIL BASTARD. HE HATES ME.
ISAAC, MY SON. I SWEAR TO YOU ON THE GRAVE OF YOUR POOR MOTHER THAT I DON'T KNOW WHERE YOUR MISTRESS IS.
SHE MUST HAVE CHANGED HER LIFE BY NOW. YOU'LL HAVE TO ACCEPT IT.
13

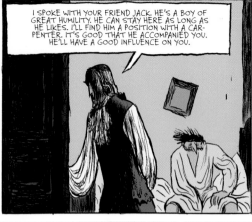

I SPOKE WITH YOUR FRIEND JACK. HE'S A BOY OF GREAT HUMILITY. HE CAN STAY HERE AS LONG AS HE LIKES. I'LL FIND HIM A POSITION WITH A CARPENTER. IT'S GOOD THAT HE ACCOMPANIED YOU. HE'LL HAVE A GOOD INFLUENCE ON YOU.

SO, MY BOY. WANNA HIRE OURSELVES THOSE WHORES?

IF WE DON'T HAVE ENOUGH MONEY, WE'LL JUST GET ONE FOR TWO.

YOUR ROBBER PALS WON'T BE COMING ANYMORE.

NO. THE WHORES ARE ALL WE HAVE LEFT.

JACK, I NEED TO HAVE SEX, BUT I WANT IT TO BE WITH REAL WOMEN.

WHY? THEY AREN'T REAL WOMEN?

I WON'T HAVE ANY SEX SO LONG AS I HAVEN'T PAINTED OR WRITTEN SERIOUSLY.

OH YEAH?

PAINTER, I'VE NEVER SEEN SO MANY WOMEN AT ONCE.

YOU'RE JOKING! THERE ARE TEN TIMES MORE GUYS IN THIS BURG

PARIS IS FULL OF YOUNG BUMPKINS LEAVING THEIR COUNTRYSIDE TO AVOID THE DRAFT LOTTERY FOR THE MILITIA.

THOSE WHORES AREN'T WORTH YOU GETTING ALL WORKED UP FOR.

HE WANTS REAL WOMEN.

YEAH.

CAN'T YOU THINK ABOUT ANYTHING ELSE FOR A MOMENT?

WE HAVE TO TALK WITH THE PIRATE.

HE STAYS.

NO, NO, I'M GONNA DRAW IN A CORNER OVER THERE.

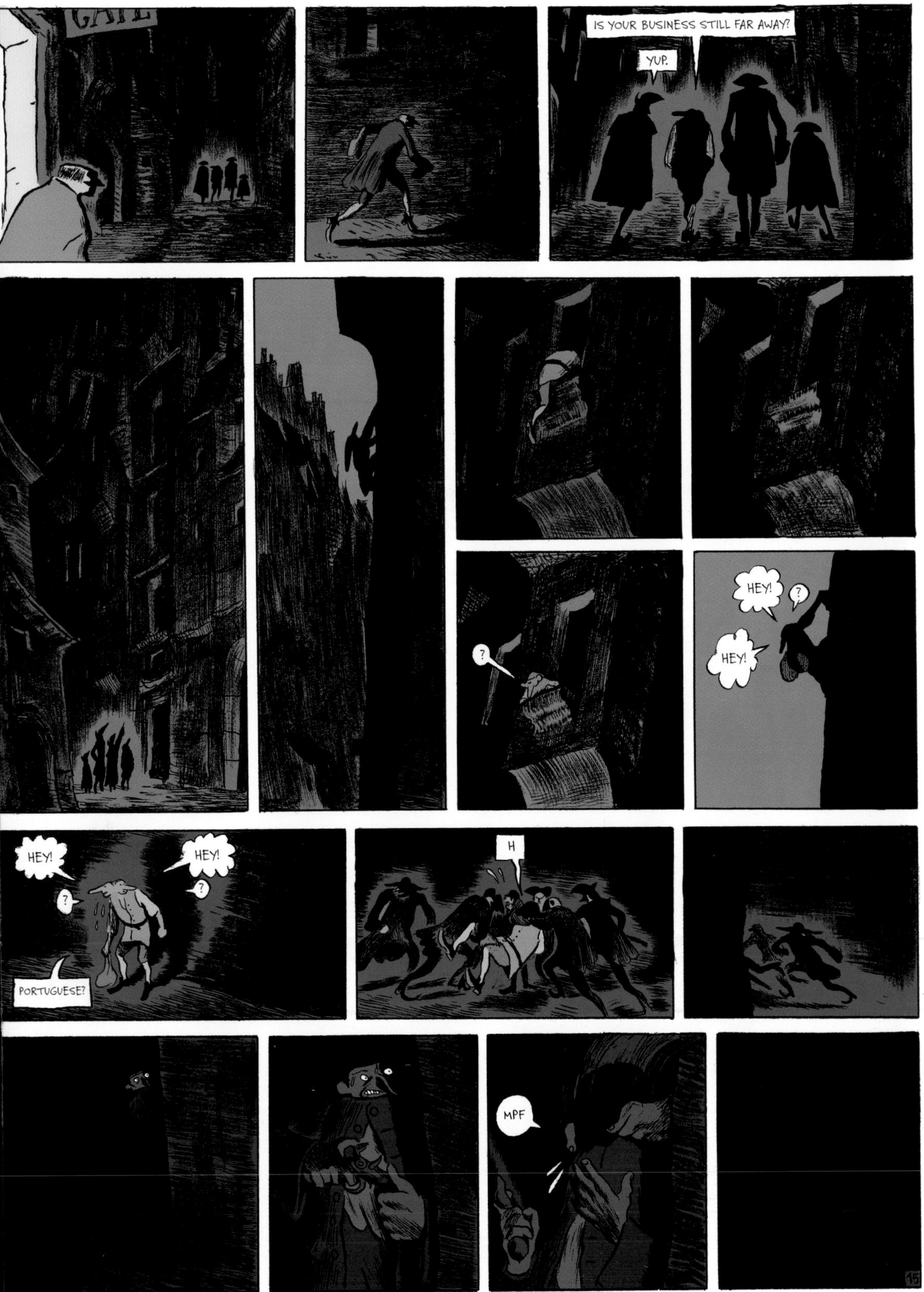
GAFE
IS YOUR BUSINESS STILL FAR AWAY?
YUP.
?
HEY!
?
HEY!
HEY!
?
HEY!
?
PORTUGUESE?
H
MPF

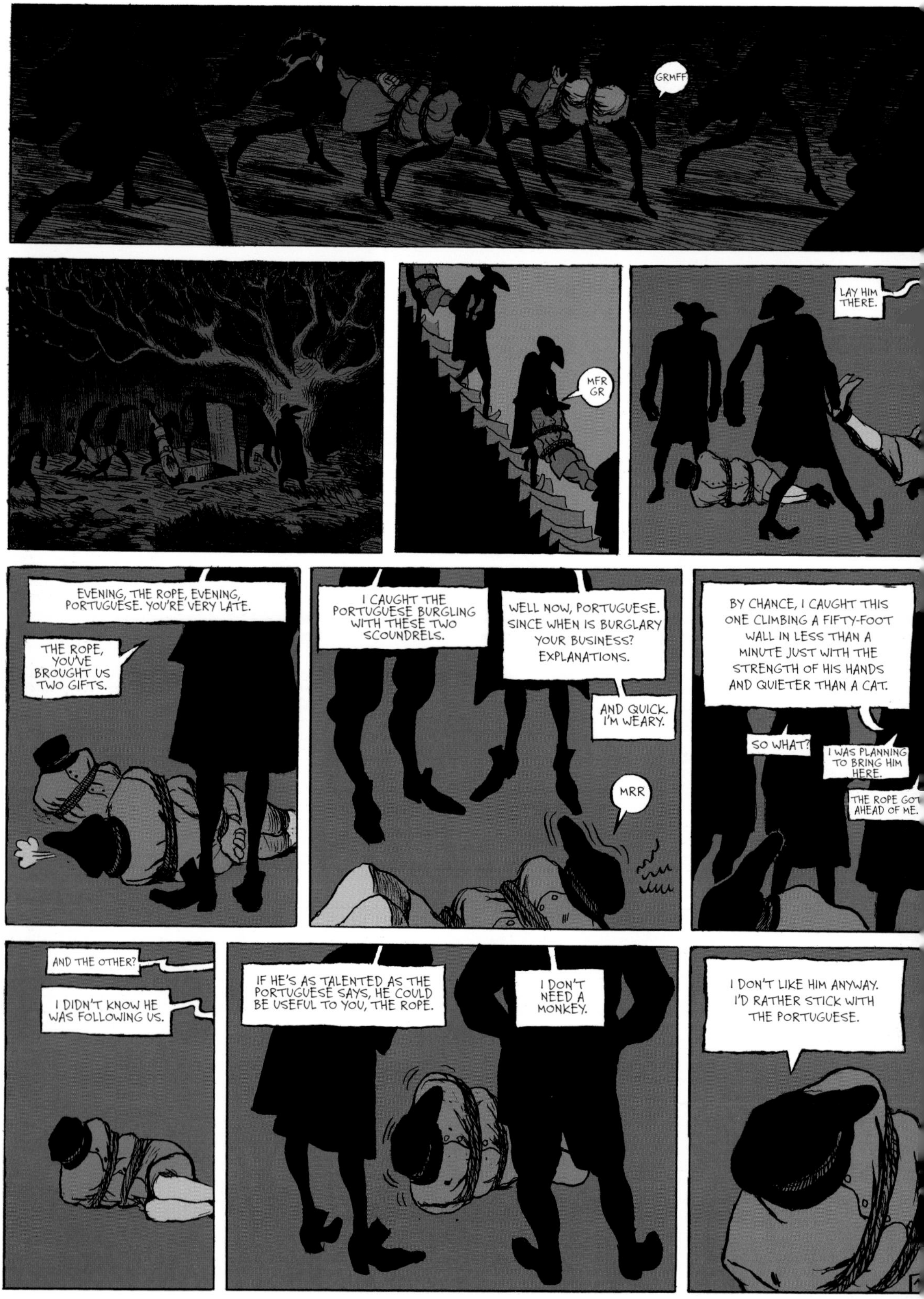
GRMFF
MFR GR
LAY HIM THERE.
EVENING, THE ROPE, EVENING, PORTUGUESE. YOU'RE VERY LATE.
THE ROPE, YOU'VE BROUGHT US TWO GIFTS.
I CAUGHT THE PORTUGUESE BURGLING WITH THESE TWO SCOUNDRELS.
WELL NOW, PORTUGUESE. SINCE WHEN IS BURGLARY YOUR BUSINESS? EXPLANATIONS.
AND QUICK. I'M WEARY.
MRR
BY CHANCE, I CAUGHT THIS ONE CLIMBING A FIFTY-FOOT WALL IN LESS THAN A MINUTE JUST WITH THE STRENGTH OF HIS HANDS AND QUIETER THAN A CAT.
SO WHAT?
I WAS PLANNING TO BRING HIM HERE.
THE ROPE GOT AHEAD OF ME.
AND THE OTHER?
I DIDN'T KNOW HE WAS FOLLOWING US.
IF HE'S AS TALENTED AS THE PORTUGUESE SAYS, HE COULD BE USEFUL TO YOU, THE ROPE.
I DON'T NEED A MONKEY.
I DON'T LIKE HIM ANYWAY. I'D RATHER STICK WITH THE PORTUGUESE.

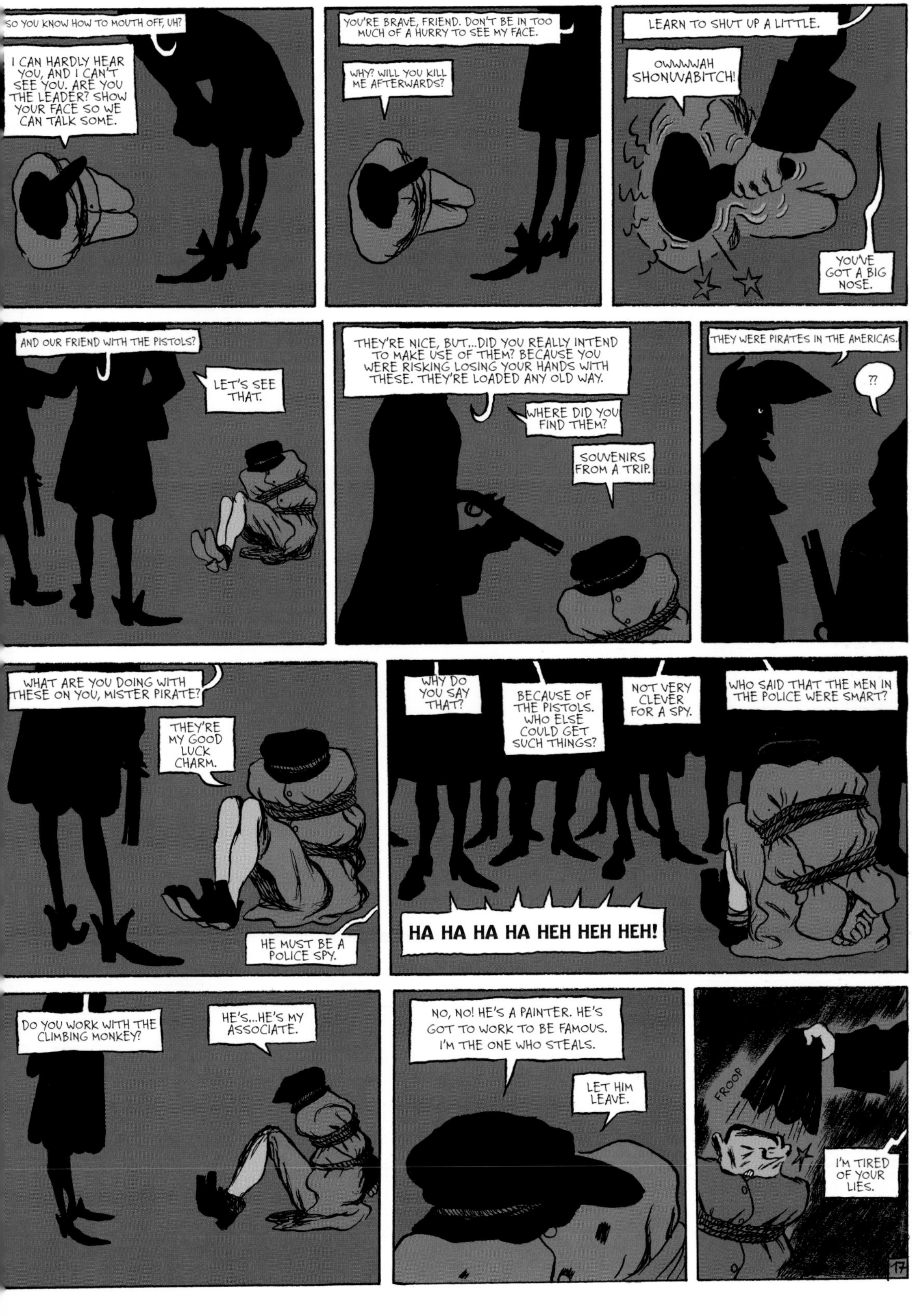

SO YOU KNOW HOW TO MOUTH OFF, UH?
I CAN HARDLY HEAR YOU, AND I CAN'T SEE YOU. ARE YOU THE LEADER? SHOW YOUR FACE SO WE CAN TALK SOME.
YOU'RE BRAVE, FRIEND. DON'T BE IN TOO MUCH OF A HURRY TO SEE MY FACE.
WHY? WILL YOU KILL ME AFTERWARDS?
LEARN TO SHUT UP A LITTLE.
OWWWWAH SHONUVABITCH!
YOU'VE GOT A BIG NOSE.
AND OUR FRIEND WITH THE PISTOLS?
LET'S SEE THAT.
THEY'RE NICE, BUT...DID YOU REALLY INTEND TO MAKE USE OF THEM? BECAUSE YOU WERE RISKING LOSING YOUR HANDS WITH THESE. THEY'RE LOADED ANY OLD WAY.
WHERE DID YOU FIND THEM?
SOUVENIRS FROM A TRIP.
THEY WERE PIRATES IN THE AMERICAS.
??
WHAT ARE YOU DOING WITH THESE ON YOU, MISTER PIRATE?
THEY'RE MY GOOD LUCK CHARM.
HE MUST BE A POLICE SPY.
WHY DO YOU SAY THAT?
BECAUSE OF THE PISTOLS. WHO ELSE COULD GET SUCH THINGS?
NOT VERY CLEVER FOR A SPY.
WHO SAID THAT THE MEN IN THE POLICE WERE SMART?
HA HA HA HA HEH HEH HEH!
DO YOU WORK WITH THE CLIMBING MONKEY?
HE'S...HE'S MY ASSOCIATE.
NO, NO! HE'S A PAINTER. HE'S GOT TO WORK TO BE FAMOUS. I'M THE ONE WHO STEALS.
LET HIM LEAVE.
FROOP
I'M TIRED OF YOUR LIES.

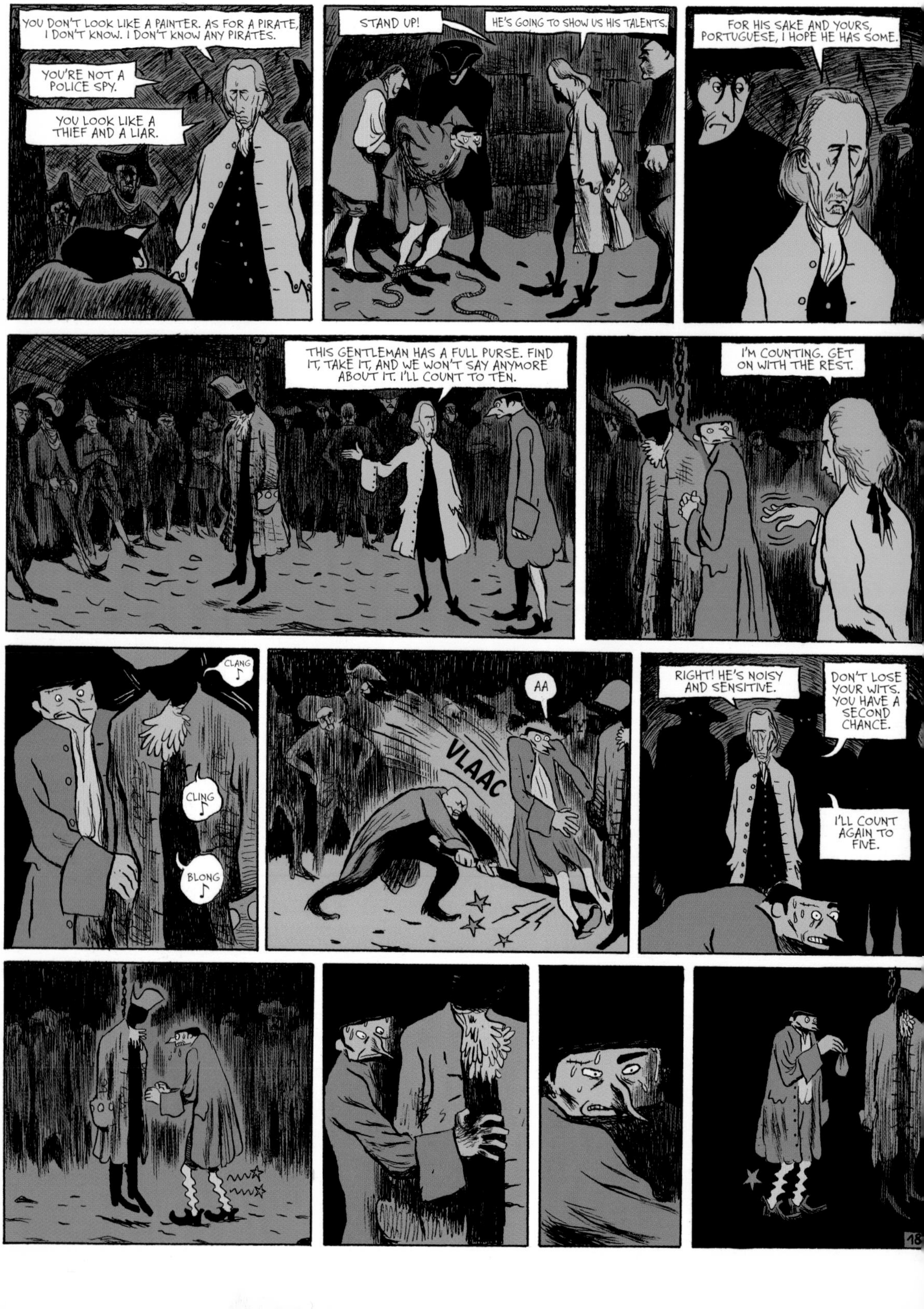
YOU DON'T LOOK LIKE A PAINTER. AS FOR A PIRATE, I DON'T KNOW. I DON'T KNOW ANY PIRATES.
YOU'RE NOT A POLICE SPY.
YOU LOOK LIKE A THIEF AND A LIAR.
STAND UP!
HE'S GOING TO SHOW US HIS TALENTS.
FOR HIS SAKE AND YOURS, PORTUGUESE, I HOPE HE HAS SOME.
THIS GENTLEMAN HAS A FULL PURSE. FIND IT, TAKE IT, AND WE WON'T SAY ANYMORE ABOUT IT. I'LL COUNT TO TEN.
I'M COUNTING. GET ON WITH THE REST.
CLANG
CLING
BLONG
AA
VLAAC
RIGHT! HE'S NOISY AND SENSITIVE.
DON'T LOSE YOUR WITS. YOU HAVE A SECOND CHANCE.
I'LL COUNT AGAIN TO FIVE.

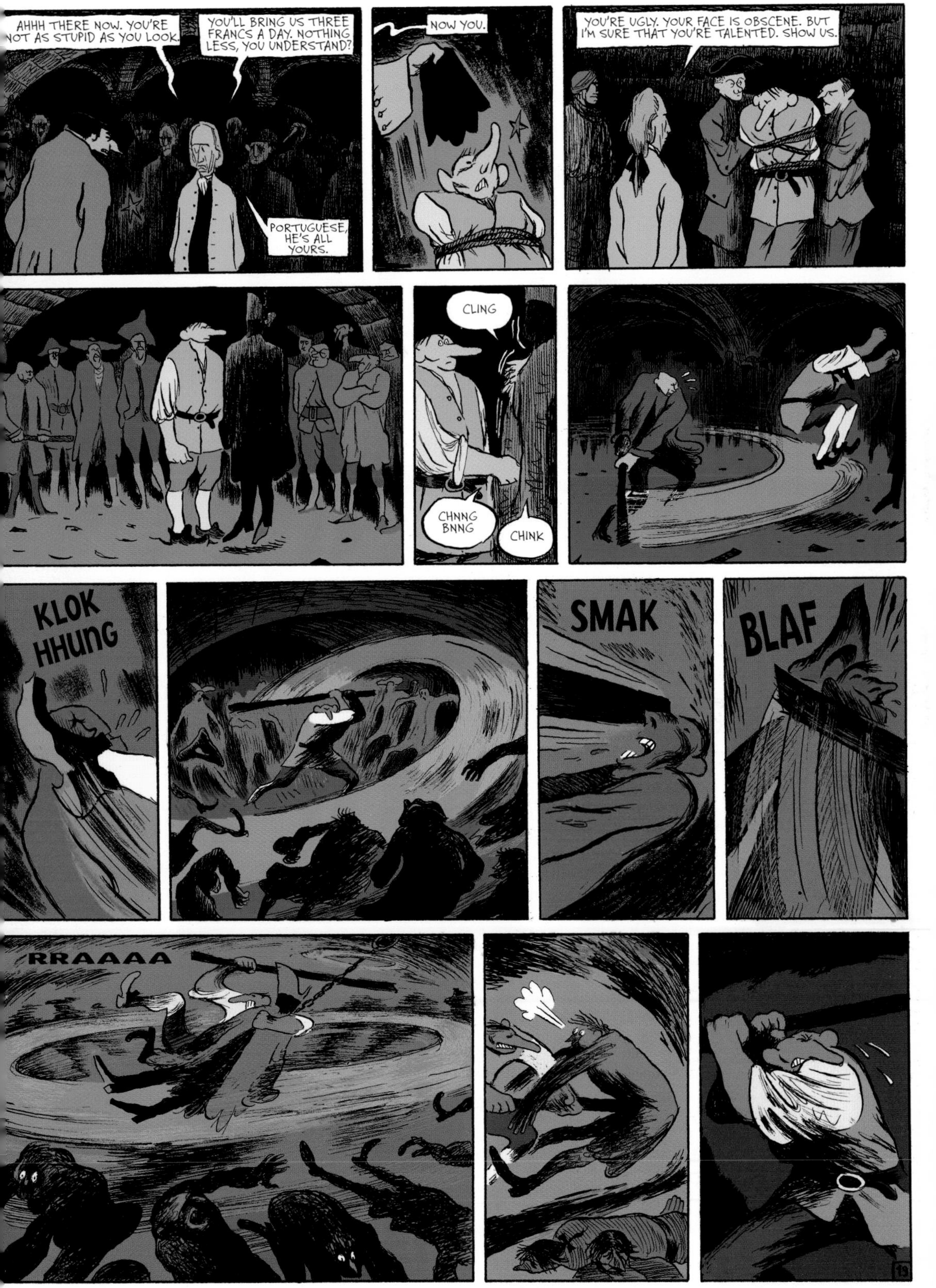
AHHH THERE NOW. YOU'RE NOT AS STUPID AS YOU LOOK.
YOU'LL BRING US THREE FRANCS A DAY. NOTHING LESS, YOU UNDERSTAND?
PORTUGUESE, HE'S ALL YOURS.
NOW YOU.
YOU'RE UGLY. YOUR FACE IS OBSCENE. BUT I'M SURE THAT YOU'RE TALENTED. SHOW US.
CLING
CHNNG BNNG
CHINK
KLOK HHUNG
SMAK
BLAF
RRAAAA

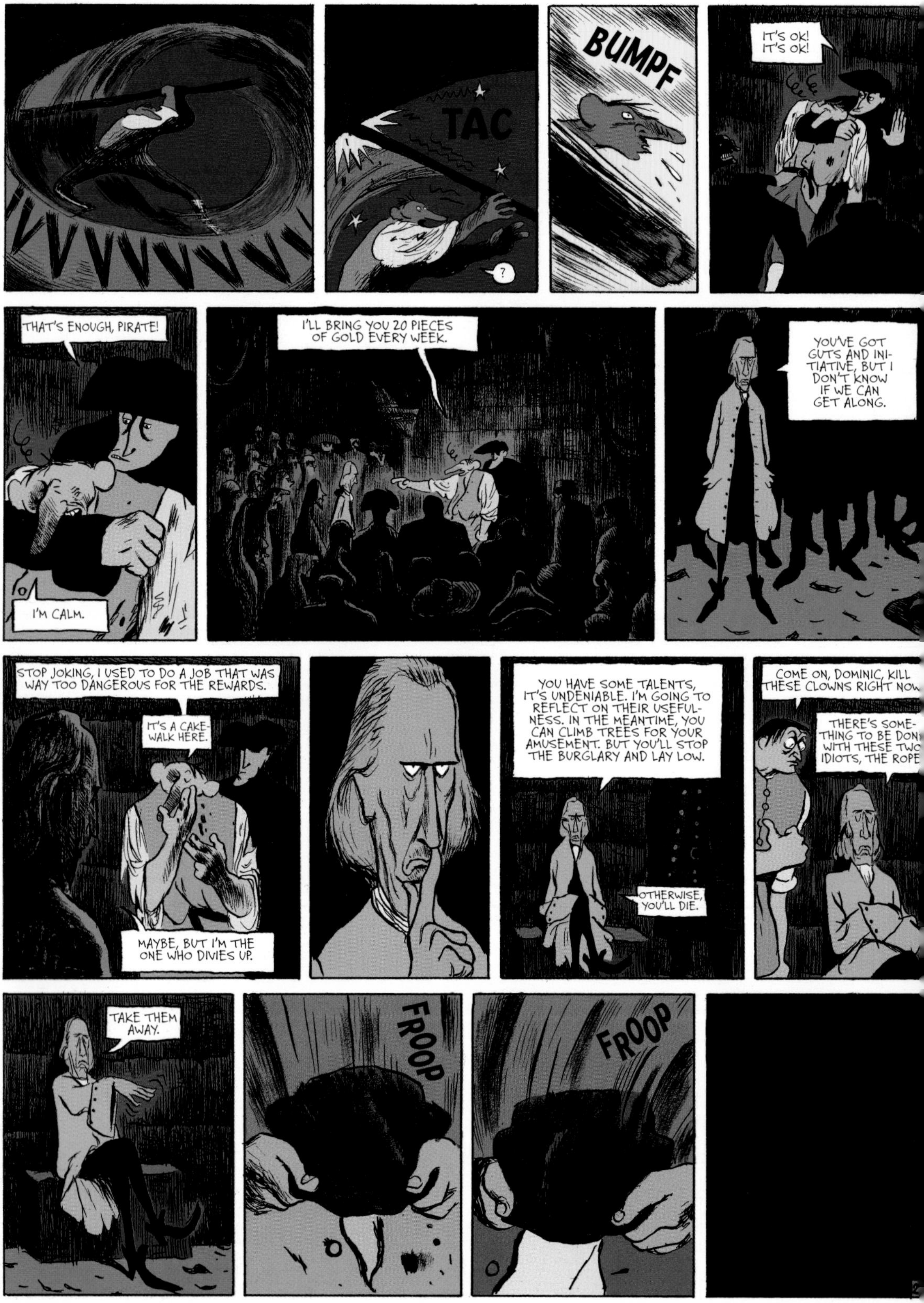

TAC
?
BUMPF
IT'S OK!
IT'S OK!
THAT'S ENOUGH, PIRATE!
I'M CALM.
I'LL BRING YOU 20 PIECES OF GOLD EVERY WEEK.
YOU'VE GOT GUTS AND INITIATIVE, BUT I DON'T KNOW IF WE CAN GET ALONG.
STOP JOKING, I USED TO DO A JOB THAT WAS WAY TOO DANGEROUS FOR THE REWARDS.
IT'S A CAKE-WALK HERE.
MAYBE, BUT I'M THE ONE WHO DIVIES UP.
YOU HAVE SOME TALENTS, IT'S UNDENIABLE. I'M GOING TO REFLECT ON THEIR USEFULNESS. IN THE MEANTIME, YOU CAN CLIMB TREES FOR YOUR AMUSEMENT. BUT YOU'LL STOP THE BURGLARY AND LAY LOW.
OTHERWISE, YOU'LL DIE.
COME ON, DOMINIC, KILL THESE CLOWNS RIGHT NOW
THERE'S SOMETHING TO BE DON WITH THESE TWO IDIOTS, THE ROPE
TAKE THEM AWAY.
FROOP
FROOP

UH, WHERE ARE THEY?

AND WHERE ARE WE?

SHIT! THE BASTARD KEPT MY PISTOLS.

UH, I WON THEM IN A GAME DURING THE CROSSING.

WHERE DID YOU GET THOSE?

IN A GAME?

WHAT GAME?

OKAY, IN FACT, I BOUGHT THEM FROM A GUY ON THE BOAT.

AS IF WE'D HAD ENOUGH MONEY! WHY DIDN'T YOU TELL ME? THAT'S BULLSHIT! THAT'S NOT WORTH A GOOD KNIFE.

I DON'T KNOW HOW TO USE A KNIFE.

OH YEAH? 'CAUSE YOU KNOW HOW TO USE PISTOLS?

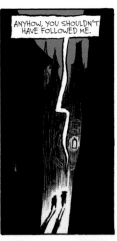

ANYHOW, YOU SHOULDN'T HAVE FOLLOWED ME.

DO YOU REALIZE?

DO YOU REALIZE WHAT YOU'VE DONE, YOUNG MAN? I WAS SKEPTICAL WHEN I HEARD ABOUT YOU. NOW I MUST ACCEPT THE EVIDENCE.

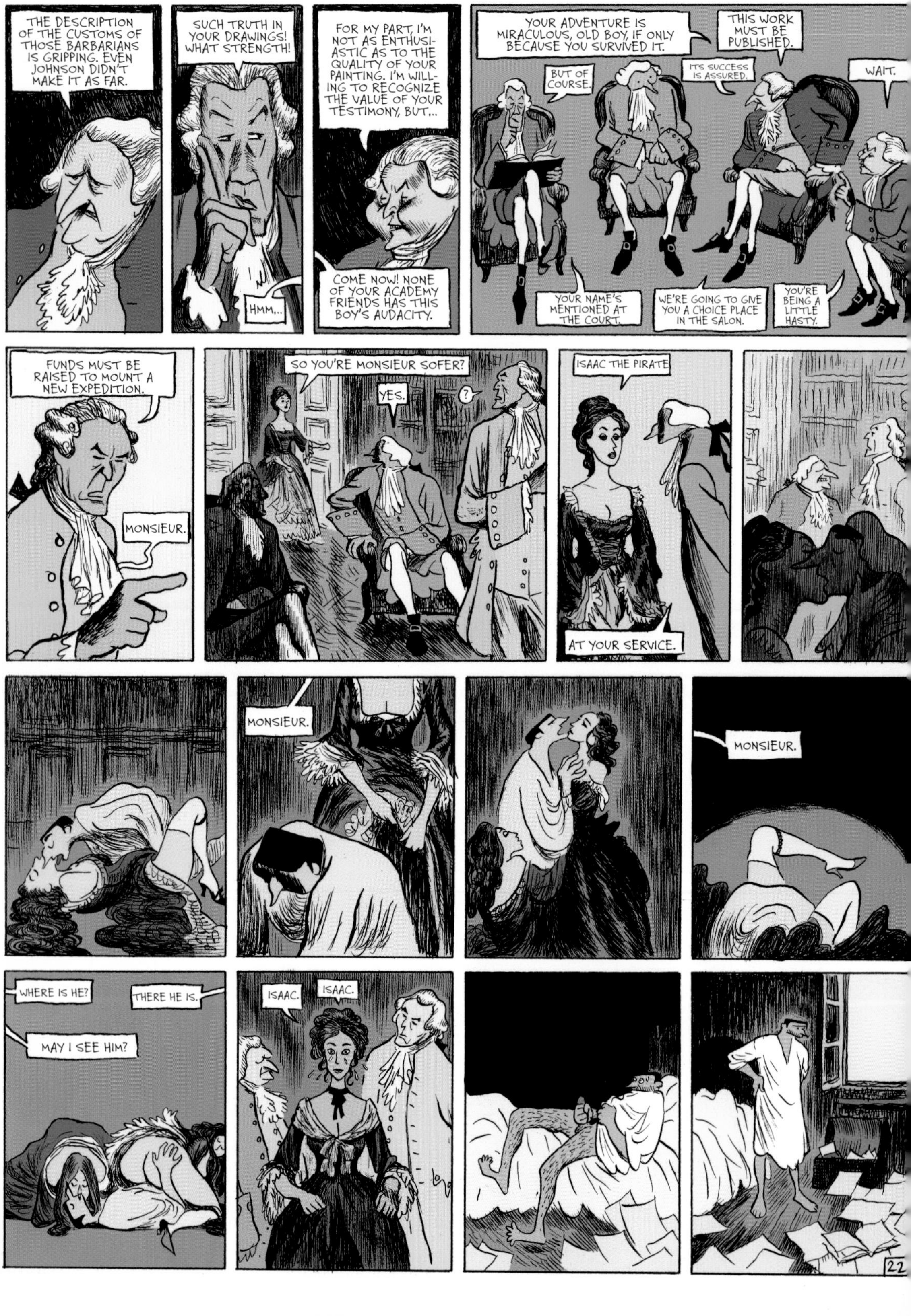

THE DESCRIPTION OF THE CUSTOMS OF THOSE BARBARIANS IS GRIPPING. EVEN JOHNSON DIDN'T MAKE IT AS FAR.
SUCH TRUTH IN YOUR DRAWINGS! WHAT STRENGTH!
HMM...
FOR MY PART, I'M NOT AS ENTHUSIASTIC AS TO THE QUALITY OF YOUR PAINTING. I'M WILLING TO RECOGNIZE THE VALUE OF YOUR TESTIMONY, BUT...
COME NOW! NONE OF YOUR ACADEMY FRIENDS HAS THIS BOY'S AUDACITY.
YOUR ADVENTURE IS MIRACULOUS, OLD BOY, IF ONLY BECAUSE YOU SURVIVED IT.
THIS WORK MUST BE PUBLISHED.
BUT OF COURSE.
IT'S SUCCESS IS ASSURED.
WAIT.
YOUR NAME'S MENTIONED AT THE COURT.
WE'RE GOING TO GIVE YOU A CHOICE PLACE IN THE SALON.
YOU'RE BEING A LITTLE HASTY.
FUNDS MUST BE RAISED TO MOUNT A NEW EXPEDITION.
MONSIEUR.
SO YOU'RE MONSIEUR SOFER?
YES.
?
ISAAC THE PIRATE
AT YOUR SERVICE.
MONSIEUR.
MONSIEUR.
WHERE IS HE?
THERE HE IS.
MAY I SEE HIM?
ISAAC.
ISAAC.

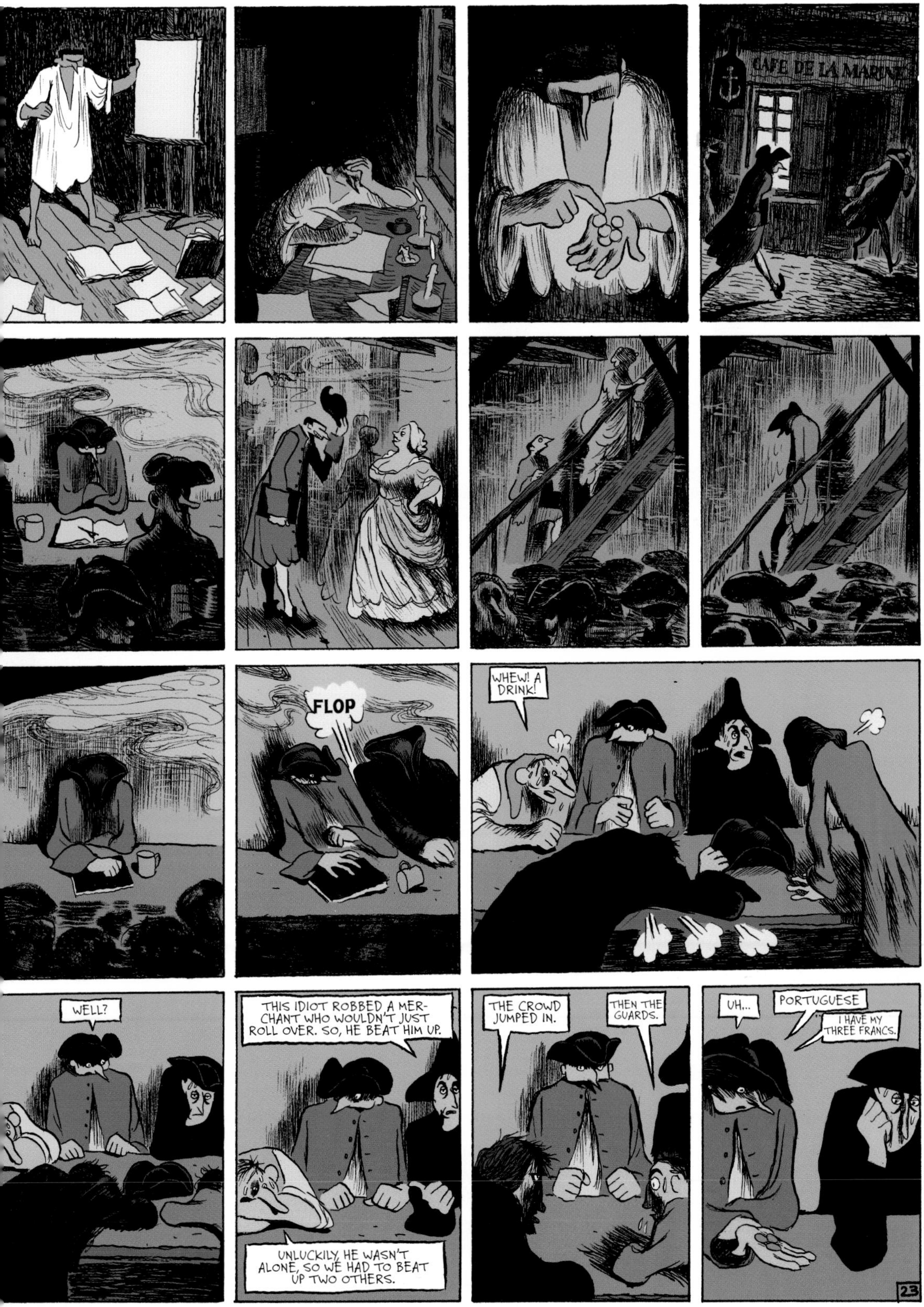
CAFE DE LA MARINE
FLOP
WHEW! A DRINK!
WELL?
THIS IDIOT ROBBED A MERCHANT WHO WOULDN'T JUST ROLL OVER. SO, HE BEAT HIM UP.
UNLUCKILY, HE WASN'T ALONE, SO WE HAD TO BEAT UP TWO OTHERS.
THE CROWD JUMPED IN.
THEN THE GUARDS.
UH...
PORTUGUESE
I HAVE MY THREE FRANCS.

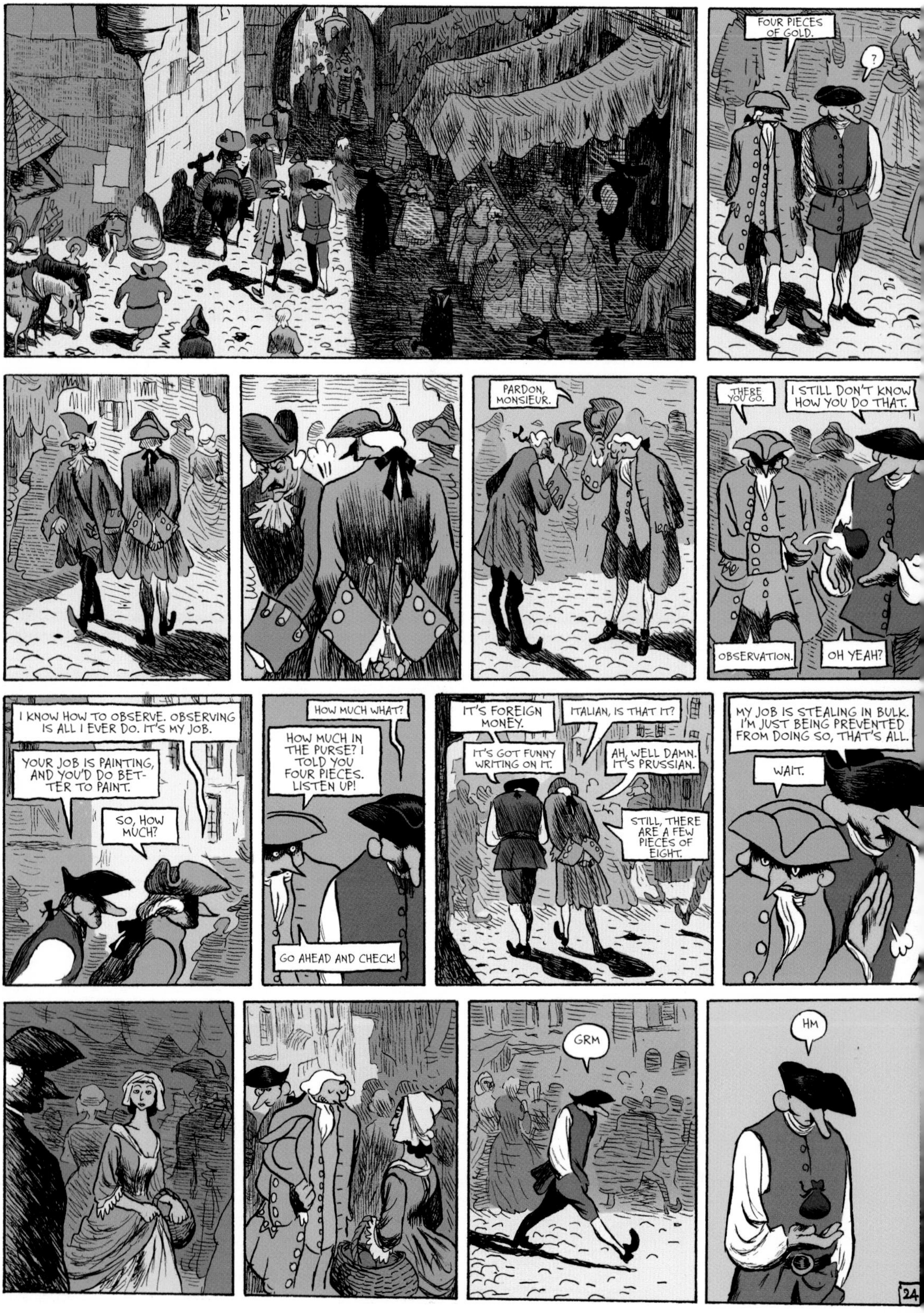
FOUR PIECES OF GOLD.
?
PARDON, MONSIEUR.
THERE YOU GO.
I STILL DON'T KNOW HOW YOU DO THAT.
OBSERVATION.
OH YEAH?
I KNOW HOW TO OBSERVE. OBSERVING IS ALL I EVER DO. IT'S MY JOB.
YOUR JOB IS PAINTING, AND YOU'D DO BETTER TO PAINT.
SO, HOW MUCH?
HOW MUCH WHAT?
HOW MUCH IN THE PURSE? I TOLD YOU FOUR PIECES. LISTEN UP!
GO AHEAD AND CHECK!
IT'S FOREIGN MONEY.
ITALIAN, IS THAT IT?
IT'S GOT FUNNY WRITING ON IT.
AH, WELL DAMN. IT'S PRUSSIAN.
STILL, THERE ARE A FEW PIECES OF EIGHT.
MY JOB IS STEALING IN BULK. I'M JUST BEING PREVENTED FROM DOING SO, THAT'S ALL.
WAIT.
GRM
HM

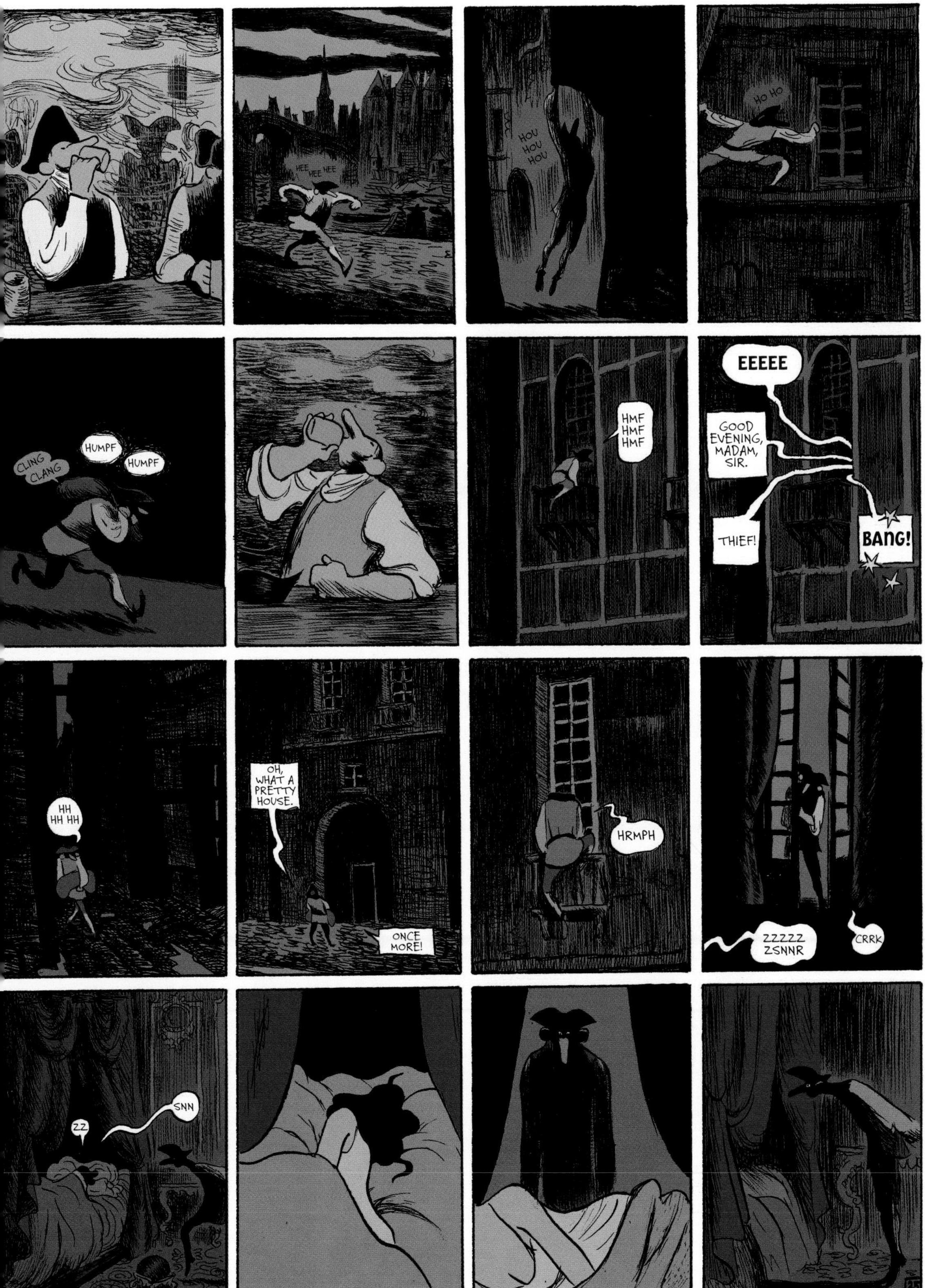
HEE HEE HEE
HOU HOU HOU
HO HO
CLING CLANG
HUMPF
HUMPF
HMF HMF HMF
EEEEE
GOOD EVENING, MADAM, SIR.
THIEF!
BANG!
HH HH HH
OH, WHAT A PRETTY HOUSE.
ONCE MORE!
HRMPH
ZZZZZ ZSNNR
CRRK
ZZ
SNN

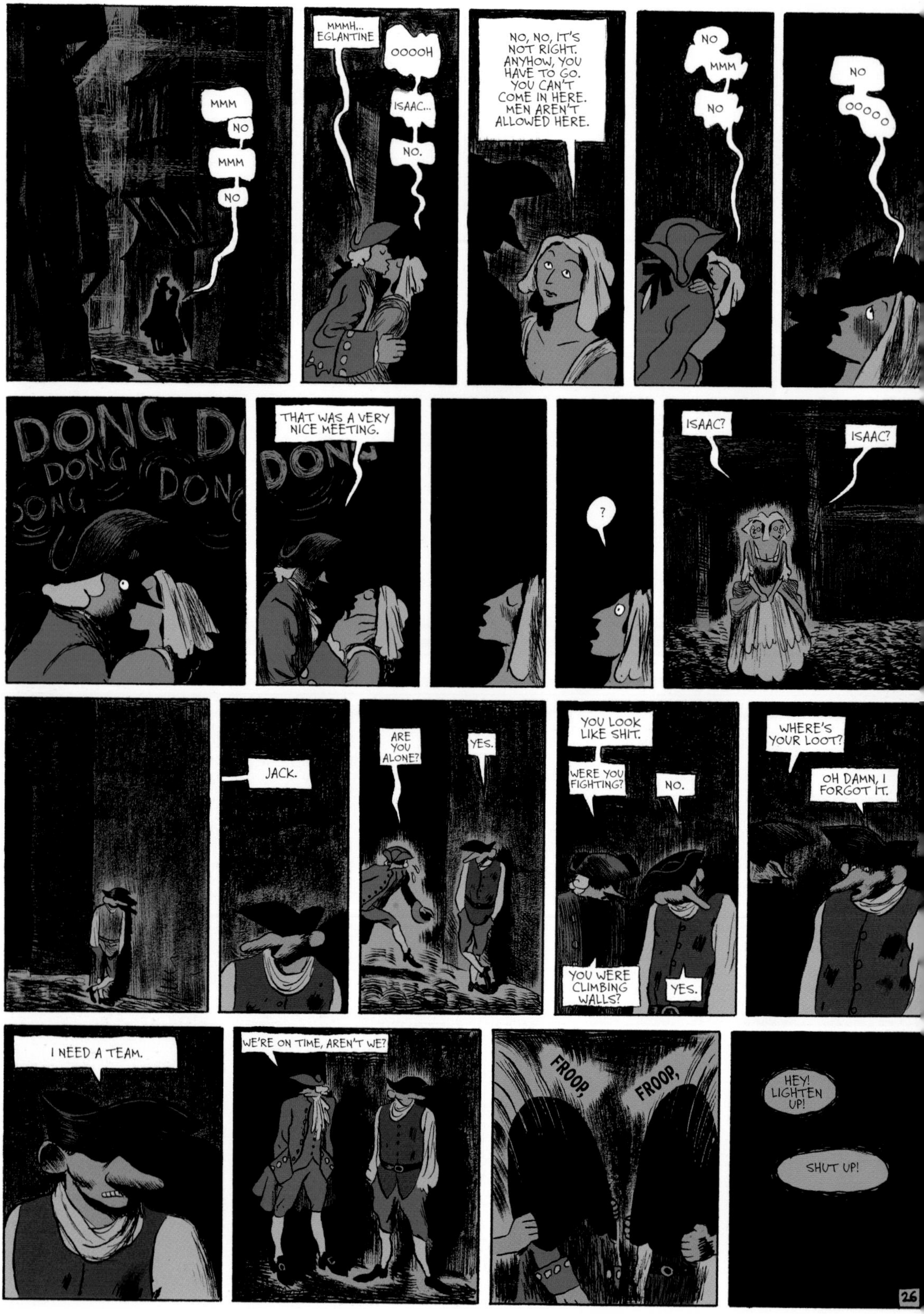
MMM
NO
MMM
NO
MMMH... EGLANTINE
OOOOH
ISAAC...
NO.
NO, NO, IT'S NOT RIGHT. ANYHOW, YOU HAVE TO GO. YOU CAN'T COME IN HERE. MEN AREN'T ALLOWED HERE.
NO
MMM
NO
NO
OOOOO
DONG DO
DONG
DONG
DONG
THAT WAS A VERY NICE MEETING.
DONG
?
ISAAC?
ISAAC?
JACK.
ARE YOU ALONE?
YES.
YOU LOOK LIKE SHIT.
WERE YOU FIGHTING?
NO.
YOU WERE CLIMBING WALLS?
YES.
WHERE'S YOUR LOOT?
OH DAMN, I FORGOT IT.
I NEED A TEAM.
WE'RE ON TIME, AREN'T WE?
FROOP,
FROOP,
HEY! LIGHTEN UP!
SHUT UP!

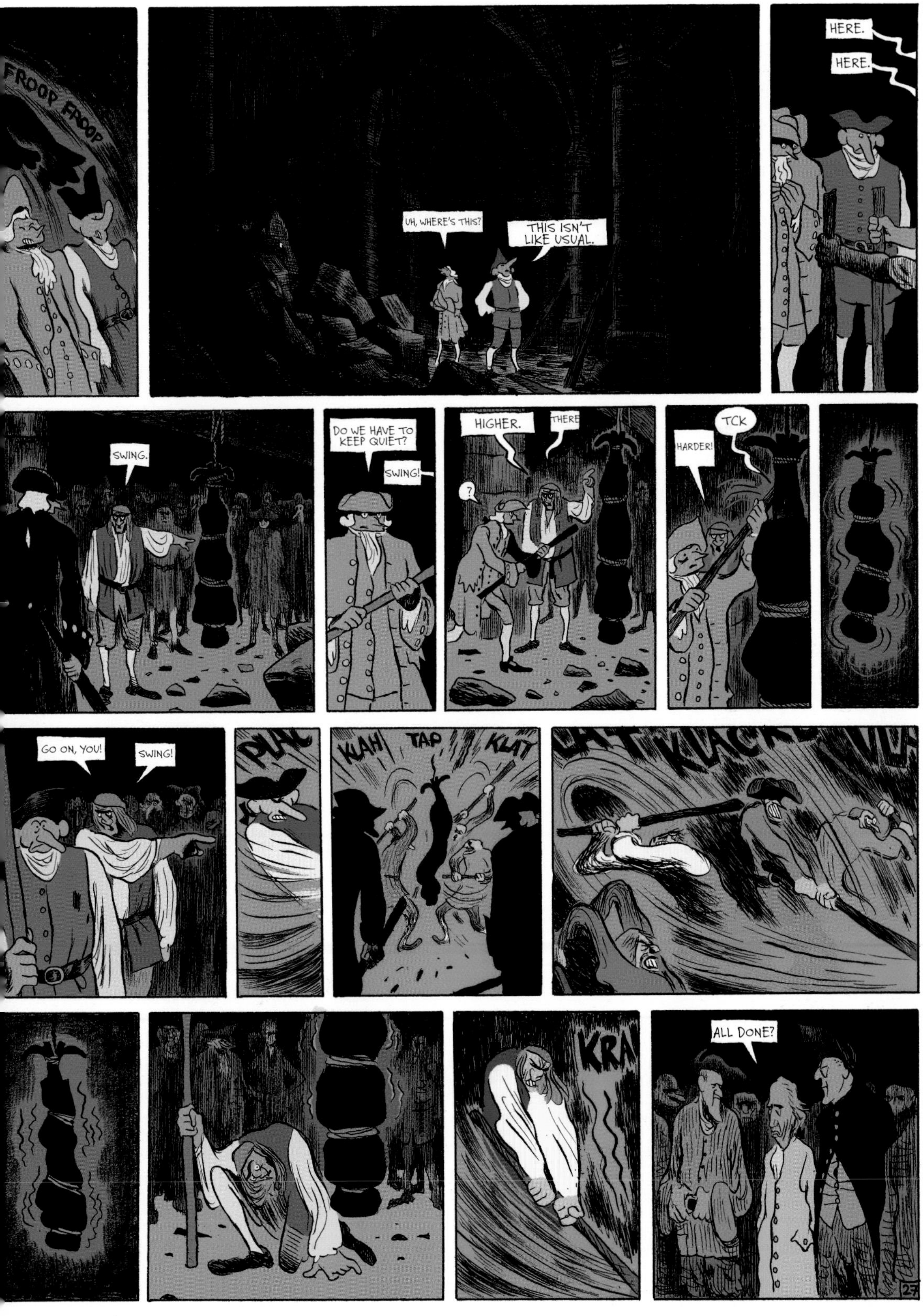
FROOP FROOP
UH, WHERE'S THIS?
THIS ISN'T LIKE USUAL.
HERE.
HERE.
SWING.
DO WE HAVE TO KEEP QUIET?
SWING!
HIGHER.
THERE
?
HARDER!
TCK
GO ON, YOU!
SWING!
PLAC
KLAH
TAP
KLAT
KRA
ALL DONE?

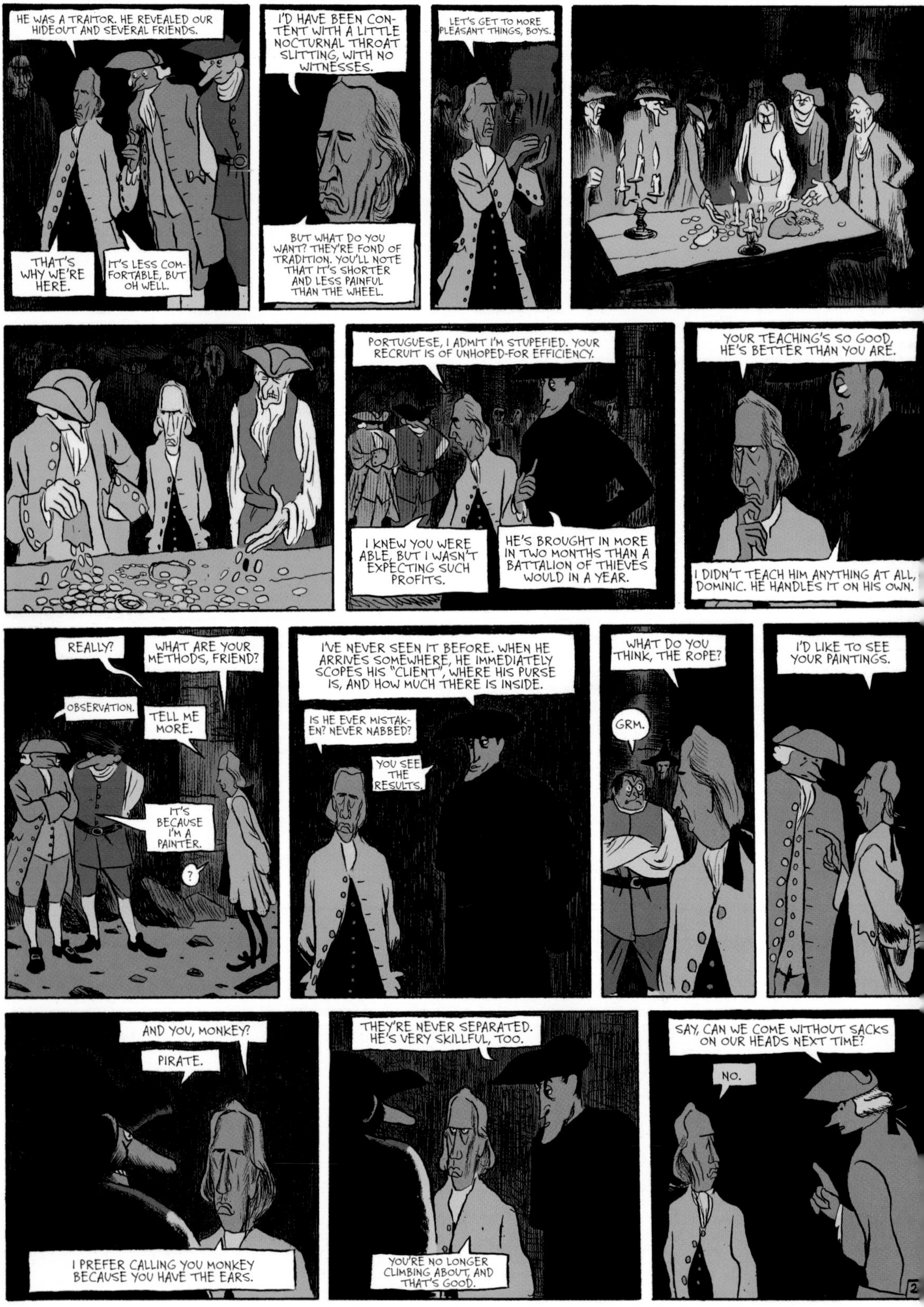
HE WAS A TRAITOR. HE REVEALED OUR HIDEOUT AND SEVERAL FRIENDS.
THAT'S WHY WE'RE HERE.
IT'S LESS COMFORTABLE, BUT OH WELL.
I'D HAVE BEEN CONTENT WITH A LITTLE NOCTURNAL THROAT SLITTING, WITH NO WITNESSES.
BUT WHAT DO YOU WANT? THEY'RE FOND OF TRADITION. YOU'LL NOTE THAT IT'S SHORTER AND LESS PAINFUL THAN THE WHEEL.
LET'S GET TO MORE PLEASANT THINGS, BOYS.
PORTUGUESE, I ADMIT I'M STUPEFIED. YOUR RECRUIT IS OF UNHOPED-FOR EFFICIENCY.
I KNEW YOU WERE ABLE, BUT I WASN'T EXPECTING SUCH PROFITS.
HE'S BROUGHT IN MORE IN TWO MONTHS THAN A BATTALION OF THIEVES WOULD IN A YEAR.
YOUR TEACHING'S SO GOOD, HE'S BETTER THAN YOU ARE.
I DIDN'T TEACH HIM ANYTHING AT ALL, DOMINIC. HE HANDLES IT ON HIS OWN.
REALLY?
WHAT ARE YOUR METHODS, FRIEND?
OBSERVATION.
TELL ME MORE.
IT'S BECAUSE I'M A PAINTER.
?
I'VE NEVER SEEN IT BEFORE. WHEN HE ARRIVES SOMEWHERE, HE IMMEDIATELY SCOPES HIS "CLIENT", WHERE HIS PURSE IS, AND HOW MUCH THERE IS INSIDE.
IS HE EVER MISTAKEN? NEVER NABBED?
YOU SEE THE RESULTS.
WHAT DO YOU THINK, THE ROPE?
GRM.
I'D LIKE TO SEE YOUR PAINTINGS.
AND YOU, MONKEY?
PIRATE.
I PREFER CALLING YOU MONKEY BECAUSE YOU HAVE THE EARS.
THEY'RE NEVER SEPARATED. HE'S VERY SKILLFUL, TOO.
YOU'RE NO LONGER CLIMBING ABOUT, AND THAT'S GOOD.
SAY, CAN WE COME WITHOUT SACKS ON OUR HEADS NEXT TIME?
NO.

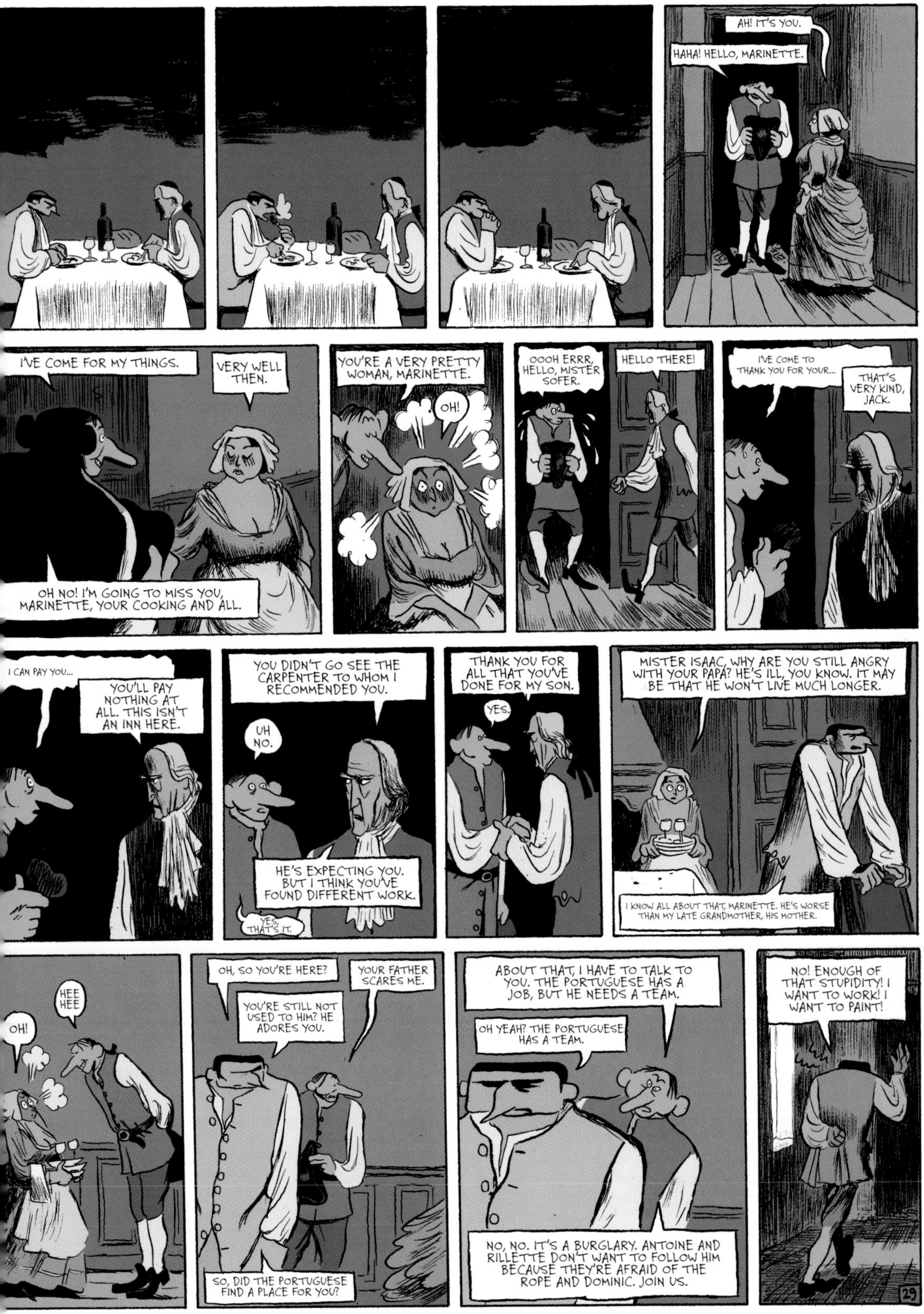

AH! IT'S YOU.
HAHA! HELLO, MARINETTE.
I'VE COME FOR MY THINGS.
VERY WELL THEN.
OH NO! I'M GOING TO MISS YOU, MARINETTE, YOUR COOKING AND ALL.
YOU'RE A VERY PRETTY WOMAN, MARINETTE.
OH!
OOOH ERRR, HELLO, MISTER SOFER.
HELLO THERE!
I'VE COME TO THANK YOU FOR YOUR...
THAT'S VERY KIND, JACK.
I CAN PAY YOU...
YOU'LL PAY NOTHING AT ALL. THIS ISN'T AN INN HERE.
YOU DIDN'T GO SEE THE CARPENTER TO WHOM I RECOMMENDED YOU.
UH NO.
HE'S EXPECTING YOU. BUT I THINK YOU'VE FOUND DIFFERENT WORK.
YES, THAT'S IT.
THANK YOU FOR ALL THAT YOU'VE DONE FOR MY SON.
YES.
MISTER ISAAC, WHY ARE YOU STILL ANGRY WITH YOUR PAPA? HE'S ILL, YOU KNOW. IT MAY BE THAT HE WON'T LIVE MUCH LONGER.
I KNOW ALL ABOUT THAT, MARINETTE. HE'S WORSE THAN MY LATE GRANDMOTHER, HIS MOTHER.
OH!
HEE HEE
OH, SO YOU'RE HERE?
YOU'RE STILL NOT USED TO HIM? HE ADORES YOU.
YOUR FATHER SCARES ME.
SO, DID THE PORTUGUESE FIND A PLACE FOR YOU?
ABOUT THAT, I HAVE TO TALK TO YOU. THE PORTUGUESE HAS A JOB, BUT HE NEEDS A TEAM.
OH YEAH? THE PORTUGUESE HAS A TEAM.
NO, NO. IT'S A BURGLARY. ANTOINE AND RILLETTE DON'T WANT TO FOLLOW HIM BECAUSE THEY'RE AFRAID OF THE ROPE AND DOMINIC. JOIN US.
NO! ENOUGH OF THAT STUPIDITY! I WANT TO WORK! I WANT TO PAINT!

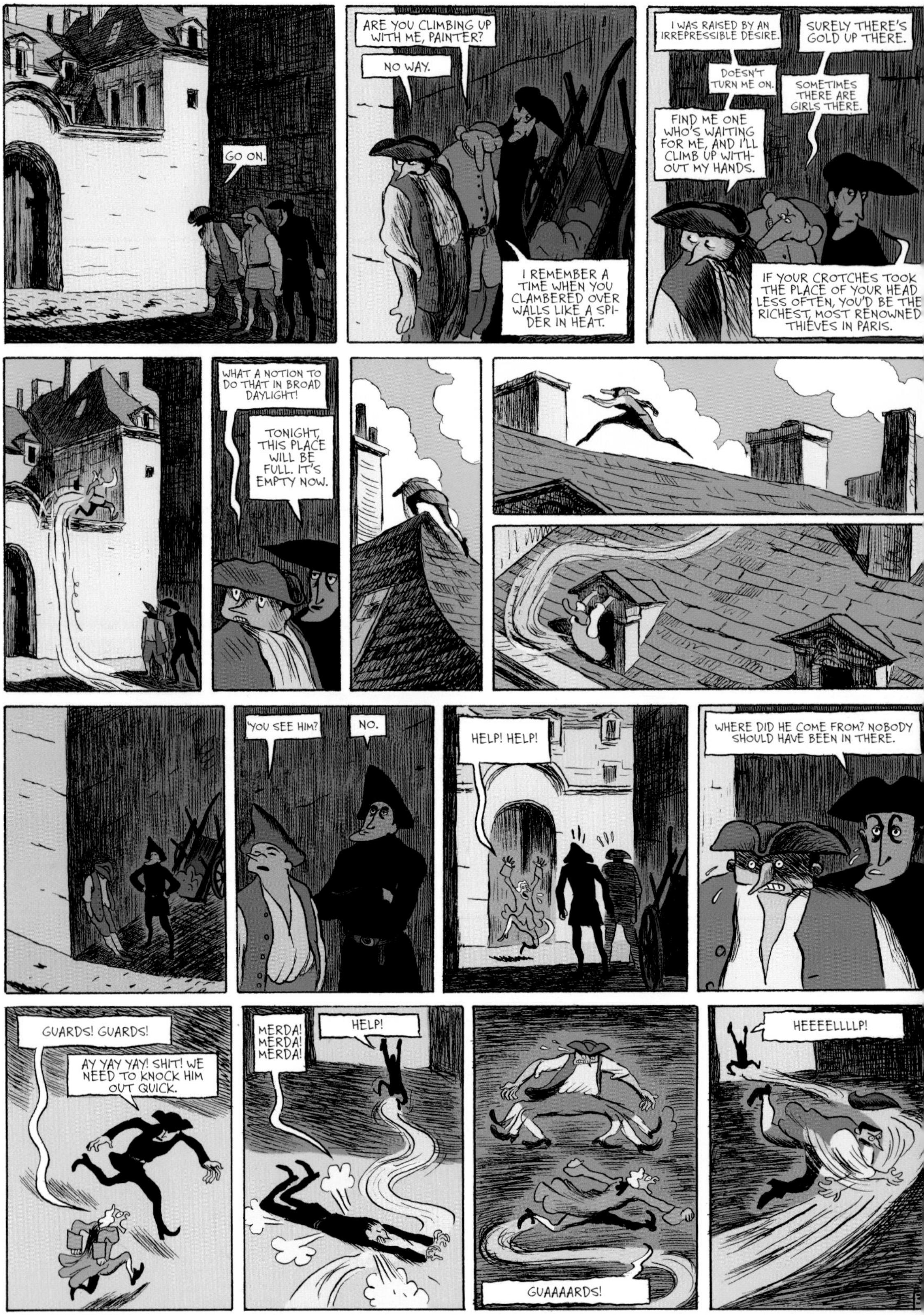
GO ON.
ARE YOU CLIMBING UP WITH ME, PAINTER?
NO WAY.
I REMEMBER A TIME WHEN YOU CLAMBERED OVER WALLS LIKE A SPIDER IN HEAT.
I WAS RAISED BY AN IRREPRESSIBLE DESIRE.
DOESN'T TURN ME ON.
FIND ME ONE WHO'S WAITING FOR ME, AND I'LL CLIMB UP WITHOUT MY HANDS.
SURELY THERE'S GOLD UP THERE.
SOMETIMES THERE ARE GIRLS THERE.
IF YOUR CROTCHES TOOK THE PLACE OF YOUR HEAD LESS OFTEN, YOU'D BE THE RICHEST, MOST RENOWNED THIEVES IN PARIS.
WHAT A NOTION TO DO THAT IN BROAD DAYLIGHT!
TONIGHT, THIS PLACE WILL BE FULL. IT'S EMPTY NOW.
YOU SEE HIM?
NO.
HELP! HELP!
WHERE DID HE COME FROM? NOBODY SHOULD HAVE BEEN IN THERE.
GUARDS! GUARDS!
AY YAY YAY! SHIT! WE NEED TO KNOCK HIM OUT QUICK.
MERDA! MERDA! MERDA!
HELP!
GUAAAARDS!
HEEEELLLLP!

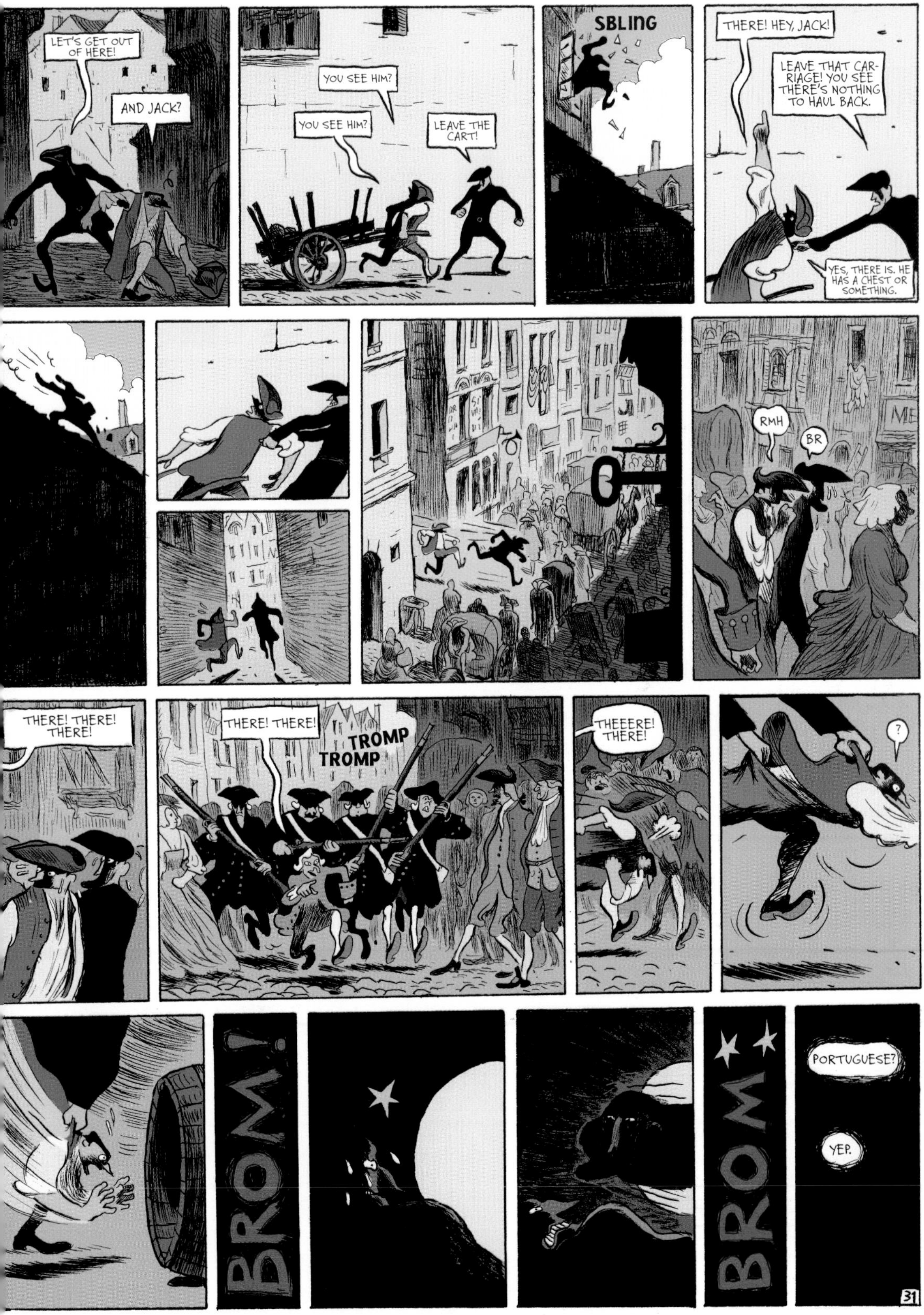

LET'S GET OUT OF HERE!
AND JACK?
YOU SEE HIM?
YOU SEE HIM?
LEAVE THE CART!
SBLING
THERE! HEY, JACK!
LEAVE THAT CARRIAGE! YOU SEE THERE'S NOTHING TO HAUL BACK.
YES, THERE IS. HE HAS A CHEST OR SOMETHING.
RMH
BR
THERE! THERE! THERE!
THERE! THERE!
TROMP
TROMP
THEEERE! THERE!
?
BROM!
BROM
PORTUGUESE?
YEP.

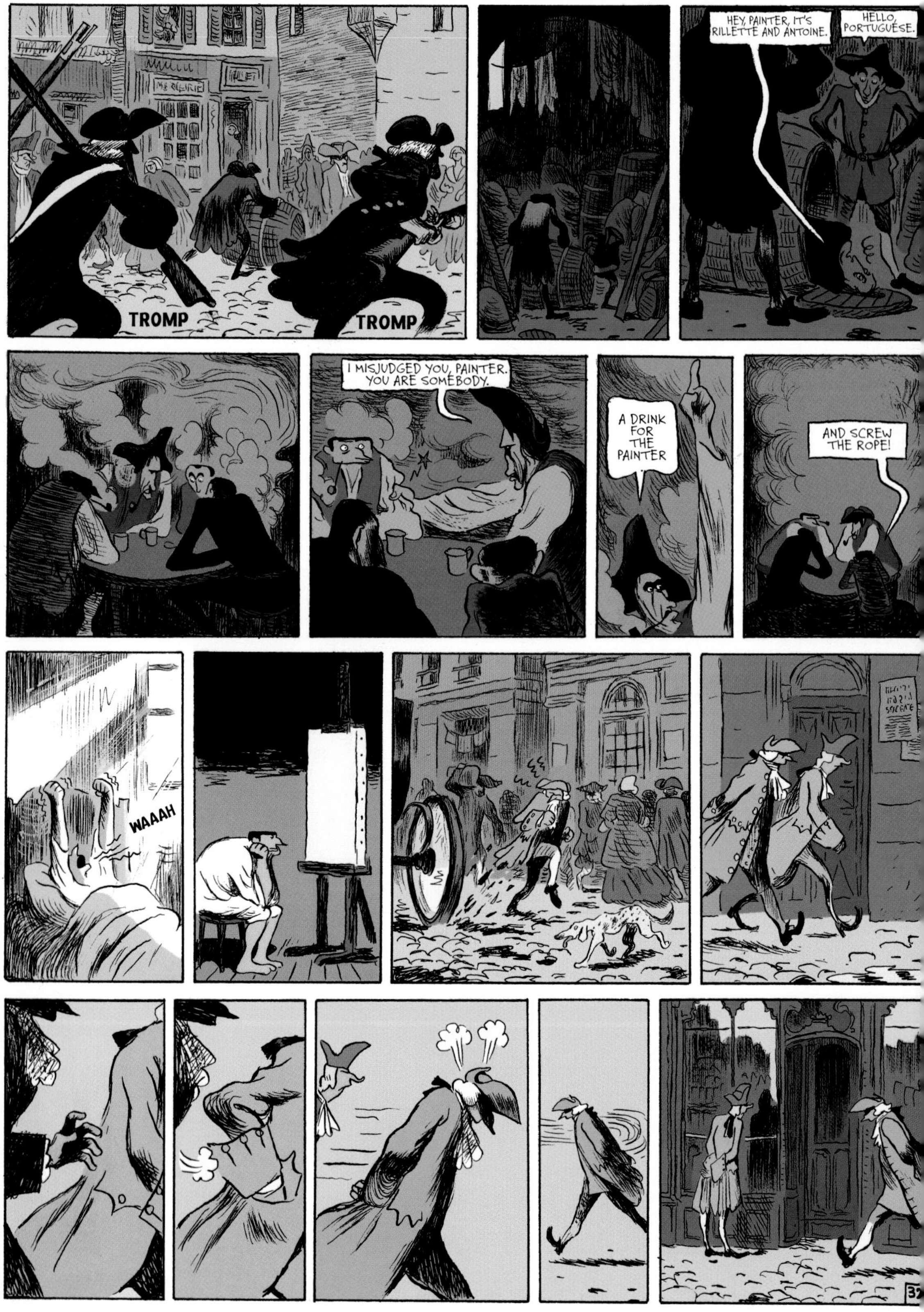
TROMP
TROMP
HEY, PAINTER, IT'S RILLETTE AND ANTOINE.
HELLO, PORTUGUESE.
I MISJUDGED YOU, PAINTER. YOU ARE SOMEBODY.
A DRINK FOR THE PAINTER
AND SCREW THE ROPE!
WAAAH

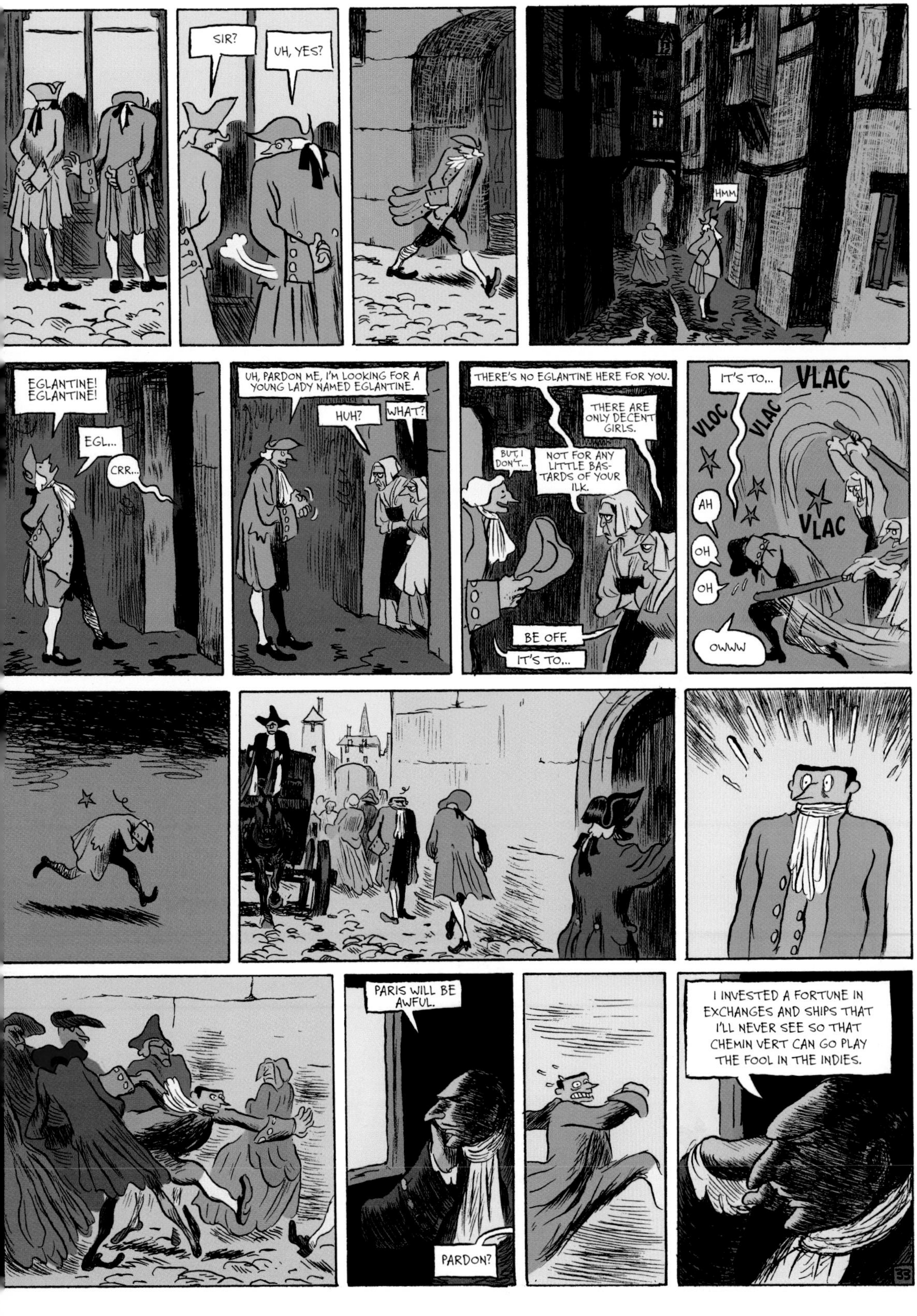

SIR?
UH, YES?
HMM
EGLANTINE! EGLANTINE!
EGL...
CRR...
UH, PARDON ME, I'M LOOKING FOR A YOUNG LADY NAMED EGLANTINE.
HUH?
WHAT?
THERE'S NO EGLANTINE HERE FOR YOU.
THERE ARE ONLY DECENT GIRLS.
BUT, I DON'T...
NOT FOR ANY LITTLE BASTARDS OF YOUR ILK.
BE OFF.
IT'S TO...
IT'S TO...
VLAC
VLOC
VLAC
AH
OH
OH
VLAC
OWWW
PARIS WILL BE AWFUL.
PARDON?
I INVESTED A FORTUNE IN EXCHANGES AND SHIPS THAT I'LL NEVER SEE SO THAT CHEMIN VERT CAN GO PLAY THE FOOL IN THE INDIES.

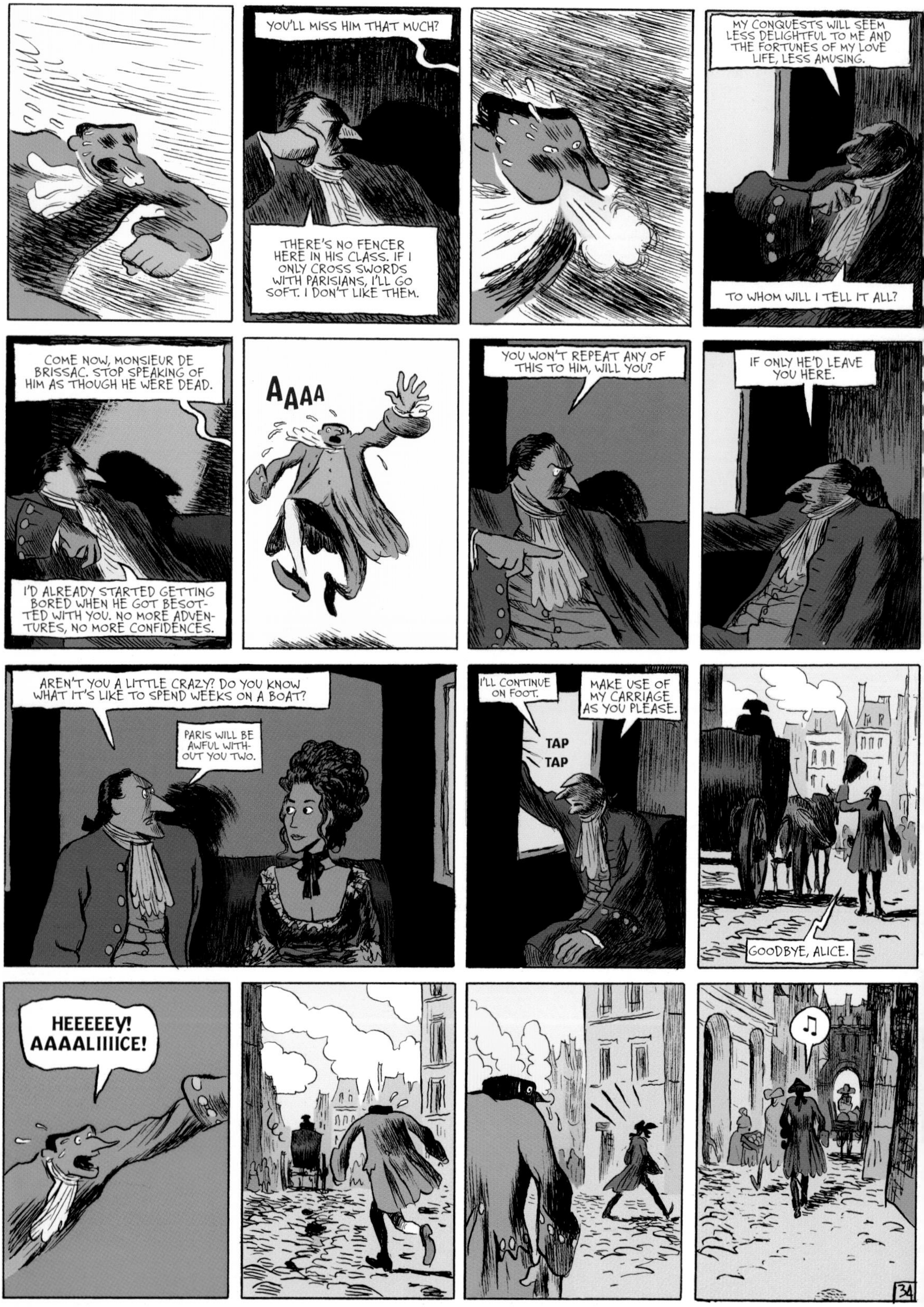
YOU'LL MISS HIM THAT MUCH?
THERE'S NO FENCER HERE IN HIS CLASS. IF I ONLY CROSS SWORDS WITH PARISIANS, I'LL GO SOFT. I DON'T LIKE THEM.
MY CONQUESTS WILL SEEM LESS DELIGHTFUL TO ME AND THE FORTUNES OF MY LOVE LIFE, LESS AMUSING.
TO WHOM WILL I TELL IT ALL?
COME NOW, MONSIEUR DE BRISSAC. STOP SPEAKING OF HIM AS THOUGH HE WERE DEAD.
I'D ALREADY STARTED GETTING BORED WHEN HE GOT BESOTTED WITH YOU. NO MORE ADVENTURES, NO MORE CONFIDENCES.
AAAA
YOU WON'T REPEAT ANY OF THIS TO HIM, WILL YOU?
IF ONLY HE'D LEAVE YOU HERE.
AREN'T YOU A LITTLE CRAZY? DO YOU KNOW WHAT IT'S LIKE TO SPEND WEEKS ON A BOAT?
PARIS WILL BE AWFUL WITHOUT YOU TWO.
I'LL CONTINUE ON FOOT.
MAKE USE OF MY CARRIAGE AS YOU PLEASE.
TAP
TAP
GOODBYE, ALICE.
HEEEEEY! AAAALIIIICE!
♪
34

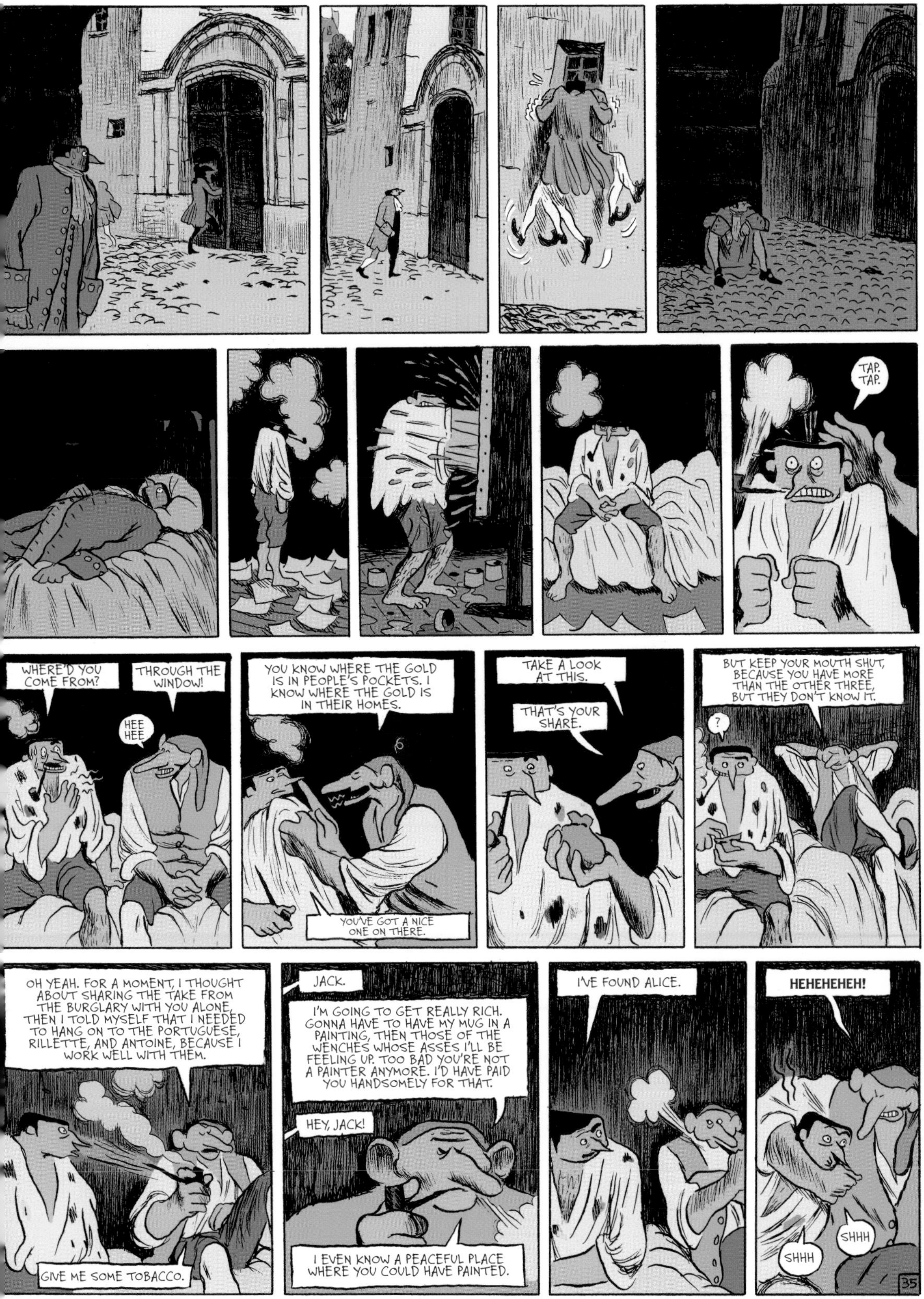
TAP. TAP.
WHERE'D YOU COME FROM?
THROUGH THE WINDOW!
HEE HEE
YOU KNOW WHERE THE GOLD IS IN PEOPLE'S POCKETS. I KNOW WHERE THE GOLD IS IN THEIR HOMES.
YOU'VE GOT A NICE ONE ON THERE.
TAKE A LOOK AT THIS.
THAT'S YOUR SHARE.
BUT KEEP YOUR MOUTH SHUT, BECAUSE YOU HAVE MORE THAN THE OTHER THREE, BUT THEY DON'T KNOW IT.
?
OH YEAH. FOR A MOMENT, I THOUGHT ABOUT SHARING THE TAKE FROM THE BURGLARY WITH YOU ALONE, THEN I TOLD MYSELF THAT I NEEDED TO HANG ON TO THE PORTUGUESE, RILLETTE, AND ANTOINE, BECAUSE I WORK WELL WITH THEM.
GIVE ME SOME TOBACCO.
JACK.
I'M GOING TO GET REALLY RICH. GONNA HAVE TO HAVE MY MUG IN A PAINTING, THEN THOSE OF THE WENCHES WHOSE ASSES I'LL BE FEELING UP. TOO BAD YOU'RE NOT A PAINTER ANYMORE. I'D HAVE PAID YOU HANDSOMELY FOR THAT.
HEY, JACK!
I EVEN KNOW A PEACEFUL PLACE WHERE YOU COULD HAVE PAINTED.
I'VE FOUND ALICE.
HEHEHEHEH!
SHHH
SHHH

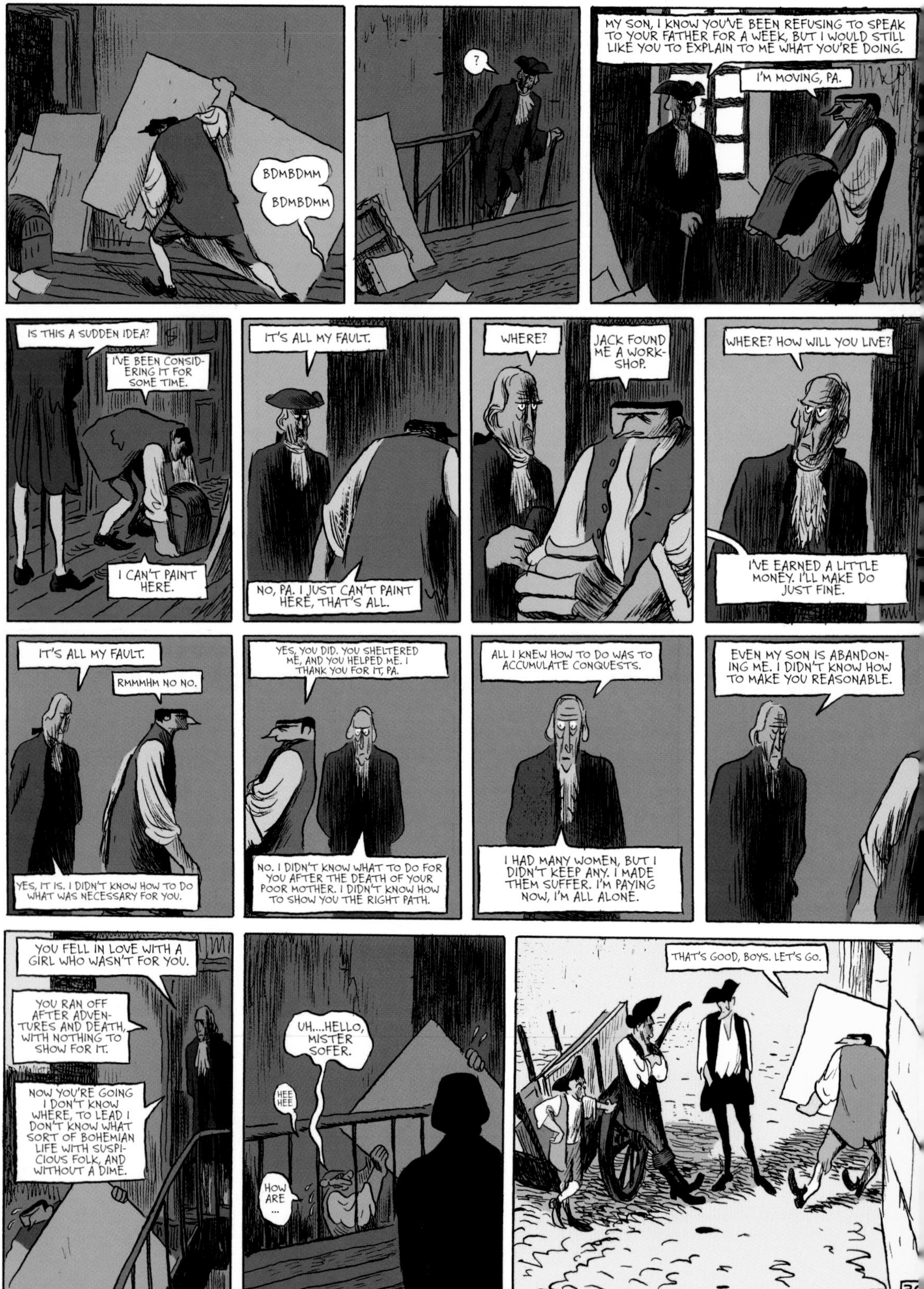
BDMBDMM
BDMBDMM
?
MY SON, I KNOW YOU'VE BEEN REFUSING TO SPEAK TO YOUR FATHER FOR A WEEK, BUT I WOULD STILL LIKE YOU TO EXPLAIN TO ME WHAT YOU'RE DOING.
I'M MOVING, PA.
IS THIS A SUDDEN IDEA?
I'VE BEEN CONSIDERING IT FOR SOME TIME.
I CAN'T PAINT HERE.
IT'S ALL MY FAULT.
NO, PA. I JUST CAN'T PAINT HERE, THAT'S ALL.
WHERE?
JACK FOUND ME A WORKSHOP.
WHERE? HOW WILL YOU LIVE?
I'VE EARNED A LITTLE MONEY. I'LL MAKE DO JUST FINE.
IT'S ALL MY FAULT.
RMMMHM NO NO.
YES, IT IS. I DIDN'T KNOW HOW TO DO WHAT WAS NECESSARY FOR YOU.
YES, YOU DID. YOU SHELTERED ME, AND YOU HELPED ME. I THANK YOU FOR IT, PA.
NO. I DIDN'T KNOW WHAT TO DO FOR YOU AFTER THE DEATH OF YOUR POOR MOTHER. I DIDN'T KNOW HOW TO SHOW YOU THE RIGHT PATH.
ALL I KNEW HOW TO DO WAS TO ACCUMULATE CONQUESTS.
I HAD MANY WOMEN, BUT I DIDN'T KEEP ANY. I MADE THEM SUFFER. I'M PAYING NOW, I'M ALL ALONE.
EVEN MY SON IS ABANDONING ME. I DIDN'T KNOW HOW TO MAKE YOU REASONABLE.
YOU FELL IN LOVE WITH A GIRL WHO WASN'T FOR YOU.
YOU RAN OFF AFTER ADVENTURES AND DEATH, WITH NOTHING TO SHOW FOR IT.
NOW YOU'RE GOING I DON'T KNOW WHERE, TO LEAD I DON'T KNOW WHAT SORT OF BOHEMIAN LIFE WITH SUSPICIOUS FOLK, AND WITHOUT A DIME.
UH....HELLO, MISTER SOFER.
HEE HEE
HOW ARE ...
THAT'S GOOD, BOYS. LET'S GO.

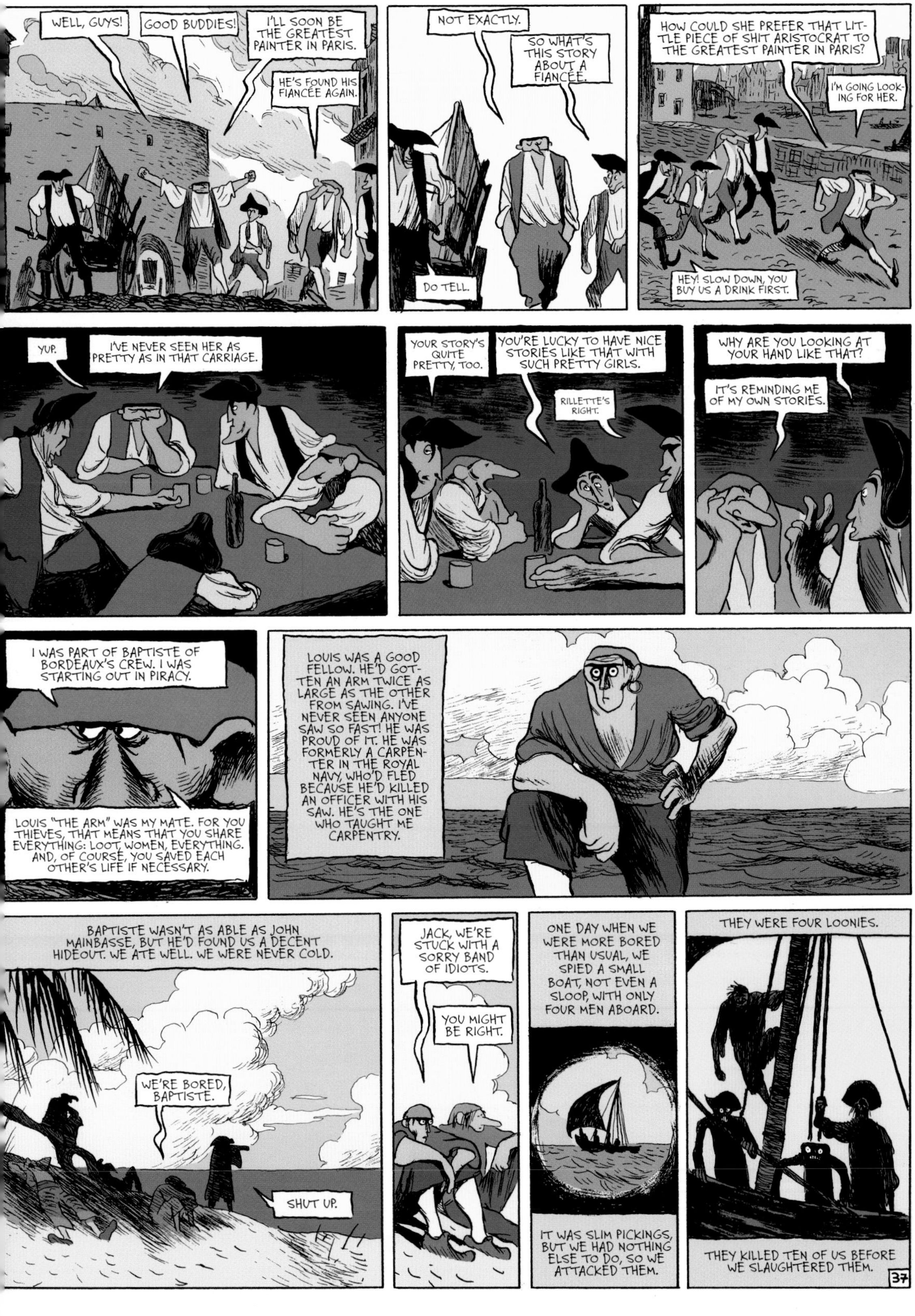

WELL, GUYS!
GOOD BUDDIES!
I'LL SOON BE THE GREATEST PAINTER IN PARIS.
HE'S FOUND HIS FIANCÉE AGAIN.
NOT EXACTLY.
SO WHAT'S THIS STORY ABOUT A FIANCÉE.
DO TELL.
HOW COULD SHE PREFER THAT LITTLE PIECE OF SHIT ARISTOCRAT TO THE GREATEST PAINTER IN PARIS?
I'M GOING LOOKING FOR HER.
HEY! SLOW DOWN, YOU BUY US A DRINK FIRST.
YUP.
I'VE NEVER SEEN HER AS PRETTY AS IN THAT CARRIAGE.
YOUR STORY'S QUITE PRETTY, TOO.
YOU'RE LUCKY TO HAVE NICE STORIES LIKE THAT WITH SUCH PRETTY GIRLS.
RILLETTE'S RIGHT.
WHY ARE YOU LOOKING AT YOUR HAND LIKE THAT?
IT'S REMINDING ME OF MY OWN STORIES.
I WAS PART OF BAPTISTE OF BORDEAUX'S CREW. I WAS STARTING OUT IN PIRACY.
LOUIS "THE ARM" WAS MY MATE. FOR YOU THIEVES, THAT MEANS THAT YOU SHARE EVERYTHING: LOOT, WOMEN, EVERYTHING. AND, OF COURSE, YOU SAVED EACH OTHER'S LIFE IF NECESSARY.
LOUIS WAS A GOOD FELLOW. HE'D GOTTEN AN ARM TWICE AS LARGE AS THE OTHER FROM SAWING. I'VE NEVER SEEN ANYONE SAW SO FAST! HE WAS PROUD OF IT. HE WAS FORMERLY A CARPENTER IN THE ROYAL NAVY, WHO'D FLED BECAUSE HE'D KILLED AN OFFICER WITH HIS SAW. HE'S THE ONE WHO TAUGHT ME CARPENTRY.
BAPTISTE WASN'T AS ABLE AS JOHN MAINBASSE, BUT HE'D FOUND US A DECENT HIDEOUT. WE ATE WELL. WE WERE NEVER COLD.
WE'RE BORED, BAPTISTE.
SHUT UP.
JACK, WE'RE STUCK WITH A SORRY BAND OF IDIOTS.
YOU MIGHT BE RIGHT.
ONE DAY WHEN WE WERE MORE BORED THAN USUAL, WE SPIED A SMALL BOAT, NOT EVEN A SLOOP, WITH ONLY FOUR MEN ABOARD.
IT WAS SLIM PICKINGS, BUT WE HAD NOTHING ELSE TO DO, SO WE ATTACKED THEM.
THEY WERE FOUR LOONIES.
THEY KILLED TEN OF US BEFORE WE SLAUGHTERED THEM.

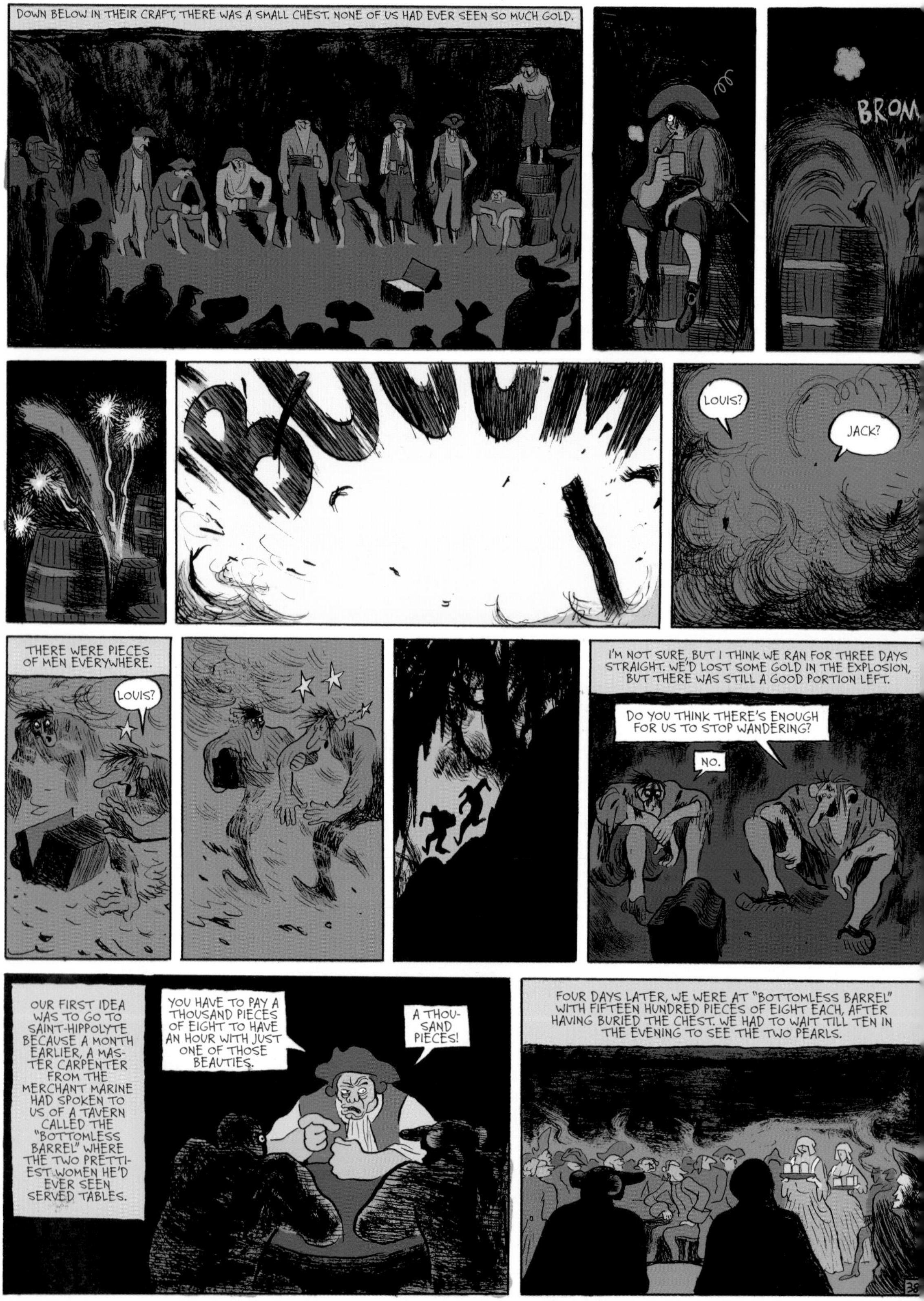
DOWN BELOW IN THEIR CRAFT, THERE WAS A SMALL CHEST. NONE OF US HAD EVER SEEN SO MUCH GOLD.
BROM
LOUIS?
JACK?
THERE WERE PIECES OF MEN EVERYWHERE.
LOUIS?
I'M NOT SURE, BUT I THINK WE RAN FOR THREE DAYS STRAIGHT. WE'D LOST SOME GOLD IN THE EXPLOSION, BUT THERE WAS STILL A GOOD PORTION LEFT.
DO YOU THINK THERE'S ENOUGH FOR US TO STOP WANDERING?
NO.
OUR FIRST IDEA WAS TO GO TO SAINT-HIPPOLYTE BECAUSE A MONTH EARLIER, A MASTER CARPENTER FROM THE MERCHANT MARINE HAD SPOKEN TO US OF A TAVERN CALLED THE "BOTTOMLESS BARREL" WHERE THE TWO PRETTIEST WOMEN HE'D EVER SEEN SERVED TABLES.
YOU HAVE TO PAY A THOUSAND PIECES OF EIGHT TO HAVE AN HOUR WITH JUST ONE OF THOSE BEAUTIES.
A THOUSAND PIECES!
FOUR DAYS LATER, WE WERE AT "BOTTOMLESS BARREL" WITH FIFTEEN HUNDRED PIECES OF EIGHT EACH, AFTER HAVING BURIED THE CHEST. WE HAD TO WAIT TILL TEN IN THE EVENING TO SEE THE TWO PEARLS.

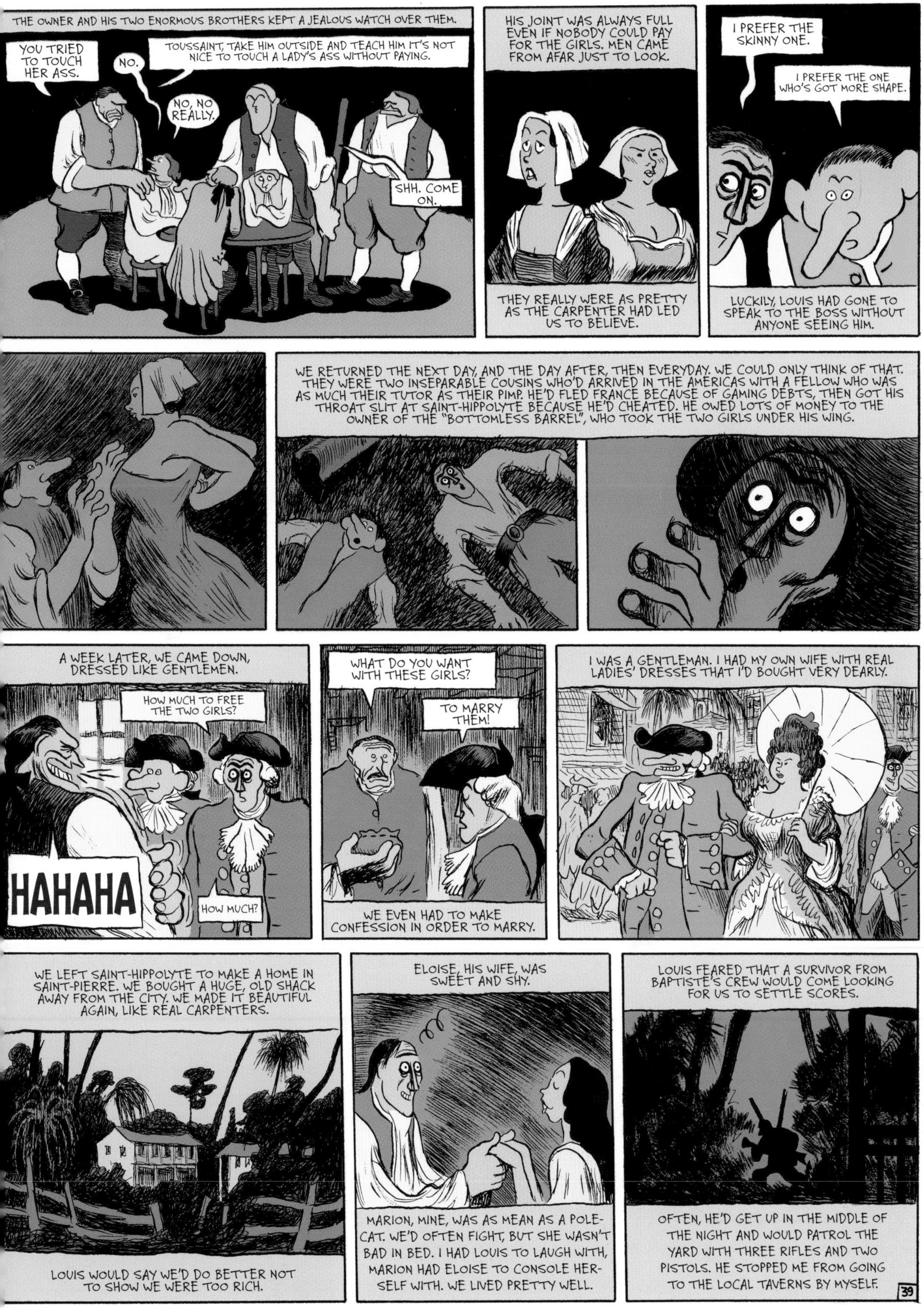

THE OWNER AND HIS TWO ENORMOUS BROTHERS KEPT A JEALOUS WATCH OVER THEM.
YOU TRIED TO TOUCH HER ASS.
NO.
TOUSSAINT, TAKE HIM OUTSIDE AND TEACH HIM IT'S NOT NICE TO TOUCH A LADY'S ASS WITHOUT PAYING.
NO, NO REALLY.
SHH. COME ON.
HIS JOINT WAS ALWAYS FULL EVEN IF NOBODY COULD PAY FOR THE GIRLS. MEN CAME FROM AFAR JUST TO LOOK.
THEY REALLY WERE AS PRETTY AS THE CARPENTER HAD LED US TO BELIEVE.
I PREFER THE SKINNY ONE.
I PREFER THE ONE WHO'S GOT MORE SHAPE.
LUCKILY, LOUIS HAD GONE TO SPEAK TO THE BOSS WITHOUT ANYONE SEEING HIM.
WE RETURNED THE NEXT DAY, AND THE DAY AFTER, THEN EVERYDAY. WE COULD ONLY THINK OF THAT. THEY WERE TWO INSEPARABLE COUSINS WHO'D ARRIVED IN THE AMERICAS WITH A FELLOW WHO WAS AS MUCH THEIR TUTOR AS THEIR PIMP. HE'D FLED FRANCE BECAUSE OF GAMING DEBTS, THEN GOT HIS THROAT SLIT AT SAINT-HIPPOLYTE BECAUSE HE'D CHEATED. HE OWED LOTS OF MONEY TO THE OWNER OF THE "BOTTOMLESS BARREL", WHO TOOK THE TWO GIRLS UNDER HIS WING.
A WEEK LATER, WE CAME DOWN, DRESSED LIKE GENTLEMEN.
HOW MUCH TO FREE THE TWO GIRLS?
HAHAHA
HOW MUCH?
WHAT DO YOU WANT WITH THESE GIRLS?
TO MARRY THEM!
WE EVEN HAD TO MAKE CONFESSION IN ORDER TO MARRY.
I WAS A GENTLEMAN. I HAD MY OWN WIFE WITH REAL LADIES' DRESSES THAT I'D BOUGHT VERY DEARLY.
WE LEFT SAINT-HIPPOLYTE TO MAKE A HOME IN SAINT-PIERRE. WE BOUGHT A HUGE, OLD SHACK AWAY FROM THE CITY. WE MADE IT BEAUTIFUL AGAIN, LIKE REAL CARPENTERS.
LOUIS WOULD SAY WE'D DO BETTER NOT TO SHOW WE WERE TOO RICH.
ELOISE, HIS WIFE, WAS SWEET AND SHY.
MARION, MINE, WAS AS MEAN AS A POLE-CAT. WE'D OFTEN FIGHT, BUT SHE WASN'T BAD IN BED. I HAD LOUIS TO LAUGH WITH, MARION HAD ELOISE TO CONSOLE HER-SELF WITH. WE LIVED PRETTY WELL.
LOUIS FEARED THAT A SURVIVOR FROM BAPTISTE'S CREW WOULD COME LOOKING FOR US TO SETTLE SCORES.
OFTEN, HE'D GET UP IN THE MIDDLE OF THE NIGHT AND WOULD PATROL THE YARD WITH THREE RIFLES AND TWO PISTOLS. HE STOPPED ME FROM GOING TO THE LOCAL TAVERNS BY MYSELF.

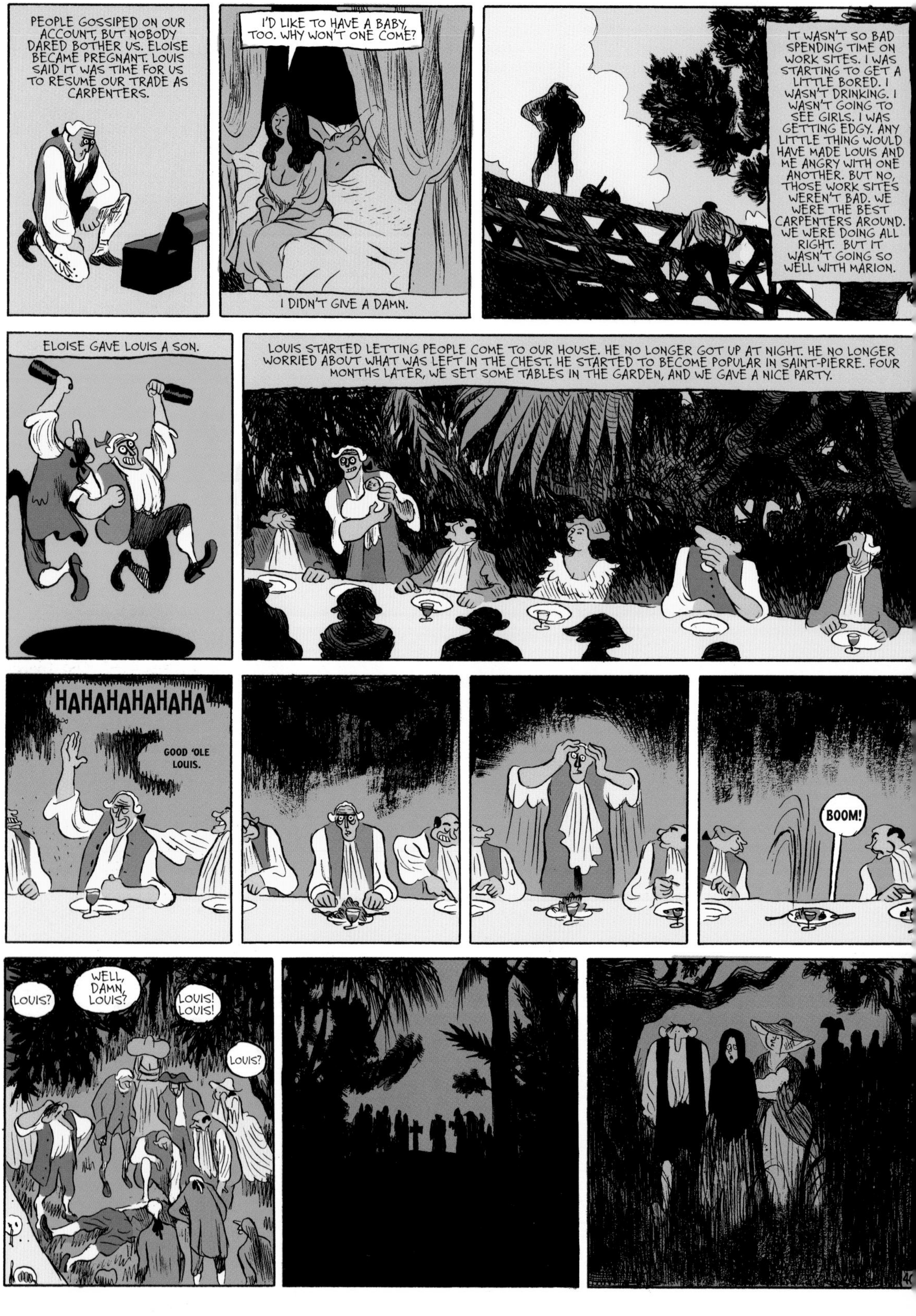
PEOPLE GOSSIPED ON OUR ACCOUNT, BUT NOBODY DARED BOTHER US. ELOISE BECAME PREGNANT. LOUIS SAID IT WAS TIME FOR US TO RESUME OUR TRADE AS CARPENTERS.
I'D LIKE TO HAVE A BABY, TOO. WHY WON'T ONE COME?
I DIDN'T GIVE A DAMN.
IT WASN'T SO BAD SPENDING TIME ON WORK SITES. I WAS STARTING TO GET A LITTLE BORED. I WASN'T DRINKING. I WASN'T GOING TO SEE GIRLS. I WAS GETTING EDGY. ANY LITTLE THING WOULD HAVE MADE LOUIS AND ME ANGRY WITH ONE ANOTHER. BUT NO, THOSE WORK SITES WEREN'T BAD. WE WERE THE BEST CARPENTERS AROUND. WE WERE DOING ALL RIGHT. BUT IT WASN'T GOING SO WELL WITH MARION.
ELOISE GAVE LOUIS A SON.
LOUIS STARTED LETTING PEOPLE COME TO OUR HOUSE. HE NO LONGER GOT UP AT NIGHT. HE NO LONGER WORRIED ABOUT WHAT WAS LEFT IN THE CHEST. HE STARTED TO BECOME POPULAR IN SAINT-PIERRE. FOUR MONTHS LATER, WE SET SOME TABLES IN THE GARDEN, AND WE GAVE A NICE PARTY.
HAHAHAHAHAHA
GOOD 'OLE LOUIS.
BOOM!
LOUIS?
WELL, DAMN, LOUIS?
LOUIS! LOUIS!
LOUIS?

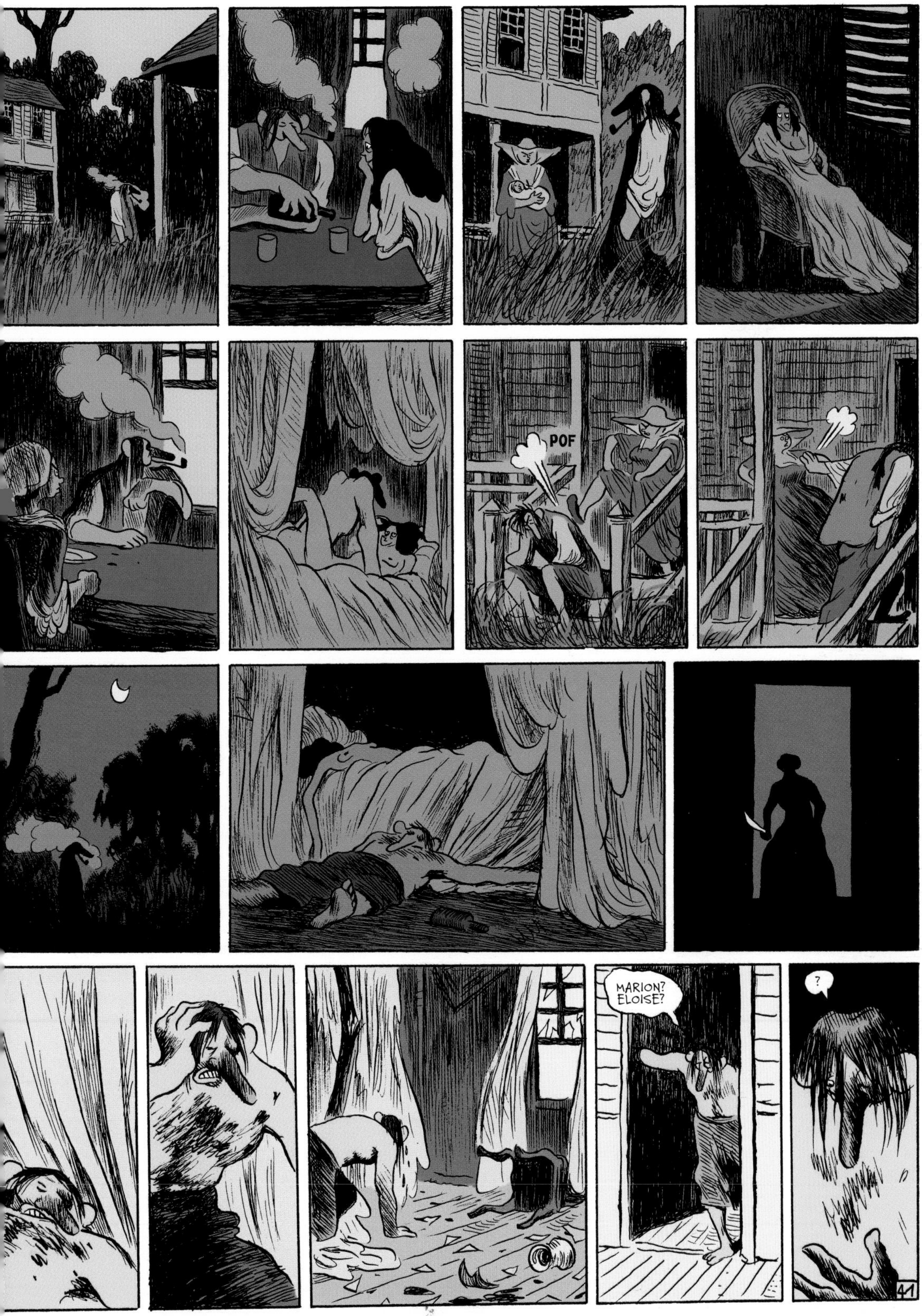
POF
MARION? ELOISE?
?

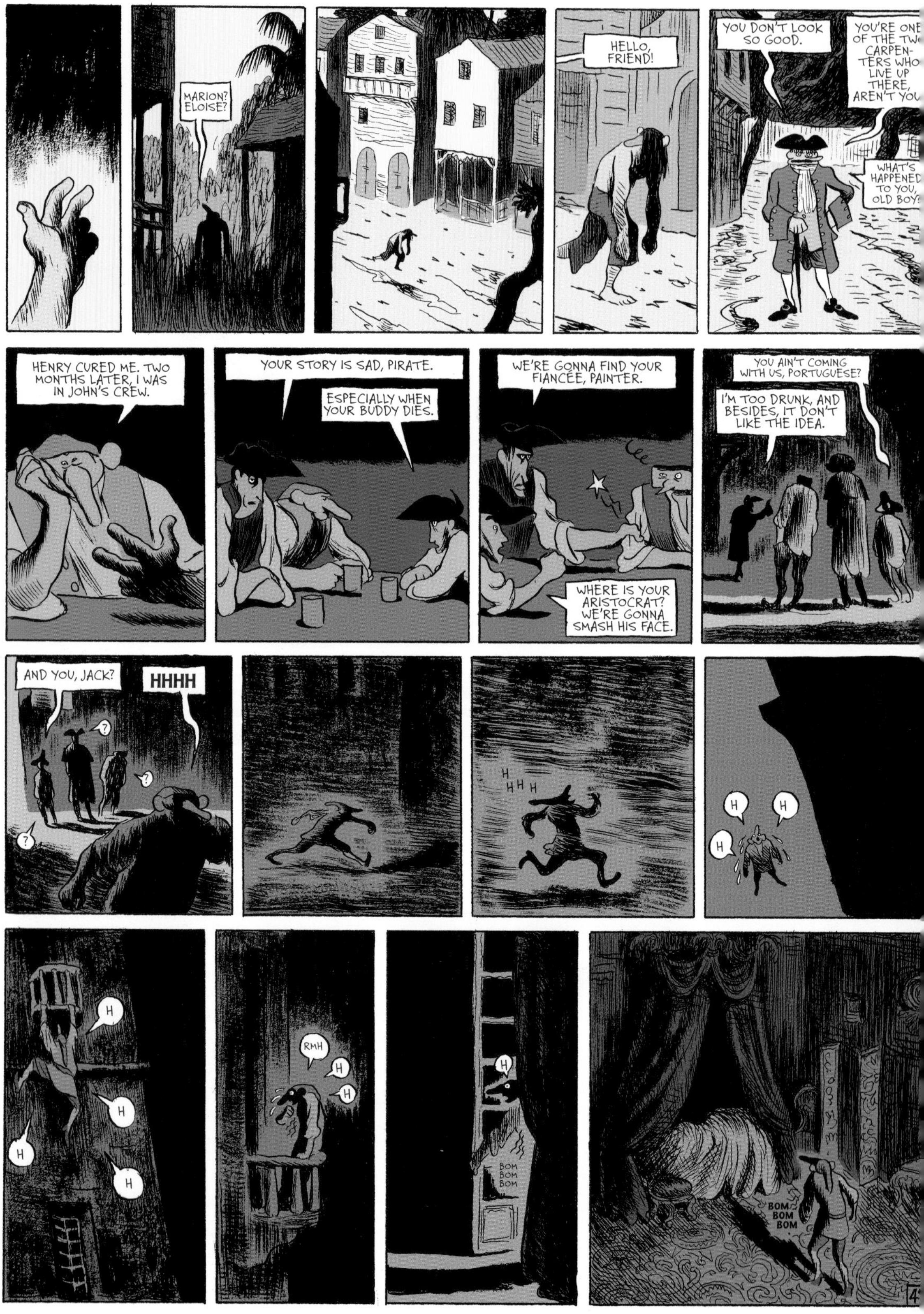

MARION? ELOISE?
HELLO, FRIEND!
YOU DON'T LOOK SO GOOD.
YOU'RE ONE OF THE TW CARPEN- TERS WHO LIVE UP THERE, AREN'T YOU
WHAT'S HAPPENED TO YOU, OLD BOY
HENRY CURED ME. TWO MONTHS LATER, I WAS IN JOHN'S CREW.
YOUR STORY IS SAD, PIRATE.
ESPECIALLY WHEN YOUR BUDDY DIES.
WE'RE GONNA FIND YOUR FIANCÉE, PAINTER.
WHERE IS YOUR ARISTOCRAT? WE'RE GONNA SMASH HIS FACE.
YOU AIN'T COMING WITH US, PORTUGUESE?
I'M TOO DRUNK, AND BESIDES, IT DON'T LIKE THE IDEA.
AND YOU, JACK?
HHHH
?
?
?
H H H H
H
H
H
H
H
H
H
RMH
H
H
H
BOM BOM BOM
BOM BOM BOM

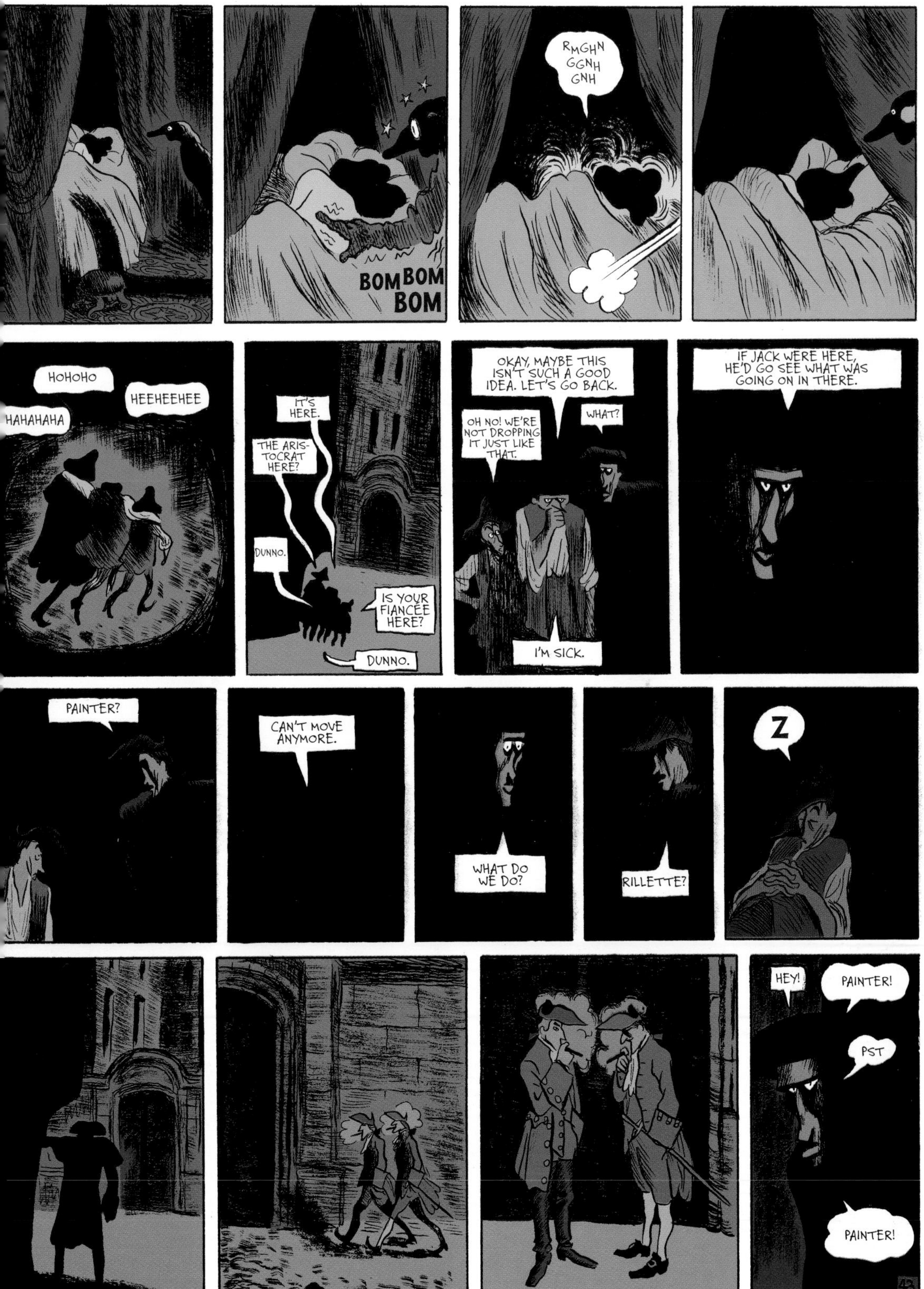
BOM BOM
BOM
RMGHN
GGNH
GNH
HOHOHO
HEEHEEHEE
HAHAHAHA
IT'S HERE.
THE ARIS-TOCRAT HERE?
DUNNO.
IS YOUR FIANCÉE HERE?
DUNNO.
OKAY, MAYBE THIS ISN'T SUCH A GOOD IDEA. LET'S GO BACK.
OH NO! WE'RE NOT DROPPING IT JUST LIKE THAT.
WHAT?
I'M SICK.
IF JACK WERE HERE, HE'D GO SEE WHAT WAS GOING ON IN THERE.
PAINTER?
CAN'T MOVE ANYMORE.
WHAT DO WE DO?
RILLETTE?
Z
HEY!
PAINTER!
PST
PAINTER!

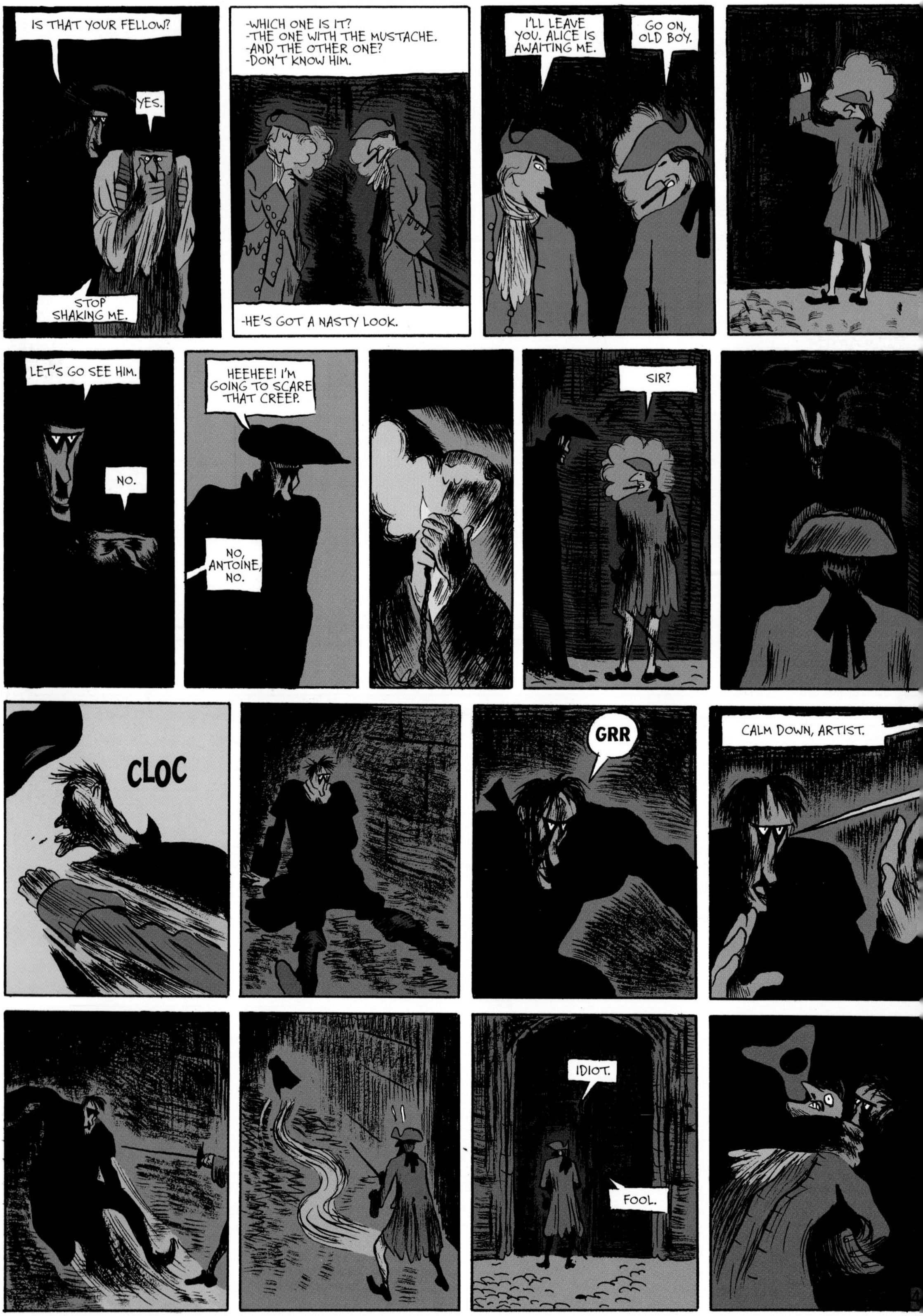
IS THAT YOUR FELLOW?
YES.
STOP SHAKING ME.
-WHICH ONE IS IT?
-THE ONE WITH THE MUSTACHE.
-AND THE OTHER ONE?
-DON'T KNOW HIM.
-HE'S GOT A NASTY LOOK.
I'LL LEAVE YOU. ALICE IS AWAITING ME.
GO ON, OLD BOY.
LET'S GO SEE HIM.
NO.
HEEHEE! I'M GOING TO SCARE THAT CREEP.
NO, ANTOINE, NO.
SIR?
CLOC
GRR
CALM DOWN, ARTIST.
IDIOT.
FOOL.

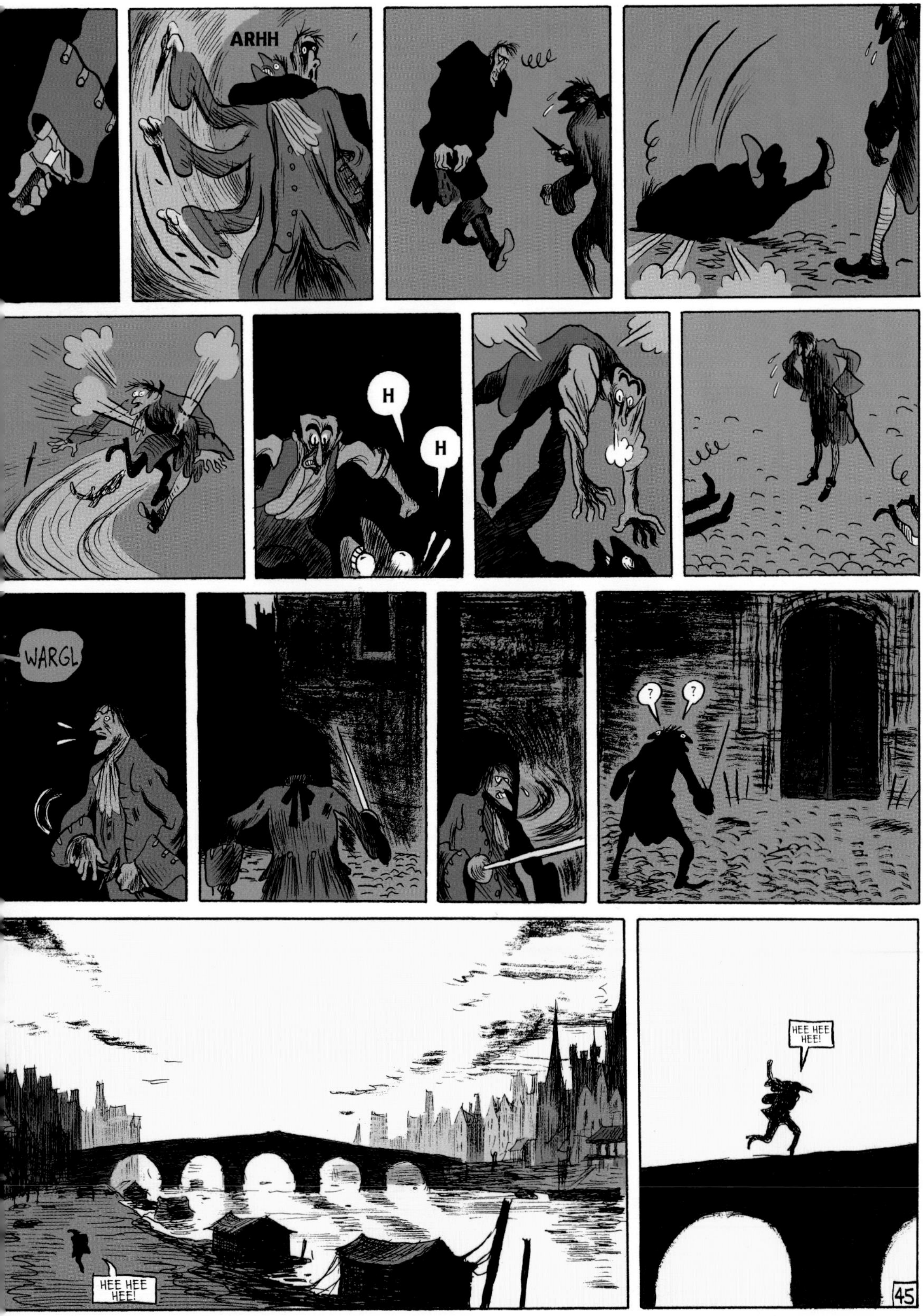
ARHH
H
H
WARGL
?
?
HEE HEE HEE!
HEE HEE HEE!

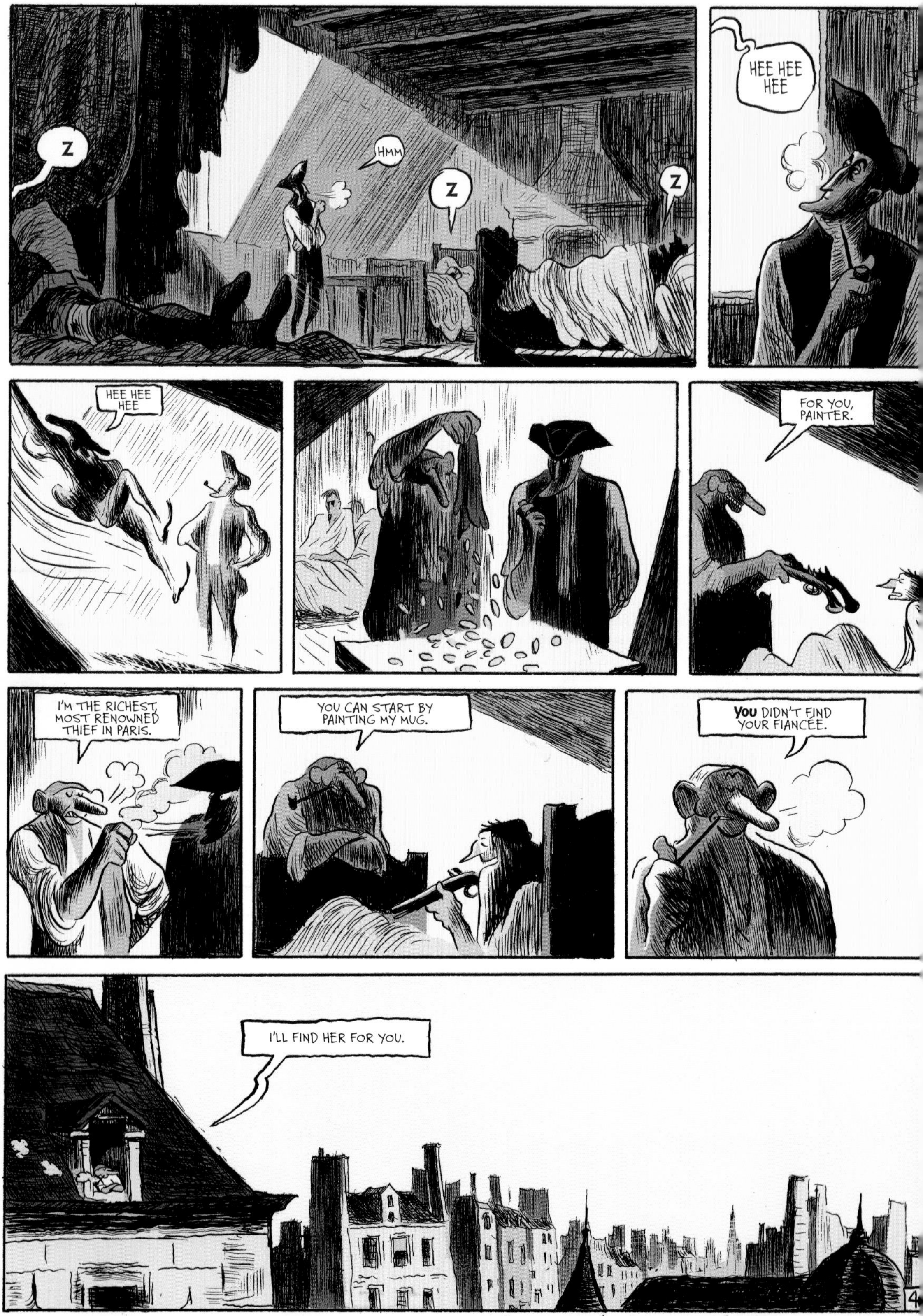
Z
HMM
Z
Z
HEE HEE HEE
HEE HEE HEE
FOR YOU, PAINTER.
I'M THE RICHEST, MOST RENOWNED THIEF IN PARIS.
YOU CAN START BY PAINTING MY MUG.
YOU DIDN'T FIND YOUR FIANCÉE.
I'LL FIND HER FOR YOU.
4

Christophe Blain avril 2004